BODY GOSSIP

tell everybody...

www.rickshawpublishing.co.uk

Published in Great Britain in 2012 by Rickshaw Publishing Ltd, 102 Fulham Palace Road, London W6 9PL

A CIP catalogue record for this book is available from the British Library

ISBN 978–0–9565368–4–6

Original cover photos by Danielle Manson

Cover design by Lee Simmons

Printed and bound in Great Britain for Rickshaw Publishing Ltd by CPI

Compiled by Ruth Rogers & Natasha Devon

RICKSHAW
PUBLISHING

Acknowledgements

Thank you so much to everyone who submitted their story to Body Gossip, we're sorry we couldn't include all of them. Huge thanks to the brave and beautiful people who came to our photoshoot.

Heartfelt thanks to the following people who understood, trusted and believed in us - Gok Wan and Mark McCullum, Siobhan Hallmark, Candy Horsbrugh at Chats Palace, Dan Freedman, Rosie Mullender and Sarah Fullagar.

To Andrew, Ben, Beth, Chloe, Chris, Dan, Imogen, Mirry, Rebecca and Rich - thank you for your beady eyes!

Sincere thanks to TTP, Harley Street, for their help and support. There is more information on TTP at the back of this book.

And special thanks to Danielle Manson, Lee Simmons, Joanna Doyle, Paul and Sam Michaelides. Without you this book could not have been made.

Foreword

In my capacity as a keen advocator of all things body confidence, I've gone the length and breadth of the country and met thousands of inspirational and beautiful people. My journey has allowed me to help women, teenagers, people with disabilities and those with eating disorders to realise that they are beautiful, just as they are, and to embrace their bodies.

In May 2011 I worked with Body Gossip on a Channel 4 documentary. They invite everyone in the UK to write something about their bodies. By exploring our relationships with our bodies and allowing real people to be given a powerful voice, they encourage acceptance and self-esteem, something I wholeheartedly support.

This book is a selection of pieces from the public, from celebs and from experts in the field of body image. No matter what your shape, size, colour, race, gender or age, there will be something in this book you can relate to.

So, enjoy these stories and through the experience of others and some of the inspirational, funny and moving pieces you will see over the following pages, I hope that you will realise that you are amazing, just as you are.

Lots of love

Contents

Introduction

In 2006 we invited everyone in the UK to write something about their body and submit it to our website. The response was overwhelming. From the hair on our heads to the state of our toes, it seems we're a nation obsessed with all things body related. You sent us poetry, monologues, dialogues, letters and raps. Some made us howl with laughter, others made us weep. We realised just how profound, sensitive and creative the British public can be.

We picked a selection of what was sent to us to be performed by a cast of well-known actors, models and musicians in live theatre shows and short films. We wanted to give real people with real bodies a powerful platform to shout "this is ME!" We live in a world where it can sometimes seem only extreme bodies are valued or given attention, so we turned the spotlight on every person in the country and said "over to you..."

Our writers reported to us that they found the experience of documenting their body thoughts cathartic and were comforted by the knowledge that their stories had the power to inspire or reassure thousands of others. Our aim was to make people think initially about their bodies more, so that ultimately they might think about them less. We wanted to free our Body Gossipers from the shackles of body insecurity and empower them to be the best version of themselves by providing a forum where they could be completely honest, or even provoke a robust debate.

At Body Gossip we have worked totally unpaid and rely on the dedication and passion of some talented volunteers, as well as our celebrity cast who donate their time for free. Over the years we have accumulated so many stories which we thought were wonderful but simply didn't have the resources to have them performed.

...Which is why we have created this book. A book full of all your wonderful, witty, moving, angry, hilarious, inspiring, thought-provoking and entertaining body stories. This is a book for the Nation, by the Nation, which documents your thoughts on everything from adolescence to ageing, via pregnancy, diets, exercise, tattoos, illness, injury and your thoughts on the pressure to conform to the 'celebrity' ideal.

And speaking of celebrities, they've contributed too. Body Gossip is one of the few campaigns which allows celebrities and the public to stand shoulder-to-shoulder in the body image debate. Because celebs are people too and they can give us a unique insight into life on the other side of the media divide. So, in the pages that follow you'll hear from television personalities like Alesha Dixon, professional sports people like Jermain Defoe, musicians, models - not to mention Mr Body Confidence himself, the fabulous Gok Wan.

Every story you will read is real. We cast our net far and wide and asked for stories on a huge range of body topics, but what unites every story is their authenticity. You won't agree with everything that's written. Or you may think "thank goodness! I thought I was the only one who..." or "I never knew some people went through..." This is a book to dip in and out of. There's something for every age group. We hope there's something everyone will be able to relate to.

Everyone has a body. Everyone has a story. We hope this book will be the first of many. To submit your body story go to www.bodygossip.org.

Love

Ruth Rogers (@BodyGossipRuth) & Natasha Devon (@BodyGossipTash)

Co-Directors of the Body Gossip Campaign

14

Chapter 1

GENESIS

You can't solve a problem until you know what it is.

Everywhere we look, the finger of blame is being pointed at specific celebrities, or schooling, or parenting, or 'the media' for our apparent lack of body confidence. Yet body image doesn't lend itself to neat explanations. If running Body Gossip has taught us anything, it's that there are many complicated factors which contribute to our body struggles. It's a minefield.

So, we asked you: WHY do you feel the way you do about your body? Is there really a problem? And if there is, what is it? What are your body ideals and do you really feel you need to measure up?

This chapter is full of your thoughts on the real root (or Genesis) of the body image debate.

Perfection

Flicking through a magazine
Really makes you think
I'll never look that good
My heart begins to sink
Showing off the clothes
These models are so thin
None have any spots
All have flawless skin
Bad hair days are banished
Bloating non existent
The models are perfection
The magazine's insistent
Why do we buy into it?
When we just get crushed
We know this isn't real life
The models are air brushed
Not everyone's aware
Poor kids don't realise
They think this is perfection
They look with honest eyes
Maybe now it's time
To tell the truth at last
And choose real people
When the model's cast!

Karen Morton, 43

Sizing up the Situation

Today I threw 237 celebrity weight obsessed magazines in the recycling bin.
And I felt better.
No longer will your images and words
Make me suffer, make me compare, make me lose hope.
You negatively influenced my weight, size and shape obsessed brain.
Size obviously matters to you,
And you tried to make it matter to me too.

Louise Brown

The Price of a Date

There was this bloke on the radio the other day having a right good old whinge:

"If there is supposedly equality now…"

…He said…

"And women are equal to men, then why are we still expected to pay for dinner on a first date?"

The radio interviewer (also a man) said that was an "excellent question". It wasn't. It was a bloody stupid question. And here's why.

Coincidentally, I was listening to that radio programme as I was, myself, getting ready for a first date.

I was clad in a towel, rubbing a lightly scented body cream into my newly waxed legs. A cream which promised to leave me with a "subtle, slimming shimmer" as well as to "tone and rejuvenate tired skin". As well it might, for the extortionate sum the sales assistant persuaded me to part with, in return for such a miraculous item.

I totted-up my preparations in my head:

Leg & bikini wax (not that I'm a first date sort of girl but, you know, just in case): £40

Professional blow dry promising to transform mane from dull, lifeless, split-end riddled nightmare into that of Amy Childs: £20

'Miracle' moisturising foundation, giving light 'flawless' coverage (making it appear as though I am wearing no make-up at all): £34 (mental)

Cream blush to give me youthful glow belying my slightly concerning 33 years (I won't volunteer that information until he asks): £6

Latest, technologically advanced mascara, so I can boast Bambi-like lashes without clumping, obviousness, or indeed looking as though I am wearing mascara: £14

Aforementioned, all over, subtle shimmer body moisturiser with 'vitality giving crystals' (will look especially good if dinner happens to be by candle light, I am told): £18

Manicure, because something I read in Cosmo once says the best way to flirt is by fiddling with the stem of your wine glass and it's probably best not to engage in this technique with manky looking nails: £12

Magic, stomach-and-thigh-holding-in pants (because men like curves, but not flab, and apparently there's a subtle distinction which, if you cannot grasp, will condemn you to an eternal life of singleness): £33 (for knickers! I ask you!).

Stockings: (because when it comes to hosiery, tights aren't sexy, apparently. That extra 4 inches of material, or lack thereof, makes all the difference, I'm told. Not that I'm a first date sort of girl, you understand, but just in case): £8.50

Book on body language: (So I can tell him I fancy him, and work out if he fancies me, without either of us actually having to utter the words "I fancy you" and suffer potential indignity of the feeling not being reciprocated): £12.99

Things I thought about buying, but decided not to, because that would be sacrificing too much of my individuality:

New, Michelle Pfieffer-esque stiletto: (I'm a chunky boots sort of girl, but according to a seminar I caught last week, men love a heel and if you don't wear heels, you're not sexy): £52

New perfume with "undertones of musk and a hint of vanilla", which a celeb-ridden glossy mag this week PROMISED will reduce any man to jelly and make my life, essentially, an inverse of what happens in the Lynx advert: £39.99

SO, that's £164.49 I've spent, and a further £91.99 a less strong-willed woman than myself might have been cajoled into spending, before we've even stepped out of the front door. Money I've invested, for me to look like the sort of woman I'm told, Mr Moaning Radio Man, that you want me to look like.

The sort of girl who LOOKS as though she isn't wearing makeup, because you tell us you don't like it when we wear makeup, but we all know you're lying, and if you saw us without any makeup at all you'd be terrified.

The sort of girl who CHOOSES to wear stockings, instead of tights, for an ordinary day at work.

The sort of girl who has effortlessly swishy hair that you'll want to run your hands through.

The sort of girl who shimmers in candle light.

The sort of girl who has no hair, anywhere, on her body. Because body hair is apparently passé.

The sort of girl with to-die-for hourglass curves, in all the right places, but no jiggly bits. Because you don't like skinny girls, you tell us, but you also think Kelly Clarkson is a 'porker'. So we have to shoehorn ourselves in somewhere, in that very tiny space, in between.

And after all that preening and plucking and moisturising and anguishing, we'll pretend we don't mind your hairy shoulders, or that fact that you talk with your mouth open, or that your mother still buys your underpants….

ALL FOR THE BARGAIN PRICE OF A NANDOS.

And THAT is why:

The idea that there's equality is LAUGHABLE; and

You're still expected to buy us dinner.

I hope that answers your "excellent question"

Anonymous

If Only

If only I had Michelle Obama's arms, I wouldn't need any other charms

If only I had Gisele Bündchen's height, then surely life wouldn't be a fight

If only I had Cindy Crawford's cleavage, and Jennifer Aniston's über-toned sleevage

If only I had Claudia Schiffer's thighs, I'd definitely have my pick of the guys

If only I had Cheryl Cole's glossy hair, then everyone would stop and stare

If only I had Kate Moss' tum, not to mention Jennifer Lopez's bum

If only I had Elle Macpherson's skin and if only I had just one chin

In short, if only I didn't look like me, surely then I'd be much more happy

I'd be out every night with a gorgeous date or married to the perfect mate

I'd have two lovely kids and a flourishing career; I'd be confident and free of fear

Because life is easy when you're pretty and slim, it's not a battle, it's no longer grim

Surely with the perfect complexion, life is simply love, joy and affection

But what if all this isn't true, and what if I didn't wish to look like you

What if I decided I was good enough and life really wasn't all that tough?

No more envy or trying to be who I'm not, because I'm me and I'm all I've got

So why not celebrate other people's beauty, but tell myself I'm also a cutie?

Why not accept myself just as I am, but also put on a touch of glam?

I have a pretty face and a shapely body, my clothes don't need to look this shoddy

Why do I hide under a baggy dress? Why not style myself to impress?

And why insist on a life of striving, when I could be out there, laughing and thriving?

So every day I'll embrace my appearance, all it takes is a little perseverance

To challenge negative thoughts when they come, and keep myself from feeling glum

Because regardless of my shape or size, I'll still be blue if I listen to those lies

So life will flow and I'll feel content and free, if only I can keep on accepting me

Katherine Baldwin, 40

Why Women Take so Long in the Bathroom

(A woman arrives on stage timid and shy wearing a comfy dressing gown. She is worried that someone can see her. She shuts a door and turns on the radio. She is transformed. In a spotlight dancing to a subtle beat, she is dancing 'like no-one is watching')

It starts with a subtle beat, something pounding low in my body. My foot just can't help it, it just wants to join in.

Quickly check the door is closed, locked: this is my guilty little secret.

(She is moving but pauses to look round quickly)

The door is definitely locked. I strike a pose – arms out, and one reaches back to run fingers through my hair. I am on the cover of a magazine, I am in a music video, I am in one of those scenes of a movie where there's lots of loud music and slow footage and the camera is on me. My hips start to understand tempo like no other person.

There is a footfall outside the door and I revert to cleaning my teeth.

(She shrinks inward, still and embarrassed. The beat has stopped)

All is quiet again. I am safe.

This time it's my shoulders that take over.

(She starts to shimmy to the beat that has started up again)

I will survive, I have freedom, I can't get no satisfaction. The toothbrush is my microphone. My lip curls and I am sexier than Mick Jagger could have ever hoped, my voice is more powerful than any Motown star could have dreamed, but I am silent.

The audience of shampoo bottles and youth preserving creams cheer and applaud.

I am a star.

(Canned applause and bulbs flash. She thanks her imaginary audience, blowing kisses and waving)

My limbs are lithe and creamy like that little bit I saw on television. I have the co-ordination of a ballet dancer, hell I am a ballet dancer. I am the most co-ordinated of any thrusting, twirling beauty. My dancing will make the flowers grow. It is inspired by the music of the universe: no, I inspire the music of the universe.

(Dances as if fascinated by her own beauty, it is almost as if she has never noticed it before)

I am the pinnacle of beauty, the blueprint for all femininity. I have it all, long glorious thighs, round capricious hips, a waist that was born to make grown men cry and breasts that float.

And they move, just how I command them. I can control them to form this physical poetry that no-one but the bathroom mirror can see.

Look at that posture, look at that spine, straight and strong, why doesn't it make it through the door?

(Pauses lost in thought)

(Turns back to audience and grabs own rear)

I can shake my ass like Cameron Diaz in that movie, only let's face it my backside looks soooo much better. Mine is a backside that asks to be grabbed, but not in a seedy way, well maybe, but only if I let them. If I want them to.

(Turns back to face audience)

And there's that smile, no one sees that smile, that's the smile that's really me. That's the smile that I would never wear in public. Only behind locked doors.

They'd arrest me if they saw that smile on public transport, that's the smile to be worn on the inside.

Remembering the way I can dance in the morning can keep me sane for the rest of the day. The fact I would never dance this way so anyone else can see me is not important. The fact that I never show the world the real me is not important. The fact that I can't is not important.

I dance in the bathroom like it is a dance floor of a club. I apply the make up to hide from the outside world. So no one looks too close to see that smile, to see that rhythm thumping down low. You know I spend my whole life hiding; dyeing, plucking, waxing, polishing, covering, revealing, pretending and locking the bathroom door. I squeeze bits in, push bits out and all to conform to something someone told me was good.

(The beat is getting a little faster, she is trying to dance and be happy but she keeps getting distracted by her thoughts)

Now this is someone else, this is what the world gets to see. This is the me that will face the day, the me that worries about cellulite, wrinkles and what people think. The me that worries what other people see. The me that doesn't dance outside the locked bathroom door. This me worries about calories, and eating too much, and that you should look like that woman in the magazine, this me wishes I had that outfit that what's-her-face was wearing on the telly, even though I hate it, even though it would never suit me but I want to be seen to fit in, be seen to try. This me wants to look just like everyone else.

Why can't I be me? Why do I conform? What is wrong with my own beauty? What's wrong with the way I look here and now? Why do I agree to hide?

But it's OK because here in front of the mirror, this sink and these bottles, I am real. Here, at least once a day, I can see just how beautiful I could really be. For the briefest, most private moments, for a little while each day, I am gorgeous.

Here alone, all by myself, I can be... a dancing queen, a rock goddess, a sex kitten.

Here I can be daring, forward, riotous, divine. Here I am allowed to be truly beautiful, behind closed doors. Here I am allowed to ooze sex, out of sight.

Here I can be anyone, anything, anywhere. I can be me.

As long as no one else can see who that is.

(She dances free and happy to a loud thumping beat as the light fades out)

Anonymous

What's in a Number?

What's in a number?
As long as the clothes feel right?
Whether your size, 6, 8, 10, 12, or 22.
All the clothes sizes are even so that means we are too.
If I'm size 14 and I don't care, why should you?
I may not look good in those shorts, but boy my boobs are bigger than yours.
What's it to you if I'm a little overweight?
What's it to you if I like eating cake?

Our society is judgemental, denying who we are.
If YOU can't expect your own body,
Why should you be the judge of mine?
SIZE IS JUST A NUMBER.

Alex, Gemma, and Jess from Year 9, Herts and Essex High School

The Perfection Plan

Susan is 36. She is dressed smartly, well groomed and slim.

SUSAN:

Sorry I'm late class, spinning over ran.

Where are we…lecture 5? No no. Lecture 6 of module P.I.A 09. Perfection Is Attainable.

Today we will be looking at how you can bag yourself a footballer.

[To audience member at back] Sorry, yes, you at the back [she listens] yes, this plan also applies for those of you want rugby players or soap stars.

Step one. [To audience member at front] Yes, at the front. This is the last question, and then we really must get on. [She listens] It will make you successful. It will make you rich. And, it will make you happy.

Step One. Image is everything.

Beauty is in the eye of the beholder. Every single one of you knows that every beholder likes a nice, thin, hairless girl with perfectly straight hair and a Californian tan. You may live in Croydon, where the sun rarely shines, but Kate Moss never let that stop her.

In order to attain perfection you will need one pair of GHD's, 600 minutes on a sun bed (I recommend Tumour Tan in Pimlico, their beds are the strongest and a ten minute session costs as little as £4), two tubes of slimming anti-cellulite cream, a short course in laser hair removal and, for those of you over 24, 3 pots of anti ageing face cream.

You cannot put a price on happiness. But the nine hundred pounds this will cost you is nothing when you compare this to the three grand you will get for your first NUTS cover shoot and the eternal happiness perfection can bring.

Another essential accessory to your image is the cigarette (preferably Marlborough Lights) and a nice expensive coke habit. Similarly to fake tanning, this does not come without risks. However, although there are links to cancer and in the case of our good friend Charlie, the odd mental health problem (and if you get carried away, a prison sentence); it's better to live thin and die young than it is to live a long, boring life as a chubby loser. And I would know.

I'd also recommend getting a gym membership with personal trainer. Although your no carb, no fat, no sugar, no salt, no nutrition, no taste diet will help keep you nice and trim, every little helps. When the greedy, lazy voice in your head is telling you to stay in bed on Sundays, knowing that you have to meet Andrea the Adonis at the gym for that 3 hour cardio session will ensure that the perfectionist that lies inside each and every single one of you wins. It will be hard, but, trust me, you will feel better in the end.

Step Two. Carbs are bad.

Now people, whilst you can avoid the baked goods section in Tesco's, sometimes you just have to walk past a bakery. When those little cakes with their chocolate icing call you and try to tempt you, trying to make you weak just repeat the mantra quietly to yourself. Carbs are bad. There's no such thing as a good carb. Carbs are bad. Come on…join in. Carbs are bad. There's no such thing as a good carb. Carbs are bad. And again. Carbs are bad. There's no such thing as a good carb. Well done.

If the urge to snack becomes too great, cross the road, away from the temptation.

If I find myself getting a bit peckish, I chew sugar free gum in and forget all about it. There was that horrible time when…There are occasions when you will want to snack. To prevent these becoming a major crisis, carry some celery or cucumber sticks to ease those cravings. Or, just have a cigarette.

[To audience member in 2nd row] Do you have a question? Yes you, the little girl in the second row. [She listens] There's a KFC opposite your bakery so you can't cross the road.

Good point. You will need to map routes that avoid eateries. The greasy fumes you ingest as a result of being in close proximity with said fast food cesspit will cause you to put on weight. And remember; the more steps you take, the more calories you burn, the better person you become.

This leads me nicely onto step 2b; Fats. If you eat too much fat, you will become fat.

Whilst some health freaks say that there are good fats and bad fats and that Omega Oils give you brain power and are promote general well being; none of these so-called gurus will ever end up on the front of Heat, they will never marry a footballer and they probably all have hairy legs, pasty skin and wear socks and sandals. So their advice should be ignored.

Step 3. Bagging your Man.

Once your image has been perfected, you are ready to start your hunt.

The preferred hunting gear is a belt length denim skirt with a white lycra top so tight it obstructs your breathing. I would not recommend these outfits until you have been on my plan for at least six weeks as otherwise you will just look like a Geordie slapper. If you're not the skirt wearing type, I'd try hot pants. They also say 'I am available and ready to be treated like the object I have become.'

To ensure he notices you, you must perfect the strut. [She demonstrates a 'sexy' walk], the hair flick [she demonstrates] the bimbo laugh [she laughs in a loud, over the top way].

Once he notices you, give him the eye [she demonstrates this]. Within a matter of minutes, any banker worth his billions will be over offering to buy you a glass of Moet. Girls, it would be rude not to accept, but your new lifestyle will mean you can no longer take your drink, so be on your guard. Those of you who were foolish enough to pursue a career, go to university or have interests outside of attaining perfection, should try not to mention your past life.

Men prefer women who can act as arm candy, smile in the right way [she demonstrates] and have very little of interest to say. You don't want them to feel threatened. Women who have become successful through genuine talent, hard work and intellect are by and large single. And miserable.

[To audience member at side] Yes, you at the side. [She listens] No. No. I. I am. At the moment. Yes. Mean. I'm fine about it. I broke up with him.

Anyway, that's why I now only buy Heat magazine. Mindless chit chat, that motivates you to attain perfection and will make you entirely non-threatening.

Step Four. Possible Side Effects.

Health Risks. As I mentioned in step one, cancer is a slight worry. But thinness is our priority, so the odd cigarette to curb those cravings is worth it. They do cause ageing of the skin, yellowing of the nails and teeth, but that's nothing a good anti-ageing crème, beautician and cosmetic dentist can't sort out. Although this does all come at a cost. Nevertheless your footballer will pay for it all and as I said before, you can't put a price on happiness. There are also the slight issue of osteoporosis and infertility, but who wants babies anyway? Stretch marks do not equal perfection.

Loss of Friends. You may find you have less and less in common with people you were acquainted with before you began my Perfection Plan. They may criticise your mood swings and blame it on the lack of carbohydrates in your diet, they may say you have become boring and obsessed with how you look and what you eat. However, they are just jealous. Your size 12 friends really do want to be just like you. When they call you weak for letting an eating disorder win, when they say you are deluded and mentally unwell, they are kidding themselves. They just don't have the same determination. In order to become one of the beautiful people, they really must give up everything they've ever worked for; friends, family, integrity and general life enjoyment. Looking this good has meant a lot of sacrifices girls.

I have had to sacrifice my career (I got sacked after I could no longer concentrate and kept falling asleep at my desk); my first husband – he said I was half the person he'd met. When I said 'thank you very much', he told me that it wasn't a compliment and walked away.

During our divorce settlement, the judge decided it was best if the children lived with him. He said my lifestyle was having a negative effect on Sarah and Ben, especially Sarah who was 10 at the time. He claimed my constant dieting and gym obsession was rubbing off on her. Rubbish. She can think for herself. And anyway, what's wrong with her becoming vegan, cutting out chocolate, sweets and crisps? Obesity is on the rise you know.

I saw Sarah and Ben two weekends ago. Ben, who just turned eight, asked me why we never eat together. Sarah told him to be quiet and he said 'No! I want to know why mummy never eats with us. Why does she not eat what we eat? What's so different about mummy?'

'Shhhhh' said Sarah. 'She's not well. Daddy said so.'

And Ben looked at me and asked me if that was true. 'Are you allergic to what we eat mummy?'

Sarah, who has grown up so much in the last 2 years looked at me and said 'No Ben. Mummy isn't allergic to lasagne, or ice cream, she's scared of them.'

I'm not scared of food, I just don't like the way certain foods make me feel.

'How does lasagne make you feel mummy?' 'Is it very different from how cottage cheese makes you feel?' 'Does it give you a tummy ache?'

I nodded. I excused myself and went to have a cigarette in the other room.

Ben's crying. 'What can we do Sarah? Can we stop mummy being scared? Daddy gave me a night light. Could we give mummy a night light?'

'She says they don't help her feel perfect'

'But Sarah, Mummy was perfect before she got smaller. She's still perfect.'

Sarah put her arms around him and said they should go and wait outside for Daddy.

And Sarah was right. I like to feel perfect. I do feel almost perfect. I feel perfectly in control of everything. I feel thin. I feel empowered. And you can too with my simple plan. Perfection is Attainable.

See you next week for our final lecture. How to survive Social Occasions and Supermarkets.

Thank you for listening and stay strong.

Abigail Graham

'Yah! (Celebs' Eye View)'

Yah, I'll have a decaf extra skinny mocha chocca latte please
My waist will be smaller to accentuate my double D's!

You see, that's the only part of me that's allowed to be big
Otherwise the press will have a field day and call me a pig

They papped me on holiday, lying in the sun
Then proclaimed to the world, "look at her bum!"

In a terrible state I rushed to the gym
Pleading with my trainer, "please make me thin!"

The next two weeks I was worked to the bone
My ass, thighs and abs, ordered to tone

My dairy became soya and steak became fish
The pounds were dropping off, I was getting my wish!

I grabbed my trainer and said, "You're my hero!
I've dropped 3 dress sizes, I'm now a size zero!"

On top of the world, I attended a premiere
Expecting the press to say, "wow, what a derriere!"

Instead though they didn't and this is what I read,
"She looks like a rake with a lollipop head"

Shocked and confused, what the hell do they want?!
I thought I'd be praised for looking skinny and gaunt

What, I get slagged for being fat and for being thin?
Well I give up, I don't know how to win

Now young girls are starving to look like me
Viewing my airbrushed pictures, if only they could see

That I have blemishes just like them
Now, if they could see that, well, maybe then

Things could change and we'd be allowed to be free
No dangerous diets, but we could just be

Whatever size we naturally are
Admired from close-up and from afar

They say that beauty is in the eye of the beholder
We should believe this, and stop looking over our shoulder

At who is thinner, prettier and who's bones sticks out most
It's time to take a stand, I don't wanna be a ghost!

When will we be happy with what we see in the mirror?
We are beautiful – let's stop getting thinner and thinner!

You know what, forget what I ordered – for goodness sake,
I'll have a full fat latte and a carrot cake!

A healthy balanced diet with a few treats thrown in
That's the way to go – that's the way to win!

So what if I have a few dimples on my thighs?
It's about time that magazines stopped telling lies!

I'm taking a stand and being happy, not just thin.
It's time to be content with the skin that I'm in.

Elizabeth Caproni, 28

Dear Diary

I'm so fed up of all the stuff in the media at the moment. They say it's not good to be skinny, about realistic bodies not having a flat stomach. They all say that boys like curves. That skinny is not good and we should be using real size models. I am real size, I'm a normal person but I don't have those curves, I have that flat stomach but not the boobs and the hips like everyone else does. Everyone in my year always seems to have bigger boobs than me and I am still basically flat chested and it really gets me down, and it's all over the media as well so people now think that if you don't have those 'curves' that you are anorexic or size zero. I've tried eating a lot to put on weight but nothing happens. I hate being my shape even though I get told so many people idolise it. I go to extremes to try and look like I have those curves. I buy underwear that is very expensive when everyone else is going to Primark and getting them for £3. I feel like I can't be confident without the gel to make the illusion. I'm fed up of people thinking it's bad to be skinny because as being bigger some people can't help it.

Emma, 14

I Love my Villain's Teeth

My teenage years, like most young girls I'm sure, were marked by a severe unhappiness with my body. I hated everything that I had acquired through nature. I loathed my pale skin, prominent hips, small mouth, and argh my feet - where to start?! Where other people saw beauty and uniqueness, I saw imperfection and flaws. My life was consumed with the way that I looked. I thought about my image almost every second of everyday, comparing myself to my peers and to the impeccably presented girls in magazines and films.

'Why do some people get to look like that and I have to walk around in this body? Surely I must have done something wrong to not deserve a body like that, after all that is what it's all about – looking perfect means that you are perfect, that you will have everything you ever wanted'. These were the thoughts constantly running through my mind.

I never thought I would be able to accept the way that I look, but somewhere between my late teens and turning 21, I changed. I didn't even notice the gradual shift from hating my body to becoming comfortable in it. Instead, it was brought to my attention by a 5 year old boy.

One day in a crèche that I helped in, a young boy was describing his affection for his primary school teacher, telling me that she looked like a Princess. He then turned and studied my face and told me that I had 'Villains Teeth'. In the instant after the child made this comment I was completely shocked, but not at his insult, at my reaction. Instead of running out of the room crying and resolving to save up enough money to get my teeth re-worked, I laughed!

That day I realised I had grown up. I stopped seeing the world, and myself, through child's eyes. I realised that my features are just that - they are mine. They belong to me, and although they don't define me, they are a part of me and no one else. It is childish to think that we are only beautiful if we measure up to the girls in the media. No one else on earth looks like me or you, that is what makes us attractive.

I grew up. It is time that our society grew up too. It's time we all understood that beauty isn't one standardised ideal. Beauty is found in our differences. Whatever size, shape, or skin-colour we are all beautiful. Don't let our Western idea of 'perfection' dictate how you feel about yourself. The ideals that our society holds are flawed, not you.

Elisabeth Reed, 21

Worth It?

In high heels and painted toe,
immaculate make-up, skin aglow,
haute couture and knife-sharp finesse,
she bestowed her secrets of success.

Commitment is the word, she said,
lipsticks in every shade of red,
sleek hair, no loose ends,
follow forecasts, fashion trends.
Pluck eyebrows with painful precision
- feel free to treat dowdies with derision.

Don't leave anything to luck,
there's nothing wrong with a nip and tuck.
If you feel the urge to give in, to quit,
don't - remember you're worth it.

So I bought the mags and watched TV,
studied the ads assiduously,
found the time to buy the right kohl,
pulled on knickers with magic control,
massaged products into my hair,

was ruthless in my regime of skin care.

I devoted my life to looking my best,
but now that I've tried it I'm less than impressed.
The effort's not worth a jot or tittle,
I'd rather look lax and live a little.

Ann Gibson, 55

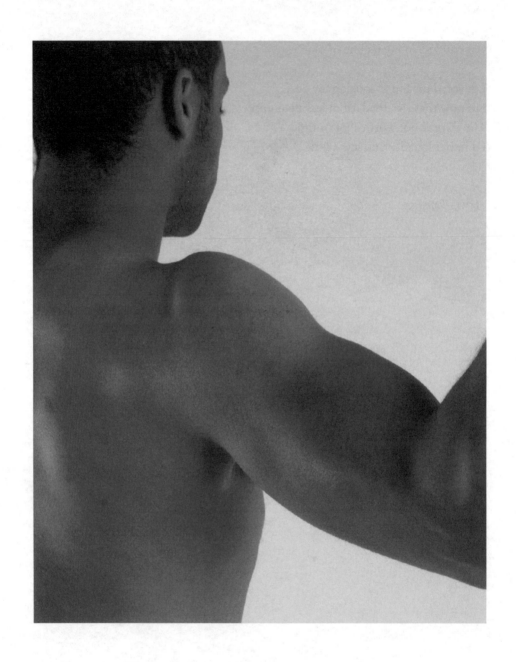

Chapter 2

SHAPING BODIES

So, now we know where our body ideals come from, this chapter explores all the things we do in our attempts to fit those ideals.

If aliens are observing this planet, we like to think they're probably laughing at some of these behaviours. Yet most of us are guilty of them. We've all been on a diet. And do we really go to the gym to 'get healthy', or is it because we harbour a secret desire for washboard abs? Where's the line between expressing yourself and expressing what society tells us is beautiful? Why do we wear makeup? What would possess someone to go under the knife?

This chapter is all about the lengths we'll go to once the desire for 'the body beautiful' has set in.

To Eat or Not to Eat

"To eat or not to eat? That is the question.
Whether 'tis nobler in the body to suffer
The pangs and torture of outrageous hunger,
Or to take one bite of that gorgeous fudge brownie,
And with that bite end it?… One bite, to eat,
To eat: perchance to be free."

Anonymous

Coming Second

A woman sits in a restaurant. She is on the other end of a conversation. Trying to seem interested.

Yes. Uh huh.

Mmm.

Ha.

That's. 'Kay.

Mmm? Wha.

I. I don't.

Sorry, what were you saying? I don't. I mean, I wasn't. I'm so sorry about this. I'm sitting here. I'm sitting here talking to you. And you're lovely. You're very. Sweet. And you have very important things to say. About religion. And art. And Brangelina. And funny! You're. Well, you're bloody charming! But all I can think about. All I can think about are the chocolate éclairs behind the counter over there. I've had them before, you see. The pastry is like air and sweetness and life. And the chocolate is deep and sensual and strong. But the cream. The cream is like. Like when the air tastes sweet at Christmastime. The cream is. That's what the cream is like. I think about them and I know what it will feel like when I eat them. Like when someone touches you in a way you haven't been touched in a while, in a vulnerable place, and you want to cry. And afterwards there's an extreme sense of wholeness and satisfaction. You're filled with it.

And I can see that there are six of them. The éclairs du chocolat. One is slightly smaller than the others, but that's okay. I'll have that one too. The runt. The baby. He's just as worthy as the rest. All six. If I pace it out right, I can probably do them all in an hour. With some coffee, or milk, to wash it down. I would usually have them at home, and put something really good on the telly. Maybe a DVD. A period drama with Emma Thompson or Colin Firth. I'll eat them quickly, but I'll savour each bite. In the middle of the first, I'll already be thinking about the second and, whilst eating the second, I'll be eyeing the third. Anticipating the final one and that feeling. The satisfaction when I'm full and the sadness that they're gone.

It's not always éclairs. Brownies are good. I like a good cheesecake every now and then. If I'm desperate, chocolate digestives. But plain chocolate, not milk. I mean, just because I like to eat a lot doesn't mean I don't have taste.

No. No, it's not just the sweets. Fajitas. Ravioli. Lamb kebabs. Cheese and pickle sarnies. Onion rings. Pesto chicken panini. McDonald's double sausage McMuffin. Fried bananas. Have you ever had a fried banana? It makes your insides shudder and quiver like…

And sushi. Oh, fuck me with sushi! Spicy sushi. So spicy the nerves in your brain jolt.

Cheeeeeeese. Brie. Cheddar. Bleu. Gouda. Red Leicester.

And curry! Oh how many times have I felt the meaning of existence in a nice korma? Hot and wet and. Oh and meat. I mean, juicy meat you can smell sizzling from a mile away. And tough meat too. Work your jaw down on it. Meat you have to work with.

I had a Sunday roast today before I came to meet you. For our dinner. Women often eat before they go on dates, so as not to seem like pigs devouring and snorting their food in front of men. I ate before meeting you because I didn't want to be hungry after my starter, soup, bread, main, and now. Well. The éclairs. They're just gorgeous, aren't they?

I don't need to look like Paris Hilton. I'm thrilled actually, that I look as opposite to Paris Hilton as possible. That's not to say I'm. I'm happy. With how I am. I tried to diet once. Melancholy. Depression. Death. It was. All of that. But then a pint of Ben & Jerry's New York Super Fudge Chunk made it go away. I'd rather wallow in it. Sit in my fatness, comfortably, than try to fight it. I fantasize about being one of those fat old ladies. Big rolls under my dressing gown. I would live in my dressing gown, naturally. With big curtains of flesh hanging from my arms like down blankets. I could just let the grease drip down my chin and a chocolate smudge stay above my lip like a moustache. Let the crumbs settle down in my cleavage like pebbles between the boulders of my breasts. Close my eyes and, mmm, just moan with each bite.

I'm telling you this now because it's only fair for you to know that this is something that will happen often. I will very frequently not be listening to you because I'm thinking about food. And I just thought. Right, you're not fussed about how I look. You wouldn't be here if you were. And you think, if someone can love you when you're fat, they can maybe really love you. But there's more than just. I don't know if I can love you the way you would need to be loved. Because I will choose an éclair over a conversation with you. There is no guarantee that you will leave me feeling whole and satisfied. But I've been eating for a long time and food and me have something special. Between us. Food is always there when I need him. He gives back, food does. It's give and take with us. And you. I mean. I hardly know you.

So, if that's not all right. If you can't handle coming second, then maybe this won't work. And I'd like to know now how you feel about it, now, so as not to disappoint each other in the future. So. You can leave now. If you want. I'll pay the bill. It's no trouble. Or you can stand up, walk over to that counter there, look that waiter in his face and order those six chocolate éclairs. And if you do. If you choose that.

Then.

Well.

I might even let you have one of them.

The small one.

Megan Ford

A Body Through the Ages

Location: The beach

Age: 4

Carefree and covered in sand, I dance with my cousins to those early beats of the 90's and splash through the pounding waves of the ocean. The Grown Ups stumble around under the palm trees, draining bottles from the cooler, trading insults and cackling with laughter. As the sun gets hotter, we get hungrier and retreat to the shady part of the beach and whine for push-pops or lunch. Finally, there are messy hot dogs on Wonder Bread, and the juices drip down our faces as we eat them as fast as our gappy, loose teeth will allow.

The Grown Ups are laughing and pinching at my stomach and legs. "Look at this big girl! Look at her eat, faster than you can blink! She looks just like Miss Elizabeth! Big girl!"

Miss Elizabeth is fat and will chase you away and eat up all your food if you don't finish it fast enough. She is happy and funny, but she is mostly fat and The Grown Ups laugh at her. Now they are laughing at me the same way.

I drop my hot dog in the sand and don't eat anything else that day.

Location: The neighbourhood street

Age: 7

Moms and Dads yell from every yard to be careful as my best friend sits on the handlebars of my first Two Wheel Bike and I peddle us up and down the streets of the neighbourhood. Peddling makes me tired fast and after we go up and down the Big Hill three times I ask if she wants to switch places.

"I mean I would", she says. "Except I don't think you would fit on the handlebars, you know? And I don't think I could push you. You're kind of bigger than me".

This is true. Parents tell us all the time that I am a Big Girl and she is a Little Girl even though we have the same teacher and our birthdays are only 4 days apart. Her Mom always gives me a whole sandwich instead of only half because I am a Big Girl. And I can never wear her clothes when we have slumber parties like the other girls can.

"But that's okay!" She says from the handlebars. "I can try if you wanna".

"No way!" I laugh. "I'm a cow, you could never push me. I was joking". My legs hurt so much that I want to cry as we go up the Big Hill again but I'm the Big Girl and big girls don't cry... they peddle.

Location: 8th grade homeroom

Age: 13

It is the first day back to school and people are looking at me as I try to find an empty chair while looking at my feet. I feel someone tapping me on the shoulder. Hoping it is one of my friends I turn around, looking for a distraction from the on-staring people. Instead, I am eye-to-eye with My Crush and suddenly my heart is in my throat. We are not friends. In fact, we've never even spoken unless you count when he was making fat faces at me, so why is he touching me? Am I in his way? Should I say something? Can't he just walk around me? My thoughts are racing as I realize he is going to talk to me. I tense, getting ready for his usual cruel fat joke.

"Hey!" He says. "You got really cute this summer". Then he smiles at me and squeezes my shoulder as he walks away.

I am shocked and astounded and happy. This summer my cousin showed me how to Get Skinny Fast. We ran 12 miles every day until we were exhausted and panting and dry heaving. She taught me that all food except salads without dressing and sparkling water were for Fatties only and she showed me how to make myself throw up in case I was dumb enough to eat a slice of pizza. We measured ourselves with a fabric measurer everyday and used sharpies to circle which parts of our bodies we needed to improve.

She taught me these things because she loves me and wants me to be popular and happy and to make more friends and to meet cute boys. I did not always like learning these things, but she had been right. I had lost 40 pounds and People liked me. People liked skinny.

Location: My bedroom

Age 16

I've finally perfected my "Glare of No Emotion" and I use it, staring straight ahead, as Mom scolds me like I am a child for binge eating and sneaking food.

I stare straight ahead.

She tells me that if she finds any more wrappers anywhere or if I gain any more weight she is taking my car keys away.

I stare straight ahead.

She reminds me that I've gained 60 pounds in a little over a year.

I know, I tell her, I was there when she weighed me every week.

She doesn't like my tone and asks me why I don't care about what I look like.

I tell her it's because I know that no one is really looking at me.

She is suddenly tearing up, and now she is sniffing, and now she is crying. She grabs my face and I stare at her red, watery eyes.

"You've eaten your beautiful face away," she says, pinching the fatty flesh under my chin. She asks why I want to be ugly. I tell her again. No One Is Looking At Me. She walks out of the room.

I wait until she is downstairs and I reach for the bag of King Size Snickers Bars I keep under my bed. There are 8 in the bag and I eat 6 and my throat burns as I choke on the peanuts and caramel and tears I refuse to cry.

Location: High school locker room, Homecoming dance

Age 18

Alone in the bathroom I glance at the mirror above the sink in front of me. The body I see in the reflection isn't anything new, even in the new dress I got at the Plus Size Store. I don't really see so much as know the reflection from head to foot. I've seen, examined and cursed this reflection thousands, maybe millions, of times. I know it has a double chin behind my perfectly layered hair, which has been teased out so that it makes my face look slimmer. I know behind the skirt there are legs that touch from the knee up. I know crammed into the strappy high heels are wide set feet. I know behind the corset there are 4 rolls of fatty flesh where my Vogue 2-week workout abs should be.

I know every angle to stand at to make my waist look smaller and every way to tilt my head to make my double chin disappear.

I know it all without seeing it. My reflection is my worst enemy.

I stare at myself and wonder how much happier I would be if I'd never seen a mirror in my entire life. I stare at myself in my Homecoming Dress, in my Homecoming Make-up, in my Homecoming manicured hands and Homecoming hair, and wonder if I even have the energy to care anymore. I stare at myself and wonder who possibly has the energy to care.

I stare at myself until the motion sensor timer goes off and sends the locker room into total darkness except the red glow of the Exit sign.

I stare at the blackness where my reflection used to be and listen to my own breathing and feel my own heart beat. I wonder if this body, which seems to be working fine, will ever be good enough for the world again. I wonder if it was ever good enough to begin with, or if I was born with things that needed to be improved. The shadow of a positive thought starts to form – maybe my reflection doesn't define me, maybe there are good things about me – but the lights come on and the door opens and two girls walk in.

I shake away that fleeting optimism with a fluff of my hair and a tilt of my chin, making sure my head is at the angle that makes my eyes look bigger and my neck look longer. I pass under the glowing exit sign and wade back into the pounding music, into the sea of dancing bodies.

Jessica McNeal-Mizell, 21

Worth it?

Getting skinny, what a feat,
All you must do is never eat.
Don't bite, don't chew and don't ingest,
You'll leave your peers much impressed.
They'll all wish that they looked like you,
And all it is that you must do,
Is give up all your favourite stuff,
And make sure you don't eat enough.
Oh and go running twice a day,
And whoopsie I forgot to say:
You'll have to give up all your friends,
When asked to dinner you pretend,
You're busy, tired, granny's sick,
You're boyfriend dumped you, what a prick.
Then you can stay at home alone,
And work more on your muscle tone.
And gaze at Claudia and Kate,
And vow to lose that extra weight.
So cut out carbs and wheat and cheese,
All you must eat are lettuce leaves.

45

Do sit-ups, weights and yoga too,
There's always more that you can do.
So empty out your bank account,
To pay a man a large amount,
To suck out all your body fat,
And make your tummy super flat.
And if you feel a hunger pain,
Drink coffee or else take cocaine,
And speed is also really great,
For making sure you're losing weight.
Of course, your heart may cease to beat,
But hey, at least you didn't cheat.
If you slip up by accident,
There's lots of things that will prevent,
The fat from landing on your butt,
Take laxatives or just throw up.
Or fast for days and exercise,
Till there's a gap between your thighs.
Keep doing what you have to do,
To make quite sure you see it through,
And when you're thin, and feeling great,
You'll probably want to lose more weight.
So now you've done it, you've got thin,
You've got the bod and everything.
And people want to look like you,
And all your dreams are coming true.
Well whoop-di-do, hurry, hurrah!
No longer do you need a bra,
Your thighs are smooth, your arms are toned,
You lift your shirt, you see your bones,
Your tummy's flat, your bottom pert,
So why the hell do you still hurt?
You still feel chubby in your head,

Despite the fact you're nearly dead.
You feel like you're in control,
But also that you've sold your soul.
Who cares if you can feel your bones?
When you're at home and you're alone.
So was it worth it? Was it fuck?
You've fucked your life entirely up,
You've ruined really everything,
But you've got this, one thing; you're thin.

Lola Frears, 23

Your Face

Your face is perfect
The stranger said
You really could be a top model
I work for an agency, I take the shots.
He was hopelessly cool,
Good looking too
He swigged his wine from an elegant glass
And moved in a little closer
You'll need a nose-job first, of course
I can organise that.
Of course, I don't doubt it, I thought to myself.

Now, I said, finally finding my voice
Can I check the size of your penis?

I stood in the wine bar, alongside friends
We laughed at the feminist retort
One up for womankind they said
I smiled, felt smug, but inside, cried.
I'd always thought my nose was odd
Had wanted one just like my friend's
Bust too small, hips too big
Not to mention the footballer's knees.
And yet, a part of me rejoiced
He'd singled me out from all the rest
Perhaps I was just the most gullible
But, nose notwithstanding,
My face had passed *some* sort of test.

Julia Davison

Silliness Makes You Sexy

Moobs, muffin tops, beer bellies and bee-sting nips can all be solved with just a wee stitch.

Or go to the gym and sweat like a beast, to make up for the double chocolate fudge brownie feast.

Look in the Mirror and poke at your fat, pull tight your loose skin and purr like a cat,

Then ping, let it go as simple as that,

Your tsunami wave of fat flies back.

Tense your pecs, your biceps, abs and traps.

Drink vitamin supplements,

Pure Protein shake for sure.

A raw egg in milk

More, More, More!

When your eyes are closed enjoying your soft pillow, you're still a child climbing up your garden's old willow, hiding from your homework, and the note that got sent home,

From Mrs Goat your English teacher, it had a serious tone.

Turn the glossy pages of your favourite magazine,

See a sensible dietician who looks like a sex god queen,

With a pointy chin at right angles to a skinny neck and chest,

With her ribs sticking out were really there should be breast.

Feel your twig-thin arms with all that coarse unnatural hair,

Feel your poor weak legs and your boney derriere,

Wish for better beauty and observe your own despair.

Perfect your slick black hair to a style to make it look like you just don't care!

Geek glasses if you dare.

A hundred and ten pound t-shirt and retro designer shoes,

All of this to cover up the fact that you feel like you always lose.

What's wrong with happiness, why is that such a sin?

What's wrong with a body that looks a little lived in?

I love chubby dimples when eyes light up with glee

I want to feel a full body lying next to me.

But not full in terms of size but full of happiness and not many lies

Engaging is attractive and focused is flipping hot.

Silliness makes you sexy but that's not the best you've got,

I hate saying clichés but this one is the truth

You look your best being you, and that's all there is to that.

Kjerstin Gruys, 28

My Fat is a Feminist Issue

This essay marks my first attempt to publicly contend with a question I've been struggling with privately for more than a decade:

If "fat is a feminist issue," does wanting to lose weight make me less of a feminist?

Why does this question haunt me? The brief answer: I'm a recovered anorexic, I'm a feminist sociologist, and I'm on a diet.

Because of my experience with anorexia, I REALLY know how horrible things can get when one starts obsessing about "bad foods" and setting (and re-setting) weight-loss goals. Not only did my eating disorder make me miserable while in the throes of it, but I have lasting health issues (osteopenia and mild kidney damage) that could eventually shorten or lessen the quality of my life. This makes me angry and sad, though I try not to beat myself up about it.

That said, recovering from anorexia (almost 8 years ago now... *Fist Pump*) made me a feminist (or, at least, a more focused one). While battling for my sanity and health, I became increasingly pissed off at the THIN=BEAUTIFUL*GOOD environment we live in. Our culture's valorisation of thinness caused well-meaning friends and family to compliment me on my rapid weight-loss, literally up until the weeks that I entered treatment. Even after entering treatment, some people didn't think I was skinny enough to be "really" anorexic, which was... unhelpful to recovery. (Worse, my appearance-obsessed-and-awful boyfriend at the time hinted that it would be great if I could recover from my eating disorder without gaining any weight, "since you're not, like, scary-thin." Ugh!) In the end, I got better, got angrier (dumped the jerk), and ultimately re-arranged my life so that I could stay healthy and continue fighting-the-good-fight as my career.

So now I'm a professional feminist with a personal (skin-and-)bone to pick with our messed up beauty culture. If you didn't know this already, we feminists typically view dieting - and, particularly, the diet industry - as an (evil) expression of patriarchy that is bad for women. As someone who studies the harmful effects of our culture's beauty standards - particularly those related to body size - I agree with this. Considering over 95% of diets FAIL, weight-loss obsessions can logically be seen as a 95% pointless and painful drain on women's energy and emotional happiness, not to mention our wallets. Add the fact that many weight-loss attempts put our health at risk, and it's pretty easy to become radically anti-diet. Hence, "RIOTS, NOT DIETS!" has become a well-known rallying cheer for many feminists (including this cute "feminist kitten". Meow!).

Another way to view dieting from the feminist perspective is to consider how dieting fits the concept of a "patriarchal bargain." The definition of a patriarchal bargain is this: a decision to accept gender rules that disadvantage women in exchange for whatever power one can wrest from the system. It is an individual strategy designed to manipulate the system to one's best advantage, but one that leaves the system itself intact. Consider that, by strategically losing weight, we accept the THIN=BEAUTIFUL*GOOD equation (which implies FAT=UGLY*BAD), and propel ourselves into positions of greater social advantage. On an individual level, claiming "thin privilege" feels empowering. (Recall, Oprah Winfrey - arguably the MOST powerful woman in the world - has described "going to the gym when I really prefer wine and chips" as her greatest accomplishment. Seriously.) Yet, these THINpowered feelings depend upon a system of inequality in which power/privilege/respect are denied to others on the basis of these standards. And that, my friends, sucks.

Considering my personal background and political commitments, you'd think I'd have an easy time giving diets a big fat (sorry, PHAT) middle finger, and then confidently going along on my way. It isn't so easy.

Given the patriarchal bargain of weight-loss, being radically anti-diet as a political stance doesn't always fit comfortably as a personal stance. Because we live in a society that so horribly punishes women for being "fat," even the most dedicated and body-positive feminists report struggles with their own body image. The threat of becoming a martyr for this cause (i.e., by gaining - or not losing - weight and, thus, giving up our "thin-privilege") is terrifying. As Esther Rothblum so plaintively stated in the title of her chapter of the (highly recommended) book Feminist Perspectives on Eating Disorders, "I'll Die for the Revolution But Don't Ask Me Not to Diet". I know the feeling.

And then there's one more little excruciating personal detail.... In the past 18 months I've gained a (subjectively) uncomfortable amount of weight by treating my body like crap.

How does this happen? Well, I've been struggling with clinical depression for the last year-and-a-half. (Depressing, I know! Sorry!) In a nod to my past issues, I've been using food to help deal with my emotions. It's wonderful that I didn't fall back into extreme food restriction, but... drinking a few glasses of wine most evenings as a "reward" for getting through the day, mindlessly eating a disproportionate amount of high-fat carbs because I crave the serotonin hit, and not-exercising-even-though-I-know-it-would-help-me-feel-better-because-shit-I'm-not-showering-every-day-either-and-I-know-that-would-help-me-feel-better-too... (deep breath)… well, these things aren't so great either. So, yeah, I've gained some weight, and it wasn't exactly in a radical feminist revolt against patriarchal body norms.

So now what is a good feminist to do? Can a feminist diet? I still don't know the answer to this question but I can tell you how I've proceeded.

Step 1: Shun Mirrors for 1 Year.

I hated seeing photos of myself, was saying mean things to my reflection in the mirror, and wanted to lose weight, urgently. My body insecurities were reaching a dangerous peak, and it scared me. Was I on the verge of a relapse? 10 years ago, if I'd gained enough weight to feel uncomfortable in 90% of my wardrobe, I probably would have gone on an extreme diet. It would have been bad. But this time something blissfully self-protective kicked in. I still did something extreme, but in a vastly more body-positive direction: I decided to shun mirrors for a year.

Yep, you read that correctly: I've embarked on a quest to go without mirrors for 365 days.

Stepping away from the mirror has been empowering and helpful. In addition to making me feel like a kick-ass renegade body-positive feminist, it's forced me to actively challenge a lot of my own assumptions about how much my physical appearance impacts my daily life and personal relationships. It also gave me a temporary reprieve from my weight-gain woes because I was able to ignore the issue a bit longer. Yet, turning away from the mirror has not been the same as stepping off of the scale. In fact, after a few weeks without mirrors I became paranoid that I might be rapidly gaining weight without realizing it, and I began to to weigh myself more frequently than before (indeed, I had gained a few more pounds, though not the panic-inducing number I'd imagined). Additional depression ensued.

Step 2: Revamp Eating and Exercise Habits to be Healthfully Moderate. Hope Some Weight-loss Follows.

With my partner's encouragement (he doesn't like depressed / grumpy / unshowered Kjerstin very much), I checked in with my beloved therapist about the situation. We decided that – given my carb-binging, lack of exercise, and weight-misery – it was time for me to set some realistic (i.e., therapist-approved) goals for food and activity. But here's the kicker: to hold myself accountable, I've been tracking these things by following the online version of… a for-profit weight-loss program (cue scary music soundtrack). I don't want to name names here, but the program-of-choice is arguably the ruling matriarch of the entire international diet industry – and, hence, kind of a feminist villain. And now I'm (cringe) paying them $18/month!

As an advocate of the "Health at Every Size" movement (which stresses the importance of healthful behaviours but rejects the idea that there is a universal "healthy weight"), I'm going to try to judge my "success" based on my behaviours, NOT by the number on my scale. The goal is to consciously re-engage in healthful eating habits and joyful activity, and then to accept my body size and shape wherever it settles, even if that place isn't my "dream body". As much as I'm still tempted to "get skinny," I know I can live with this, and (more importantly) I know my body can live through it. But I still hope I lose some weight.

So, yeah… despite being a recovered anorexic and a feminist sociologist, I'm on a flipping diet. Does this make me a hypocrite? Should I be stripped of my feminist merit badges and laughed out of the club? I don't know the answers to these questions, but someday I will.

Anonymous

Finding Miss Maybe

So how does a nice girl like Lisa find the wicked, mischievous Miss Maybe?

I was on my first diet at the age of 9 – of course there was no need – but I did think my legs looked fat in my ski pants (forgive that fashion sin – it was the eighties!). So armed with crispbreads and apples, as I had seen my Nan and mum do, I embarked on what was to become a 24-year battle with my body.

I 'blossomed' early – getting a pair of boobs overnight, not just little teenage ones, but at the age of 9 proper boobs that needed a bra that looked more like something a builder would use to hoist bricks! Of course this caused much hilarity at school – though of course I wasn't laughing.

I moved schools at the age of 12 and my first lesson was something called 'drama' – a wondrous subject. I seemed quite good at it – in fact my ability to make my new class mates laugh was I think the only thing that stopped the prim and proper, naïve new girl from being bullied. However, by now my boobs were definitely coming into the room before me so I was always the subject of bra-twanging, grabbing and comments.

So what does a girl do when she thinks her boobs are making her stand out? Well this girl went on a whole series of diets, you name it – I tried it. Meal replacements, groups – all the time wishing I could be the skinny one of the group.

My dreams of being an actress were met with this response from one of the old ladies I looked after in my after school job: 'Well dear...I don't suppose you have to be pretty and slim to be an actress'

If we move forward a few years to uni, my disappointment in the way I looked led to me doing the opposite to dieting, I began consuming large quantities of bread, pasta, cereal, and chocolate because, try as I might, I could not seem to do this magic thing of losing weight. The highlight of uni was when a friend offered to lend me her MATERNITY dress to wear to the ball as none in any of the shops would fit my chest!

At drama school it did not get any better – 'gems' of advice included:

'You're not exactly pretty, or slim, but not fat enough to be cast as the comic figure, your teeth are a bit wonky, best thing you can do is go into an audition tits first.'

Oh, and the classic from an agent:

'Well...I'm not sure what I'm going to do with you – I mean you're not leading lady looks-wise, but you're too young to play the dragon, you've got to make a decision – are you going to get yourself sorted, or are we going for the hattie jacques? Oh, and your eyes? They're different colours, you might want to get contacts to fix those!'

So, still dieting and now in no doubt that if I ever made it onto a stage it would be a miracle, I happened one day about 6 years ago on a workshop called 'Remove a glove in 6 ways'. It was near my birthday and every year I set myself a personal challenge – and this I felt was it!

This is my response to the questionnaire I had to fill in: My Background: Wanted to be a dancer (as lots of young girls do) but started to develop boobs early and was told that I was 'the wrong shape' to be a dancer'. I then did not dance for 10 years.

All through my adult life people have felt that it was okay to make comments about my figure/face, often making me feel very ugly, and physically unattractive and that my chances of being a successful actress would be hampered by these things – leading to me always being on and off diets and not having much confidence, despite appearing to the world a confident person!

So I did the workshop and it was a light bulb moment! I could move, I could celebrate my curves, I could be powerful and joyful in using my body to express myself (oh and I could have a blooming great time!!!).

Since that time I've slowly started to dip my toe into the world of burlesque – buying the frilly underwear, the vintage clothes, researching, doing workshops wherever I could find them, and finally, 2 years ago, embarking on a decision and action to get fit through dance and exercise and to finally ditch the bloody diets! It was about that time I met Miss Maybe.

Now how shall I describe Miss Maybe?

How does one describe Miss Maybe?

Charming, powerful, sensuous, glamorous, unpredictable, cheeky, fearless, fickle, feisty?

She's all of those and to those minxes that know her best, she's great fun. She even shares her chocolate truffles.

She believes in bubble baths, wind up clocks that chime, steam trains, fountain pens, plenty of high-heeled shoes, veiled hats and red lipstick. But most of all she believes in spreading the word that we should celebrate ourselves, enjoy what we can do and have rollicking good fun doing it!

About 9 months ago I looked in the mirror and started to feel ok about the woman who looked back – and though I am certainly not 'fully there' in the belief that I am great as I am (there are days when I will compare myself to others, or not feel so great), I am the furthest along in believing that I have ever been and now, through my one woman show and my workshops, I want to make other people feel that same sense of joy. I begin my workshop by passing round chocolate or cake and asking the ladies to 'feed their curves' – then I ask them to allow themselves to turn off their inner critic for the next hour, I don't want to hear any one complain about their 'lack of boobs', 'big hips', 'wobbly tummy' – and I ask them instead to celebrate whatever they have and to ENJOY it! My workshops are the highlight of any week for me because of the way I see these ladies change in their attitude to their body.

Lisa Payne

Changing

I have sweaty palms. I can't believe I have sweaty palms. This is ridiculous; people do this all the time. Great – now my legs are weak and the sense of fear is beginning to stifle me. I can't breathe; seriously, I don't think I can breathe. Stay calm; keep composed, everything's going to be fine. My feet reluctantly make their way towards the offending area like a lamb to the slaughter, and I'm greeted by an eighteen year old drop dead gorgeous stick thin waif girl child by the name of Lucy. I know her name is Lucy because she is wearing a 'My name is Lucy' tag above her left, soft – so perky that I don't need to wear a bra – breast. My breasts never stood so firmly on my chest even when I was that age. I think I hate Lucy. She smiles a sickening smile and chirps "How many items do you have?". "Just four", I manage to reply, hoping she'll quickly give me the coloured disc with the big four on it. No such luck. "I'll just check", she twitters, and takes the clothes from my hand and with each item she inspects, she looks at me as if to say "we both know you're not going to get into this size 12 skirt, and red definitely isn't your colour. Who are you kidding?". I crumple as she smiles again and guides me toward the smallest fitting room cubicle imaginable.

I ease out of my clothes and look at my semi-naked body in the 360 degree mirror – yes, now I am able to see how much cellulite my bottom and thighs contain from all angles. Ok, I have the skirt around my knees, but the mission gets harder as I fight with my thighs, I don't understand how this could happen… I only had a Shapers sandwich for lunch. Squeeze, squeeze. Rip. Shit. I stand there looking at my pathetic reflection and I nearly cry as the walking stick approaches my cubicle and asks "Is everything all right in there?". No, everything is not all right in here. "Everything is fine", I tell her. The next few minutes are torture. I now know how magicians feel trying to escape something too small for them. I need some magic to happen now…or at least a miracle. With one almighty tug, the skirt is ripped from my body and has kind of split in two. I get dressed as fast as I can, although the artificial luminous lights send me slightly dizzy, and I fumble out of the cubicle and into Twiggy's stick arms. "Is there anything wrong with the items?", she enquires. "No", I lie, "it fitted perfectly. I'd just prefer it in navy blue."

Charlene James, 26

The Fat Girl in the Corner

Katie: Olivia...
Olivia: Yeah?
Katie: Rosie just said...
Rosie: *Laughs* Shut up Katie...don't...
Olivia: What? ...?
Katie: Rosie just said your ass is huge *laughs*
Rosie: *laughs*
Class: *laughs...and laughs...*
Olivia: *cries...inside*

I am "Olivia" and this was age 13. I was scared. I was scared of me, of how my body was changing, of how other people now judged me because of it. To the world I was - and still am - a toughie. Say anything to Olivia, she doesn't care. It's just a laugh. She's popular, she always has been. She's sports captain, leader of the netball team. Olivia gets top marks in everything, and she's funny, she's sooo funny. *Whispers* But...but Olivia is fat. Olivia is huge...who would ever look twice at Olivia? Well they wouldn't. Not aged 13...14,15,16,17...18, because Olivia is fat. Who cares that she's popular, one of the pretty plastics? Sports captain? Really? Have you seen her! No one cares that she's clever, that she's artistic and smart, and funny? Well duh...she's fat - aren't all fat people jolly? Who cares? No one...because Olivia is FAT. This was me. I never actually said these words myself - "I am Olivia and I am fat". I've never said those words out loud. Because inside I wasn't "fat". I was beautiful. I would sit and listen to the world discuss their weight. "Oh my god I'm sooo huge, I need to stop eating", my size 8 friends would say. But I've never been able to say it to anyone. Maybe... I used to wonder - if I just said it, admitted it, maybe then I could deal with it? But as puppy fat turned to actual fat I closed ranks. I shut the world out. The less I saw people the less they could judge me.

My room became my sanctuary. There was only one person in my room and that was me. I could deal with me. I judged myself yes, but I cared. I judged my attitude, the way I spoke to my mum, I cursed myself for both of those things. I pacified my anger and comforted my hurt, telling myself some day, one day someone will see through all the barriers, the physical and mental barriers that my body, my person puts out. Because deep down I knew, I have always known that the fat exterior hides the beautiful self-assured person deep inside. I would watch as my friends got boyfriends. They would argue and complain about each other. They would cheat, lie, humiliate and disrespect one another. I became the mediator. A "mate" to the boys and a caring friend to the girls, I soon settled in to my inevitable role. I watched as my best friend dated my best mate. He told me the truth as he lied to her face. I saw them all fall in love, in lust, in anger and hate. And throughout it all there I stood as the fat girl in the corner. It didn't matter who I was, who I was friends with, how much I achieved, what I did or how I was.

Because when you are fat, to the world you are simply just that. I am 23 now and I still battle with my body every day, but I'm working on it, I'm working with it and I'm working because of it. That 13-year-old little girl is gone. I've found the confidence to break the cycle; I no longer hide and I'm proud to be me. I still haven't found my prince charming but I've found my body and ultimately I've found myself.

Elle Homer, 23

My Battle with a Wedding Dress

How amazing, I am getting married! The rush of excitement telling the world is huge as I get planning. Not in a Bridezilla kind of a way, I assure you.

I am an independent and hard working woman in my 30s. But I have to say I am still a bit tearful when I think of the proposal. I guess we all have our softer side and my partner certainly brings that out in me.

The wedding however has also seen the worst of my insecurities return. The dress is all anyone wants to talk about and the one thing that I am dreading the most. Now, to put this into perspective, I work in an all girls' school! So you can well imagine the topic of most of the conversations that I have had over the last few months. Everyone has an opinion and this adds fuel to my secret fears.

I overcome the initial terror and book appointments to try on dresses. The 48-hour build up is a ritual of no carbs, super tea and anything else that may help. I purchase some nice but slimming underwear to help me…..

I can't sleep, I am dreading this. The alarm sings like the mocking sales assistant's voice in my ears as I wake and start to feel sick. I am not going to be sick. I promised myself years ago that I would not return to that.

The shop is covered in mirrors, I feel inadequate. The many angles of my face, my bum, my huge boobs…. I start to sweat. Not a good look I tell myself!

Having picked several dresses, I go into the small room to be helped on with the first one. OK, can someone explain to me why sample sizes are so small? I feel huge, unattractive and vile. The assistant pulls and pokes me and then says, "You are going to have to hold it to get an idea". My heart is broken now. This is not how it is in the films. The dress fits, they look amazing and everyone cries. The only person tearful is me. In five minutes, I am feeling fat and ugly and humiliated. The dress is all wrong. The next few dresses follow the same pattern. Then finally, one fits. I hate it and look like an oversized doll, but it fits. I am so happy that I am willing to forget the fact I hate it. The sheer joy at fitting into the dress is overwhelming. Lucky for me my friend tells me that I should look at more.

I leave the shop and I am crushed. How has the most wonderful celebration turned me into a nutter? I start to plan ways of losing weight and looking at how I can hide, as the assistant put it, "my rather huge boobs!".

Well, a good friend and some common sense saved me. I have found a dress and I love it and, more importantly, I love me in it. But it took several more unpleasant and hurtful visits to wedding shops with rude staff. Then I found a shop that made me feel great. The power of words should never be underestimated, so I say to all you bridal assistants in shops across the UK…be nice, be careful and don't judge. We all have our own body image issues, and this is supposed to be a great day not a torture.

To all the brides, I say this…you are so lucky to have found someone who loves you just the way you are. Don't think that he would love you anymore if you were half the size. You would be half the woman he loves and half the fun.

Sarah Spicer, 35

By the Time it Got to the Mantelpiece

I remember when I was a teenager, my mum used to pack me off to Ireland for the summer to my Gran's. She said she needed to not see me for two months to remember how much she couldn't be without me and that I was getting 'a bit English on her' and that a month or two with my cousins would be the right kind of bad influence.

I used to work in this gift shop. This Irish Fiddle-Dee-Die-My-Eye sort of place. We sold stones and bits of flat leaf parsley to Americans telling them it was good luck. Americans or 'poor eejits' as my cousins called them. And they probably called them the same.

It was like the Americans were all made out of rubber. And if rubber could speak it would probably speak in the same high pitched drawl that each (putting on accent) 'Barb', 'Nancy' and 'Drew' did.

Handed over the visa cards with pictures of their grandchildren on them, which were happily accepted. Boom, Boom, Boom.

But we weren't complete sell outs in the shop, we also had the good stuff.

The 'Watherferd Cryhstal' for example. And you couldn't stick that into your carryon luggage, we had to ship that.

I was sort of proud of the Waterford Crystal. It's just timeless. Unique, hand-crafted, Irish and beautiful. Just beautiful. And even though each piece was similar to one of the others, there was always something that set each one apart; a number, an edge, a slant, a pattern change. Each one the same but totally irreplaceable.

So you really had to 'handle with care', 'this side up'.

And it's got this crazy heaviness to it, the Waterford Crystal, this wonderful importance to the glass. This delicate yet enormous weight to each piece and you can just feel, just holding it, that you could puncture someone's brain with it if your aim was right…but it's also got this nerve wrecking fragility to it so that if you, God forbid, dropped it say, or…(smiling) threw it, it would smash into a million pieces (Beat).

I mean there were some less complicated pieces or some with separate bits like a lid or a base, that could be fixed or replaced if it got chipped…but then some of them, a lot of them - well, if they got damaged or (remembering) thrown around… (pause) well they could never be fixed…so you really had to make sure that they were kept safe going into the boxes. And so you did 'handle with care', your job depended on it. No point arriving to 'Barb' or 'Nancy' in bits because some Paddy had been a bit shoddy with the packing.

Each piece, all shiny and new and sparkling, full of possibility, of the possibility of the person who would own it and what they would fill it with or who they would give it to or where it may end up.

And then you got the brown cardboard box from the store room with the right bar code at the side to put it into…always seemed like such ugly packaging for it to start off its journey.

Like throwing icicles into a muddy field and watching them melt…but, you had to keep it safe somehow.

And so then you have to cover them with these Styrofoam nugget things to pad it out.

You know them, they come with everything and you never know how to get rid of them and you still find them stuck to your bloody jumper or clogging up the Hoover three months later.

So anyways, you've got to make sure that you've enough of these shitty little things inside the…shitty box, to keep the not-shitty-at-all thing, safe.

You've got to…stuff them inside to keep it safe and keep it protected.

You've got to make sure that you get hundreds of these stryrocrap pieces of foam

and stuff them two thirds inside the box

and then put the vase in

and then stuff more inside the vase

and then outside the vase

and around the base of the vase

and then keep filling up the box around the sides

and have enough of these things in and around and on top of the vase

so that even if it moves about or it's stored upside down, the packaging is all safe and soft

and no matter which way you turn the box,

or if it's dropped,

or something falls on it,

or someone forgets that what's inside is beautiful and kicks it about… (Pause)

that the vase…inside, the crystal…inside, is safe.

Because it's your job to keep it safe, that's your job.

Who cares how shitty the outside looks, you have to keep what's inside good and safe and intact and together.

So you keep packing it and packing it and stuffing it, thinking you're doing the right thing and the sides of the box begin to bulge and the seams begin to give from the shitty sellotape and soon you just don't have any room for the vase anymore!

So you take it out and put the vase to the side trying to get the packaging right!

Well because no one would want what's in this shitty, bulging, box now.

Who'd give a shit that there's a Waterford Crystal fucking vase in there looking at this? Who'd know that there's a Waterford Crystal fucking vase in there looking at this?

A big, brown cardboard box covered in brown packing tape with stamps and stickers and barcodes and addresses all over it so randomers in the Post Office think they know where it's going and where it's been, but really you have no fucking idea.

So then you try to make it look better so it won't look so crap, so that you wouldn't take one look at the box and not bother to open it up.

You put bows on it and wrap it up and you write all the addresses in gold pen and you wish there was a better box that you could squash it into. Or even better, one with a big picture of the vase on the front so that by just looking at the outside the whole fucking world would just presume that something fucking AMAZING is inside and they'd fucking take their time to bother with it then, wouldn't they?!

But by the time you realise you've spent your whole day there, down on your knees...it's too late to get the post, the box is wrecked and almost as fragile as the vase.

And it's just a piece of tired cardboard full of squeaky white shit with nothing else inside...and you've such a fucking headache trying to make sure someone you don't know is happy.

And I guess what I'm saying is that as long as you get there and no one bothers to open you up, as long as no one looks and you look right, as long as they don't get close enough to see or try to look at you...as long as I'm thin...well, it doesn't matter that I'm full of shit.

Aisling Bea

The Biscuit Tin

The biscuit tin is very near my desk.
I don't have to stand up to reach the biscuit tin.

In my mind I seem to have oversimplified
my condition. And I can petition

the goddess of my worth,
my love, my charity, my mirth,

my words quoted in theatre lights,
distressed friends who can call me at midnight,

finding my way across the US
alone with a map book and a bus pass,

and the catalogue of wondrous men I've loved
and who, too, have loved me.

I have oversimplified my condition.
Conversations rehashed

and in the small of night the penitent lash
(or, at least, the metaphorical sense).

While I inch myself through the sweat
amongst the weights and shoulders,

the treadmill conveyor belt and the spray
every second day,

the biscuit tin is very near my desk.
I don't even have to stand up

to reach the biscuit tin.
I cannot mitigate myself with where I've been,

with what I've done or dreamed.
The truth is, the way my soft stomach looks to me

can signal emotional melt down, even in obscene-
ly expensive jeans. So maybe you can tell me

how in the hell I can create such fervent guilt
if I should dare to sin so cardinally and eat a cookie?

Sarah Alison Wells, 32

Another Way to Be

Fat, fat, fat… Jeez, will you look at the size of that stretch mark!… Two hundred and fifty-seven calories, if I eat that I'll have to skip pudding tonight… Thirty, thirty-one, thirty-two, just one more lift… A fourteen? Since when am I a fourteen?… 'The desert menu? I'd better not, thanks'… Hark at her, skinny bitch… Oh God, he's gonna kiss me; I should've waxed my bikini line… Six biccies. Six. Well, that's blown it. Might as well finish the pack… Keep on running, keep on running, keep on running, keep on running… Good grief, is that a whisker!… 'Yes, I did notice Jen had lost weight. Yes, she looks amazing. Atkins was it?'… Stupid, pathetic, weak… How much fat in a frappuccino?… Yes! Result! If I lie down and breathe in hard I can do up the old jeans!… 'So I said to her, you want to watch how much you eat now you're pregnant; that eating for two thing's a pile of…' I hate shopping. Nothing fits. I'm the wrong shape… Da da da da da da DA, da da da da da DA, wineshgood but sh'very naughty… Urgh, that podgy bit spilling over the top of these stockings looks minging! How can he possibly find this a turn on?… Oh wow, this chocolate cheesecake's orgasmic; a laxative'll clear it… No, no, no! It's meant to be dusky blonde! Why's it gone green? I should've gone to the salon… 'What are you getting? A burger? You're right, I think I'll go for salad too'… A hundred and fifty quid? Are you kidding me? Ah well, it'll be worth it when those crows' feet disappear… 'I'm fine, I'm fine. Just a dizzy spell. What? Of course I'm eating enough. It's my time of the month, you know'… This abs class is torture. Repeat after me: no pain no gain… Jesus, look at her. She's stunning. I'm keeping this cardie on all night. No way is she getting a peek at my bingo wings… I want a cheese sandwich. No, naughty. Oh but I want it. No, it's too late in the evening to snack. Oh but the cheese is calling to me. Get a grip, woman!... These heels are killing me; at least my calves look good... So that's three hundred cals for the porridge, two hundred and fifty for the sandwich, fifty for the apple and four hundred for the diet ready meal; hmmm, perhaps if I just have one square of chocolate... 'Close your eyes. Because I don't like you watching me get dressed, that's why'... Just two more pounds, just two more... Ouch, damn you, stairmaster burn... Whoever said beauty's only skin deep was talking bollocks... Tomorrow'll be a good day. It's all about structure and control... What. The. Effing. Heck. Is. THAT. On. My. Chin!... A velour tracksuit, I mean, what is she thinking?... 'I could've been a ballerina, you know, but my arse is too big'... He says my cellulite is cute, like little dimples. Is he teasing me?... 'She lost forty kilos and then she married a footballer'... He can't stop staring at my lopsided boobs. Yes, I'm a freak show; buy a ticket, why don't you?... That's it. I'm buying a balaclava ... There's nothing for it: it's all-in-one-control-body-suit time. Who needs to move/bend/eat/wee/breathe anyway?... 'Yes, I'm aware my bikini line is fast approaching my knees. Just wax it, will you'... Childbearing hips? What the devil does that mean?... Oh crap, a Christmas buffet. I feel a tactical vom coming on... Bloody Swiss ball, why do they have to be so rolly'... Blimey, she's let herself go since she got with him... I mean, would Edward love Bella if she was stout and sturdy?... Bad girl, bad girl... Ha! I showed you, huh? Now who's super skinny?... 'Another diet coke, please'... He's gone. Thank God, now I can stop holding my tummy in... Camel hoof! Gah!... My head aches. Man I'm hungry... Not good enough, not good enough... A rib! I can see a rib!... Disgusting pig... Just a few more pounds, then I'll be happy...

Continual.

Controlling.

Crippling.

Consuming.

Draining.

Depressing.

Demoralising.

Disempowering.

But what if there was another way to feel, another way to think, another way to be? What if, instead of food and body and beauty and exercise and calories and fat, there was just calm? Quiet. Peace. Acceptance. Joie de vivre.

What if there were no limits and no judgement – no naughty, no bad, no fat, no ugly, no not good enough? What if there was time and space and energy for so much more in life? For laughing. For loving. For sharing. For creating. For experiencing. For being all that you can be and all that you want to be.

What if there was just you, just you, just as you are? Lovely, loving, loveable you.

Just you.

Pippa Wilson, 31

I am Fat and that is Fine

As a 'big girl' I go through phases of questioning, worrying about, agonising over this state, and very long periods of not thinking about it at all. Recently, I've found myself in a questioning phase; a problem of definition. I have no problem with calling myself 'fat'. I simply am. To my ears, my own voice using this term isn't hateful or self-loathing, it denotes nothing but the truth of my body. I have no problems self-defining as fat. Everyone else, however, seems reluctant to afford me the same luxury. I remember, maybe 5 years ago, referring to myself as fat in front of a friend. 'But you're not!', he cried, 'you're not fat!'. He seemed to think he was reassuring me, appeasing me, whether or not he was telling the truth. What I couldn't muster the energy to say to him then, and what I've since learnt to say succinctly and with dignity, is that denying my fatness is denying me the right to be attractive. When I say 'I'm fat', I'm making a pronouncement on my size and my body. The colour of my eyes, the way I look after my nails, the shape of my lips, the length of my eyelashes; none of this has anything to do with my size. And besides, what if I like my thighs, my chubby upper arms, my fleshy, surgery-scarred stomach? Denying that I'm fat is denying me the chance to find any beauty in it.

I feel uncomfortable when bigger girls talk about how they wouldn't want to be skinny, how they would never want 'hips like a 12-year-old boy' or a flat chest or how much they like being 'womanly' because that's just the same, confidence-crushing bullshit they've put up with all their lives but flipped over against some other girl. I don't want to make anyone feel bad about their body, I don't want to pronounce on what is, in general, an 'acceptable' size or shape. I want everyone and anyone and their aunt and their puppy to feel like it's ok to be the way they are, and if they're already happy with it, then that's even more ok.

When magazines or, indeed, other humans talk about 'real women' and their 'curves' it makes my blood boil. Ok, so we've had years and years of one 'heroin chic' look, and now we're trying to atone for it, but I don't think that Kate Moss circa 1994 or Gwyneth Paltrow or Amy Winehouse are holograms… are they? I mean, they're real in the sense that I haven't just made them up for the purposes of this blog post. And they're anatomically women as far as I know, right? So where's the beef? Is it guilt and shame that makes magazines so keen to call Christina Hendricks 'real' because they know that until a couple of years ago, her and Adele and… well, that's about it, would never have got a look in?

I don't think I'm somehow superior because I'm fat. I just like being me. I find waking up in the morning and looking in the mirror satisfying. I enjoy my appearance, whether or not you do. And that's priceless.

However: fashion magazines, the media, our global culture teach us that thin is preferable to fat, which is why it seems so much harder for fat girls to realise they even have the option to like themselves. And I mean girls like me or Beth Ditto, who are actually fat, not girls like Christina Hendricks or Lara Stone who seem to exist solely to make fash mags feel like they're good people because they're using pictures of someone above an A-cup. It is hard to be fat and to like yourself. Fatphobia, fat-shaming and plain old fat hate are so, so ingrained in our culture that people don't even think twice about the fact they, instinctively, attach a lower value to 'fat' than 'thin'. I'm speaking as someone with friends who think Keira Knightley has 'big thighs'. I work in an environment where it's assumed that fat people don't wear high heels. Even plus-size retailers don't have the respect or common sense to use appropriately sized models or mannequins to promote their clothes. To paraphrase, (I believe, correct me if my memory has failed me) Lionel

Shriver in 'We Need to Talk About Kevin', the greatest thing a Western woman can achieve is a protruding ribcage or a visible spine: she wears it as a badge of honour. We are trained to hate fat. By rights, even I should hate fat. I should hate looking at my fat legs, I should be ashamed of my fat arms, I should be wearing a tent-like apparatus to conceal my fat stomach, I should grow my nails long to elongate my fat fingers.

But that's bullshit.

I live once. I am blessed with one body, and one mind and I've worked hard to reconcile the two. I'm 21. I wear what I want. I seek romance with people I find attractive. I got over my heel-dragging and nerves and took an internship at a women's glossy fashion magazine where I look like no-one on the staff, because I want to be a journalist and I want to be fearless. I stand up for myself. I stand up for others. I write my blog to help other people understand that you have a choice, that you only live once, that regret and resentment and denial are a life wasted. I have trained myself not to assume that the fat on my body means I am worth less, deserve less, that I appeal to no-one, that I shouldn't wear what I want, that no one will want to date me or sleep with me or be my friend, that it will always be me who gets rejected, that as a fat girl, I can't be fussy about who I'm kissing. As a wonderful man said to me over dinner in Montréal one night, 'For some people it's a deal-breaker; for others, it sweetens the deal'. It's a sign of weakness on my part that I had ever assumed that potential partners would be deterred by my fat and that the same men or women would love me any more for weighing less. But the man was right; as well as doing myself a disservice, I'm doing a disservice to anyone that would potentially find me attractive.

Do people think I've never looked in the mirror? Do they think I've never seen a photo of myself, or bought clothes? Are they so keen to push their terror of fat onto me by denying me the right to be fat, and telling me I'm not? Are they conscious of the fact that by denying my fatness, they're implicitly unpicking years and years of hard work, of hard knocks and of blows to my confidence to find the courage to enjoy being myself in the face of overwhelming opposition? Their cowardice in not being able to acknowledge that I am fat translates to disbelief that I am or could ever be attractive or beautiful or stylish or deserving of romance or a personal style. No one in the public eye that's considered beautiful or a positive role model looks anything like me. At least slim girls know they're doing ok because they see, every single day, photos of models and actresses and singers that basically look like a variation on their theme. Not me. I had to figure this all out for myself. Up against all this bullshit, it'd probably be easier to lose weight than to develop any kind of backbone or self-love.

I'm going to wear horizontal stripes, tight skirts, short dresses, weird textures, a blunt fringe, high heels, skinny jeans, small florals, and whatever else takes my fancy, even if a fashion editor would vomit with disgust on sight. I have the choice and I choose to be fat and fucking marvellous, not one or the other.
I am fat. That is fine.

Bethany Rutter, 21

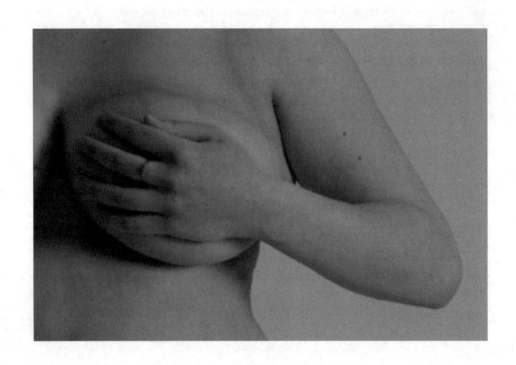

Chapter 3

BOOBS

When it comes to body parts, nothing seems to hold our collective attention more than the allure of the bosom. Their appeal, we've learned, is universal. Male or female, gay or straight, we're a Nation obsessed with norks.

At Body Gossip, we're at opposite ends of the chest divide. Whilst Ruth's are small, perky and in keeping with her athletic frame, Tash owns bras which could double up as a tent for a family of badgers.

So we were interested to hear the stories in this chapter, which focus on those things literally closest to your heart...

My First Bra

So I'm 14 years old and I'm in a small room with a tiny Thai woman, taking my clothes off.

Now, this isn't as bad as it sounds. For starters, we're in the changing rooms in John Lewis, and the little woman is a professional 'boob-measurer', and we are here because despite last getting fitted for a bra 3 months ago, already I'm having to clutch my bosom with both hands whenever I make any sudden movements to stop it escaping.

I turn around, topless, to face her and she gasps. Actually gasps.

'How old are you, sweetheart? 14?? You ARE very well-developed, aren't you? My daughter, she is nearly 25, she isn't near your size!' She continued to exclaim loudly over the size of my chest, whilst people wandered up and down the rows of cubicles outside, and my face turned beetroot. Then she sent one of the shop assistants out to find something with enough reinforcement, probably from the section entitled 'Matronly and constructed by shipbuilders – Size DD+'

I am DD+. I'm actually an E cup, and bordering an F. Busty-ness runs in my family, and I've learnt in the 8 years or so since I was first visited by the puberty-fairy that with large boobs, comes certain problems and expectations.

Number one is that no one who doesn't themselves possess a massive pair will ever understand why you would complain about them. Smaller-busted ladies wave their wonderbras with extra padding in your face and cry 'But I'd give anything to have them naturally! You're so LUCKY!' And guys...at best they look at you with utter incomprehension (I mean, big boobs = good, right?) Or, you get treated to 'If I was a girl with boobs like yours, I'd just look at them in the mirror. All day. I'd never go out again.'

Tell anyone over a DD cup, on the other hand, and you're likely to get nods of recognition. There's the back pain, for one. Having to wear a bra at all times, even in the house, to stop everything poking out and ensure that you don't have to clutch one boob in each hand every time you go up or down some stairs. There is the knowledge that, as you age, they will head so far south that you will eventually be able to play 'keepie-uppie' with them, gently bouncing them off of your knees.

The fact that, if you're under 30, very few shops for your age group will stock many tops and dresses that will suit you. Backless dresses, anyone? Crew-neck tops? Loose smock-tops and t-shirts, seemingly specially designed to hang off the end of your boobs like a shelf, giving you that '6-months pregnant' look that is so very, very popular.

Dressing them for a night out brings its own set of problems. Large boobs do not suit high or restrictive necks as a rule, so often the only way to dress attractively with a large bust is to get it out. Scoop and v-necks are where it's at. Ditto sweetheart necklines. If there's a bit of cleavage on show, if the area immediately below your collarbones and ideally a bit lower is out, then that improves your outline considerably. This does however mean that every time you bend over to fix your shoe or lean over the bar, a certain kind of man in the vicinity will take this as his cue to grab you, stare at you unblinkingly, or make comments that you didn't ask for and don't need to hear. Their reasoning? 'Her cleavage is out, so she's clearly asking for it.'

I've experienced this first hand since I was 14 years old – at school, in the pub, on the street – shouted from vans and bus stops, often by men old enough to be my dad. To a young teenager, it felt frightening and complimentary at the same time, as though I was being congratulated for the momentous achievement of growing a large chest, something which I had no control over. Now I'm in my twenties, it's irritating. And sometimes still frightening. I've encountered men who think nothing of posting things down my front, asking if they can cop a feel or if it makes it hard to run for a bus. Hell, I've had women come up to me in the toilets of clubs and pubs and compliment me on them, sometimes by patting or cupping them - as though by virtue of having big breasts I'm giving the world permission to comment on them, and by dressing in a way that emphasizes them (rather than trying and failing to hide them), I'm actually inviting those comments.

There is disproportionate importance attached to these two pieces of fat and tissue stuck to a woman's front. They are taken to be indicators of everything from promiscuity to intelligence, particularly in younger women. I joke about them a lot because I don't want others to get in with their jokes first, and try to dress in a way that embraces them, rather than swaddling them in layers of oversized jumpers, as I did when I was 14 and still slightly embarrassed by them. I've accepted that, whilst I'm slim, I'll never be one of those waifs who can waft around in a loose backless top, and mine is a figure that needs to be dressed with a narrow waist and lower front - regardless of the reaction that this may elicit from idiots who think that I'm dying to hear their every thought on my body. I am largely happy with the way I look, even though it brings certain practical problems, as it's a healthy body, and the one that I grew into, and yes, very occasionally I may be guilty of leaning a bit far over the bar, so that my friends and I get served quickly.

That said, I do think that I'll have a reduction if I can afford it in my middle-age, so that I can go on the treadmills at the gym without doing myself an injury. It would be quite nice to be able to run without hitting myself in the face.

Megan Evans, 21

I Hate Big Boobs (and I Cannot Lie)

I hate big boobs and I cannot lie
People laughed and I just cried
It really smarts
When the builders laugh
And you're only
Fourteen!

Yep – that's my story. I've worn fully under-wired bras since the age of 10 and at 21 it still gets to me a bit. High Street clothes just don't fit girls (or women, for that matter) with "novelty" proportions – having a teeny waist and giant boobs sounds idyllic, but when that teeny waist is drowned in a size 16 top the effect is somewhat lost! Also, when you're upset because you have back pain nobody gives you any kind words – just "Shutupatleastyou'vegotboobs!!" As if that's a comfort! I weighed mine once for a laugh: 8kgs later and I felt the joke was on me.

There's a dark side to this story too however. At the age of 17 and having been ignored by doctors who told me I was "lucky" to be a HH cup (yes, they do exist),

I tried to lose weight. I lost three stone in one year and went from weighing 10st to 7st by throwing up 3 times a day. I was desperate: my back ached, people stared and my 6th form shirt would randomly burst open and reveal whatever matronly maternity bra I managed to find in my price-range. I felt even more ashamed when I started fainting at school and nobody knew why because I still couldn't fit into clothes smaller than a 14. I got more and more depressed and began drinking and smoking heavily and come August 17th 2007 I failed all my AS Levels and realised that I jeopardised my whole future just because I couldn't wear the same pretty, feminine tops my friends wore.

After a lot of hard work and an extra year at school I did get into university – not the one I wanted, granted, but I realise now (with the clarity that only hindsight can bring!) that I am different. I could probably make a fortune as a page 3 girl if I wanted to and that I've just got to accept that what your shape is doesn't matter and that no amount of celery and vomiting in the school toilets is going to make you become your idea of "perfection". I wouldn't shout out what I did from the rooftops but I want you (yes you, reading this!) to know that you aren't the only one, and that one day you will realise that you've got dissertations, or meetings, or children, or bills and mortgages to worry about and life will slide into a more comfortable perspective. And besides, celery tastes vile.

Sophie Power, 21

I Just Want to be Normal!

I'm Jess. Also known as Tess. Going to a high school is a very weird situation. You get the fake Barbies, the real friends which you love to bits and then there's me, I'm very individual I love the way I look but sometimes I wish I never had a big bum and biggish boobs. I will tell you why. When you constantly have boys touching you up in lessons and at break on the stairs it gets very annoying. I put up with it every day and it doesn't get on my nerves no more because I'm used to it but I wish I had no bum and small boobs at times, who would think that? Being quite pretty and attractive in my year at school I also find it hard as well because I constantly have boys making up lies about other boys and all I want is to have a proper boyfriend who treats me right and doesn't like me for what I look like!! Is that too much to ask?

I don't think it is and now I am fed up of being treated like this I start to tell the boys who do it to me and to be honest they do not listen, even giving a hug they have to touch my bum and why the hell - is it like a magnet? No it isn't!! :(I just want to be normal!!

Jessica Packman, 14

Ode To Small Boobs

While other bosoms rise like lusty seas,
Upon the chests of bootylicious girls,
Now mine are less like melons more like peas,
Or at a push like mini Viennese whirls.

They hardly earn the common name of baps;
A secret I like to keep under-wraps.
So, under-wiring and a padded bra,
To make them more desirous from afar.

But at some point the armour must come off,
How can I feel even slightly yummy?
I'm full of fear my boyfriend might just scoff,
Cos my boobs are smaller than my tummy.

Although it seems my cares could be misplaced…
They say more than a handful is a waste.

Anna Cookson, 30

Breasts, bangers, boobs, baps

This is a story about my breasts, or rather The Breasts, as I like to call them. This makes them sound almost as though they don't actually belong to me. They do, they are attached and everything but they seem to have a will of their own. They were just normal breasts until around the time I turned 17 and then they took over my body. I was my breasts, my breasts were me. People, and by people I mean men, stopped looking me in the eye. Their gaze never left my chest area. I took to looking down and feigning surprise, dusting off an imaginary speck of dirt from my cleavage, trying to shame them into looking where I wanted them to look. I wore huge baggy tops and started hunching my shoulders in slightly, anything to draw attention away from the damn things. I resented them; resented the identity they gave me. I refused to be defined by my breasts. I wanted to be taken seriously. I felt like my body was conspiring against me. I had long blonde hair and big breasts, was this some kind of joke? I tried too hard to sound intelligent and assumed everybody thought I was an idiot when in actual fact I'm sure nobody cared. They were too busy worrying about their own issues, their too small breasts, enormous nose, wonky knees (I have those too), funny toes, etc.

In the media we are bombarded with mixed messages. We see breasts everywhere, lovely big, shiny surgically enhanced ones, popping out of tight dresses in the gossip pages of magazines, always with the assumption that if you have big breasts you are only about one thing. That one thing is sex and I wasn't sure I wanted to be carrying round such a huge sexual statement. People assume certain things about you when you have breasts the size of mine. One woman accused me of 'always sticking them out'. I ignored her, I really couldn't be bothered to explain that when they are the size that mine are they are quite capable of sticking themselves out with no extra help needed from me. Men assume they have permission to comment on them as you walk past, like I've stuck them there for that very purpose, for their entertainment. In books and films you never get a serious/interesting/clever character with big bababbas; they are always the flighty one, the ditsy secretary, the femme fatale. If a character has big breasts then that is what she is, there's no room for anything else in her personality. If a character is going to be murdered, it'll be the one with the double d's.

I never attracted the kind of boyfriends I wanted when I was a teenager; the moody, skinny goth boys all went for the moody, skinny goth girls. I made a point of having boyfriends who weren't that interested in what I had down my top but that backfired too as I wanted it both ways. I wanted someone who loved my body AND my mind. It was a case of 'pay them attention, but not too much, unless I want you to and that depends on how I'm feeling on that particular day'. They didn't stand a chance.

I grew up a bit, got myself some self-confidence and a decent fitting bra and stopped obsessing quite so much. They were still there though. Tolerable on most days, hated on others. In the winter they made my jumpers look awkward and bulky and meant I couldn't fasten my coat up properly. In the summer they were too hot and prevented me from wearing little vesty tops with no bra and playing volley ball. (Not that I've ever had a desire to play volley ball in my life, but it would be nice to know that I could if I wanted to, ok?) Clothes that could look quite classy and stylish on the hanger could look positively indecent once these babies were stuffed inside them. From Audrey Hepburn to page three lovely in one swish of the changing room curtain.

Then I got pregnant. My breasts grew but then so did my stomach and for once they seemed small compared to my huge bump. I felt in proportion. At a time when most people start wearing long baggy tops I started wearing tighter clothes, I was proud of my shape. It felt natural. I gave birth and suddenly my breasts weren't just there to irritate me, they had a job to do, they were keeping a person alive. I regularly 'got 'em out' (albeit discreetly) in public and didn't care, they finally had a purpose. I was now faced with the paradox of breasts. It's apparently acceptable to have them displayed across advertising boards if they are trying to sell us something but those same men who ogle them in a magazine often take offence at the sight of you breastfeeding in public, as if to say 'how dare you?

Didn't you know that breasts are sacred?!' This all helped feed the feeling that actually, they don't belong to me at all.

I breastfed my daughter until I got pregnant with my next daughter, and then fed her too so all in all I was probably breastfeeding for about 3/4 years. When my youngest stopped I actually felt pleased about having my breasts to myself again, I'd missed them. Admittedly they had changed shape slightly but they were still all mine. My tops stayed tight, my necklines low. I felt womanly and curvy and they were a source of pleasure. We finally seemed to be able to inhabit the same body without too much conflict.

Recently a good friend of mine was diagnosed with breast cancer. She's facing a double mastectomy and now my earlier angst seems shallow and pointless. It seems crass to moan about my breasts to someone who is about to have hers taken away. Talking to her about her operation has made me think about how I would feel about losing mine and as much as they have annoyed me over the years they are such a huge (excuse the pun) part of me, I'd be lost without them. As I've got older I feel proud of the identity they give me.

So now I love them. They may jiggle when I walk and attract unwanted attention. They may cost a small fortune to support (no pretty little dainty bras that cost a tenner for me, my bras have a suspension system to rival the Humber Bridge).They may disappear under my armpits now when I lay down (there is not a sexual position in the world that makes your stomach look flat AND your boobs look pert without the help of an intricate pulley system) and they may mean that my career as an international volley-ball player will never quite hit those dizzying heights of success. But they are mine, they are healthy and they are completely adored by my boyfriend. My breasts and I may have had a bit of a rocky start but we are beginning to enjoy our journey together and although they may have caused me a certain amount of embarrassment (the supermarket delivery man who was treated to an impromptu wardrobe malfunction as I bent down to retrieve my shopping may never recover) I wouldn't be without them for the world.

Tracy Tidswell, 38

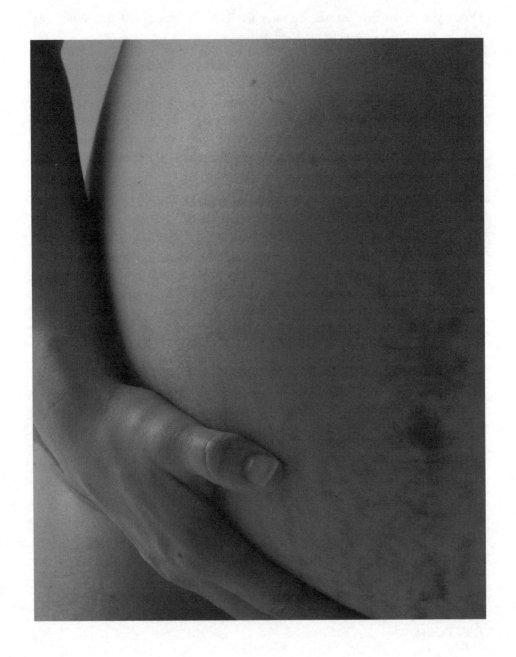

Chapter 4

MAKING BODIES

For all our musings on the breast front, as seen in Chapter 3, often we forget that they have a practical purpose (i.e. feeding babies).

Neither Ruth nor Tash are Mothers, but we've often suspected that women who go all misty-eyed when asked about the realities of pregnancy and childbirth and tell us it's "just magical" might be...well, lying.

So we're fascinated to receive pieces which reveal the realities of creating life and the diverse experiences of women all over the country (turns out there are a gazillion ways to have a baby - who knew?) Get ready for a candid chapter.

Losing Control of the Machine

Pregnancy triggered in me emotions familiar to those I suffered in puberty.

My body took on a life of its own, underwent changes I never gave approval to. I lost control over this machine. These physical changes, which in puberty testified to a blossoming sexuality and in pregnancy to an active sexuality, an innately private matter, were to my horror manifesting themselves overtly.

In both cases, my fumbled attempts to conceal these changes were betrayed.

Anonymous

Pregnant Goddess

I never used to like my body. I tolerated it and it tolerated me. My brain always felt like it was operating separately with a vague contempt for the lumpen practicality of the flesh, its boring, predictable and repetitive needs. I felt it was my enemy, taking the focus off the me inside, the real me, the one that was just underneath and begging to be noticed. It was a traitor - never looking the way I imagined it did in my head. It wouldn't be ignored, it wouldn't go away, it wouldn't let me think and dream and learn in peace.

Then I got pregnant, not once, but twice in five years. The needs of the body increased, doubled with the growing burden inside. I was forced out of my ivory tower and into practical reality. But I liked it. To my surprise the more I grew and swelled, the more uncomfortable it was to sit and lie and stand, the happier I felt. I was a goddess, I was a queen, I was doing something amazing - my body was doing something amazing. I stroked my belly, oiled it, talked to it, enjoyed the fact that my body was doing something so simple, so complex, so natural. I displayed it in tighter clothes than usual, strutted proudly around in a way I had never done before, full of this pure simple joy in what I was accomplishing.

When it came to the birth, my previously neglected body showed a natural talent I had never suspected. Birth was the greatest pleasure of all, a deep, dark, primal experience that left me smiling for weeks, months, years. Inside my head, with the help of my body, I reached a place previously unreachable, untouchable. I completely escaped from the world around me, at one with the child attempting to breach the confines of my womb and we worked together, in peace, to bring them into the world.

Now I love my body. I love the lumpy bits, hairy bits, scarred bits, the long scars on my stretched stomach that are a reminder of my child's first home, the journey that my body and my brain went on together. I want to show my daughter that a body, a real female body, is a thing of great beauty and power and is never something to be ashamed of. I feel so sad that I passed all those years barely tolerating my form, unappreciative and unhappy with myself. Now we are a team. Now I love myself completely.

Sarah Drew, 29

Turning the Light On

(Bethany, a woman in her late thirties, enters in a panic pushing a shopping trolley.)

Bethany: I'm holding the fish fingers when here it comes, a wave of heat snaking through my body and all of a sudden I'm trebling head to toe. The woman in the pickle aisle is watching me and I can feel her eyes hot on the back of my neck, but I can't stop myself and the fish fingers seem to slide away from my hands. And the beeps from the checkout counters seem to rise in volume (The sound of a price scanner's beep becoming her heart beat, it gets faster and louder as she continues). And I'm hot, I'm terribly hot, and I seem a long way away from half fat, low fat, low calorie, low sodium. I'm in high cholesterol territory now! And the fluorescent strip lighting seems to burn down on me and I'm choking under my coat and my top's clinging to me in a sweaty death lock and I'm sure the skirt's cutting off circulation. I can't breathe and a terrible thought comes over me, what if I die?! So I'm tearing off the coat and ripping at the top, it has to come off because I cannot die with a cart full of ice cream and Yorkshire puddings. And I'm wriggling out of the skirt (the scanner beep tails off). And it takes just a second, a second for mothers to stuff nappies into their carts to tug off their toddlers from their ankles, for the guy stacking the shelves to stop picking his nose and the old lady to notice the weight of the jar she'd pulled from the shelf, and let it fall, smashing as it hit the sticky floor, pickle corpses rolling out, indiscriminately bumping into children and shop assistants. It took a second more for the noise of the shop to stop rolling in, as people stopped, stunned, all looking at me standing there in the frozen food aisle. And I finally realise it, I'm naked in Asda.

Normal people do not do naked, they especially do not do naked in a major supermarket and I especially don't do naked! I haven't looked at myself properly since I had children. It's not like I intentionally planned to avoid my body, it just happened slowly over time. At first I put it down to being too busy with the children; I stopped going swimming I told myself because I was too tired. I had got out of the habit of taking showers when I was pregnant, standing up with a huge bump and trying to reach round for the soap is near on impossible. I'd take bubble baths as it was more relaxing. Then the light bulb went out in my bedroom so I had to change in an out of my pyjamas in the dark. I didn't even contemplate clothes shopping. Fashion seems to ignore the post pregnancy body. This is all the stuff I told myself. All the reasons I explained for everything below my neck to become a stranger to me. The real reason is I caught sight of one of my breasts while feeding Jack in a cafe window, I glanced up and there was this alien thing, something which used to be my breast. But it wasn't the shape I remembered; instead it flapped down like a deflated balloon and the nipple stretching out like a broken yolk. From then on nakedness became the enemy. My baths were bubble filled so the foam would skim over my lumps and bumps and the light bulb in my bedroom was never replaced. It started off with little things like that but after a while me and my body kept missing one another. I'd catch a glimpse of my veined thighs occasionally on the toilet, or of my belly as I pulled off a jumper in a rush. But other than that, me and my body were quite happy to be acquaintances, catching each other only on the odd occasion.

I thought all this quite normal until I met Gary. He asked me out for coffee, after I apologetically handed over a fist of his daughter's hair, which Jack had torn out over a dispute for play dough. At first I thought he was being polite, but coffee turned into dinner and dinners turned into movies. Then something awful happened. Something me and my body hadn't conceived. Sex. There we were – me, him and the body. And even though it was in the dark, I could feel every wretched piece of me as I felt his hands caress me. I imaged myself as a small, inflatable bouncy castle, or rather like the Michelin man. After that the diets began, low GI, low fat, low calorie and with them came the panic attacks.

Then came the episode in Asda. After that I realised I needed help. I've started going to therapy. I get set tasks. On Wednesday Gary had to tell me what he liked about my body and I had to listen. I wanted to cry when we did that. On Thursday I had to talk to my breasts. I laughed at that one. Today I changed the light bulb in my room and for the first time I turned on the light and took off my clothes.

Amber Dodd, 21

A Few Home Truths

I thought giving birth was the most painful thing my body would ever go through. I couldn't believe it when I went into labour, I thought something must be really wrong – surely it wasn't supposed to hurt this much. Women give birth every day and I assumed it would be a bit painful, but no amount of maternity classes or reading baby books could have prepared me for the reality. Afterwards when the midwife (who I did not like) told me that it had been an "easy, uncomplicated birth" I held my peace, what would she know after all? So, I was fairly confident that I had been through and survived the worst my body would ever have to take.

Six weeks after my daughter was born I started getting intense stomach pains and horrendous wind. I went to the doctor and was told I had adult colic, then IBS, then gall stones. I subjected myself to all the advice and medications they suggested, but nothing seemed to affect the pain. The doctors at my surgery thought I was time wasting, the look of "Oh no not this one again", was something I became accustomed to seeing. I started to feel really down, no-one seemed to think that there was anything much wrong with me, but the pains were so bad that I couldn't eat or sleep. I managed to go to work, but spent very little time with my husband or daughter as all I could do when I came home was go to bed. The pain went on for eighteen months. I had always had a problem with my weight and had never been slim, but after eighteen months of being unable to eat much I became thinner and thinner. My hips stuck out and you could see my ribs.

Eventually I was in so much pain that I convinced my husband to call an ambulance. I believed that I was dying but the first hospital I went to just gave me some strong painkillers and sent me home. By this time I was on the list for an operation to remove gall stones so the medical staff assumed that this was the problem. A couple of days later I had to call an ambulance again, this one took me to a different hospital where they decided to do exploratory surgery as my white blood cell count was so high. This told them that something was wrong, even if they could not work out what. Scared but mostly agonised I agreed to the surgery. When I woke up they told me that they had found a huge abscess inside me. An infection had started on one of my fallopian tubes and developed and grown. It had taken over my gall bladder, appendix and large parts of my bowel – all of which my surgeon had removed. The infection had grown and mutated over the months I was ill, developed into the abscess and basically "eaten" my bowel and organs, hence the horrendous pain I had been in.

It was very difficult to adjust after the operation, physically and emotionally. I had spent so long telling myself that there was nothing wrong with me that to find out the truth was quite shocking. It was not easy for many of the people around me either as they had been given the same information I had. My body was so weak from eighteen months of being ill and barely eating that it took me a long time to recover. As large portions of my bowel were removed, I had and still have digestive problems that will be with me for the rest of my life. I also have a huge scar on my stomach and a mutilated belly button.

Would I change anything that happened six years on now that I am well and coping? If I could, I would but as it is I am just happy to be alive. I am healthier and fitter than I ever was before my illness and the pain and inability to eat have taught me to think about my relationship with food in a very different way. Now I understand that it is fuel, of course you can enjoy it, but essentially you need it to keep your body going. Would I have surgery to hide my scar and beautify my belly button? No – after my experiences I would never willingly volunteer for an operation that was not strictly needed.

Steph Edwards, 33

Not So Perfect

One last big push and a massive yell and finally it's all over. The alien that's been growing inside of me for the last 9 months flops onto the bed and I lay back exhausted. For 9 whole months my stomach has been slowly stretched to the size of a space hopper and my breasts are like a couple of water balloons. Now space hoppers and balloons don't look half bad when fully inflated, but 10 minutes after giving birth the half deflated look is not very attractive. My hair is plastered to my head and my cheeks are crimson. I am covered in a variety of bodily fluids, some of which I'm sure are not mine, and I have been yelling the most obscene things at anyone who even dared pop their head round the door. The image I had of the birth of my first child was so not like this. I was meant to pop out a rosy cheeked little angel whilst remaining serene and glowing. It hadn't gone quite as planned. And yet despite all of this my partner, Stuart, looks lovingly at me, and tells me I look absolutely beautiful and that our new baby daughter is perfect just like me. Tears well up in my already blood shot eyes and I sob uncontrollably.

Stuart holds my hand as I lie there with my legs in stirrups while a nice little doctor sits with his head between my legs sewing me back together. He calls Stuart round to show him his handy work and both of them tilt their heads to one side and Stuart says, "that's perfect" and smiles that loving smile once more. Later in the hospital bathroom, I balance with one leg up on the basin and angle a compact mirror between my legs. My goodness, it's hideous!!! How can anyone in their right mind find that even the slightest bit attractive.

20 years on, I have lost most of the baby weight, having had 2 more since, and I keep myself fairly fit. I get my hair done and I still have all my own teeth. So why is it that I'm not so perfect now?

My breasts are still a reasonable size, although they are a bit more like sand in socks now. And my hips aren't quite as slim as they were then. "How do I look?" I ask, having spent an hour in the bathroom attempting to persuade my face and body to look mid thirties and not mid forties. I successfully managed to squeeze into size 14 jeans and with a lot of persuasion with hot irons and hair gel, my hair was looking reasonably fashionable. I stand in front of Stuart waiting for his approval. I should have known not to have asked him just as Ronaldo got possession. "For God's sake, woman, it's the quarter final!" I still stand there waiting for a sliver of a compliment. Ronaldo misses and the half time whistle goes. "Well?" I ask. He grabs his crotch and rearranges himself (men have to do that because it's complicated down there, apparently) and all he manages to say is "Did you mean to have that roll of fat hanging over the top of your jeans?" I leave the house completely deflated while he goes for a pee before the second half.

I meet my friend Mary and after a few bottles of Chardonnay I feel a lot better. We end up chatting to two very good looking young men. Mary and I nip off to the ladies, not for a wee though, we need a bit of a breather having held our tummies in for so long. Both the men stand as we return to the table. "You look storming", James said to me. I'm not sure what it means but I take it as a compliment.

Over the next few weeks I see a lot more of James and eventually we become lovers. It's all very exciting at first, but then I experience a comfort which I haven't felt since that day on the delivery table. James strokes my skin and tells me its soft, he finds the bulge of skin that is forced up under my arms by my bra strap, very sexy, and he loves to grab the fold of my stomach and fondle it. And as for my bottom and breasts… Well, he cannot get enough of them.

It won't last with James I know. He will soon tire of me and move on to someone else, he is that sort of person. I will, however, be eternally grateful to him for making me realise that most men do not look at women's bodies the way women do. They see curves and a good handful of flesh as being incredibly sexy. They want to bury their heads in an ample bosom. They need something to play with and boys like big toys. As James once said "It's much more fun on a bouncy castle than a wash board."

I am happy being a bouncy castle!

Hazel

My Boy

I love my body. It's not perfect – far from it – but it's mine and it tells my story. From my hair, greying at the temples just like my mother's, to the rounded hips from my love of food, to the hardened soles of busy feet. But I didn't always love it and it's the parts that people don't see that say the most.

I've never been all that slim. Since reaching adulthood I've not been smaller than around a dress size 14, which at my entirely average height is a little heavier than we are told is healthy and a lot wider than fashion and media tell us is beautiful. I've never considered myself all that pretty. I don't tan, my skin is dry and the shape of my face is just nothing special. As a teenager I was a loner and didn't exactly have an army of boys chasing after me. Then I fell in love with someone wonderful who loved me back. I'm not sure which of us was more surprised. Several years later we were married and starting a family.

Having kids is never easy and difficult births are commonplace. My experience was a long, painful, terrifying one. Illness and slow progress conspired to see me facing my biggest fear: an emergency caesarean. I'll spare you the details as they don't really matter here, but suffice to say that it was the most traumatic thing I have lived through.

My body was damaged by the experience. I had purple stretch marks across most of my abdomen and round my hips, a long scar across the top of my pubic hair from the operation, and a number of little spots on my hands and lower back from drips and epidurals. In a way, these scars represented everything that had gone wrong, all the pain and indignity I had suffered, all the things that were done to me about which I had no real choice – not if I wanted my baby to have the best chance at being born healthy.

In the first few weeks after the birth I had some terrible nightmares. Mostly they focussed on my baby being disfigured or disabled, not the perfect little boy he was. Sometimes they focussed on me. I recall one particularly vivid image of my caesarean scar being a wide, gaping, festering wound.

Slowly, the scars began to heal. With counselling, and support from my husband and friends, so did my mind. I began to believe that my baby was growing and developing normally, nourished only by the milk my breasts provided. The evidence was there in front of me every day that this wounded, scarred body had produced life and, even more miraculously, was still sustaining it. As my little boy grew, so did my confidence in my parenting abilities. I began to believe that I was a good mum, but somewhere in amongst it all I had lost me.

In the early days I had all but hidden away from the world, but slowly I came back to it. I was overwhelmed with how much it welcomed me back. Friends that I hadn't seen for months, if not more, offered smiles, hugs and kind words. Some of them even flirted with me a little, which at first I had no clue how to respond to. I began to remember that they loved me and the scars under my clothes and in my mind made no difference to that.

As my boy started to eat real food I started to cook better, healthier family meals, thinking more about what I put on my plate because I'd be putting the same on his. Rather than rely on the car for every journey, I walked, often with my child on my back, safe and snug in a sling. I also took up yoga, strengthening my core muscles and improving my flexibility. I was the slimmest, fittest and happiest I had been in years. It glowed through everything I said and did, even in the way I stood. An old friend even commented that he had never known me sexier.

Through all of this I came to the realisation that my body, scars and all, was amazing. The folds of puckered skin on my belly tell the tale of how my body carried a child inside. The thin line underneath tells the story of how I was prepared to face anything for my son. The solid, toned muscles hidden inside tell of the inner strength I found with the help of my friends. I carry these stories with me everywhere. It doesn't matter that nobody else sees them because they are part of me. They are part of the woman who can fight her own corner, who can stand up and be counted, and who can draw so many positives from the most terrible thing she has ever experienced.

Jen Philips, 32

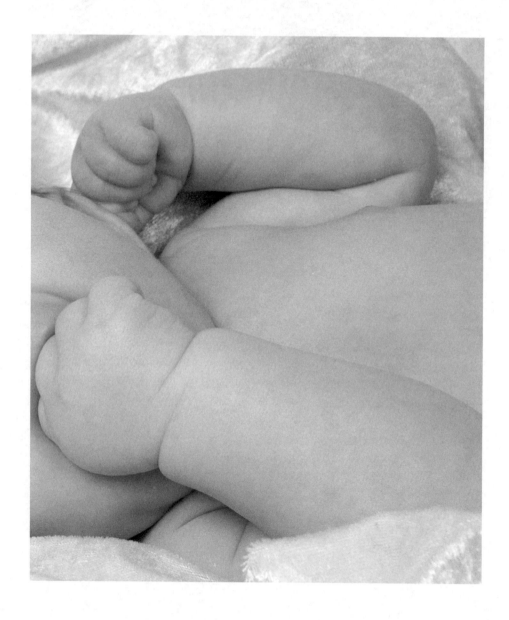

Chapter 5

WHAT ARE WE PROTECTING OUR CHILDREN FROM?

Confusing, aggressive, seductive and conflicting body messages are fired at us from all angles in the 21st century. Body image is big business and so it can sometimes seem it's on every billboard, every TV ad, in every magazine and dominating every discussion.

Dealing with this and finding your own unique brand of gorgeous is tough enough when you're an adult, but what about the effect it's having on British children?

In this chapter, you'll hear from parents on the realities of trying to provide the right body guidance for their children and then it's over to the kids themselves...

Dear Body Gossip

This is a poem about me and the past three years of my life. I have been suffering with Anorexia and through this have found my best friend in the world, my mum. She has helped me so much and she has been so understanding through all my many ups and downs. I chose to write this poem in an attempt to try and thank her for never giving up on me, though I know it would take me a lifetime to try and make it up to her for all the stress, heartache and pain I have caused her. This really is a family illness and I don't think anyone ever goes through it alone, although is regularly feels like it.

Thank you very much for considering my entry.

Yours gratefully,

Katie McBain

Be a big brave girl

Why can't I be pretty mummy, like all the other girls?
They have such lovely dresses mummy and pretty little curls.
They all go out to parties and dance with all the boys
While I stand in the corner and try hard not to cry.

I feel so all alone, whilst looking across at them
I wish for just one day, mummy that I could be the same.
I felt so crap when I was big and now that I am small
It's now all plainly clear, I don't feel different at all.

I lost so much weight mummy, to try and be the best,
Lost my bottom and my hair and what was on my chest.
I found my spine, my ribs and coccyx too, aren't I a clever girl,
I can be like all the rest, I can dance and spin and twirl.

What do you mean I'm ill mummy and that I have to stop this now?

I can't go back to how I was; that ugly, lazy cow.
I was stupid, grotesque, I served no purpose
Look at me, I'm fat, I'm worthless.

Today I saw you cry mummy, you wept your tears for me.
You told me to be strong and please just try to eat,
But mummy you don't get it, I cannot take it back
I've come so very far now, too far to just relax.

Where are we going mummy, I've not been here before?
We're going to meet a lady, who will help me eat some more?
My body won't stop shaking is that the cold or is it fear?
Mummy, please don't do this, please don't bring me here.

PAUSE

A year has passed and so it seems I may be on the mend,
Though you and I both know mummy, this isn't quite the end.
I still have to weigh it all, both myself and all my food.
But I no longer cut things out, tell me that, that's good.

Prom came and went and I had fun, I finally could say
That I was just like the other girls, dancing there that day.
But a few days later the voice came back, the voice that made me ill.
It made me walk to town today and then choose a smaller meal.

Mummy, please can I be normal, can you make this go away,
Can you take my thoughts and feelings and bring Katie back to play?
People starred when I was fat mummy, now they stare because I'm thin.
Will there ever be a time mummy, I time when I will win?

I'm back to see the lady now, the lady that made me eat
And hopefully this time, the illness I can beat.
But mummy what if when I'm better, people still are mean?
What if when I'm rounder, they make me feel unclean?

Feel again that I am worthless, that I'm a leper of the town.
Let them get a sneaky punch in then proceed to kick me down.
You tell me that I'm clever that I've got so much to give
If only I could see that mummy, then I would want to live.

But I've got to be your big brave girl and just try to let this pass,
For when I reach the other side I will see the greener grass,
The clouds will lift the goggles will go and I will see what's real.
I'm the same as all those other girls, I know just how they feel.

Katie McBain, 17

Don't Tell the Youth to Change; They're Perfect as They Are

My Mum says I'm pretty,
But then why do I feel like this?
I try and try again,
But it's a game of hit and miss.

They say wear makeup,
Its glamorous and a simple task,
But when I decide to do it,
It just reminds me what's under the mask.

They say natural hair is boring,
Dye it - it's easily managed.
Oh, now you did it too many times,

Now it's just greasy and damaged.

They say don't dress like that,
You look like a right drag,
Shorten your skirt and your top,
Oh you look stupid now, like a right slag.

They say lose weight right now,
That top shows all your fat through it,
It's no ordeal or anything,
All of the models seem to do it.

No, you're too skinny,
Eat this, oh and that.
Well now you're just chubby,
Verging again on fat.

They say be exciting,
Someone interesting and fun,
But I try and fail,
And end up feeling more like a no-one.

I wish I'd seen before
That the expectations are impossibly tough,
That you get it, and then they move it,
So you never will keep up enough.

All I ever saw was this other me
That was better, I wanted to be different and vary.
Following these I didn't realise that everyone was after the same goal,
But being your happy self is already extraordinary.

Ellie Payton

Dear Dad

When I was a little girl I loved you. I loved spending time with you, you made me laugh, you were warm and loving, you were the centre of my world.

Then I hit puberty. Then I started to gain weight. I no longer had the thin body of a child. I was changing, developing large legs, a rounder belly and I was getting tall. I was broad shouldered, one of the tallest in my class and I had fantastic legs, strong and muscular.

I began to notice that I wasn't as slim as some of the other girls in my class. I had a bit of a double chin. My waist was bigger and I had the aforementioned belly. It became evident that I was only going to take after my small, slim mother in one regard – my thighs. You pointed out to me that my Mum had "short, fat legs", which she agreed with, and I noted mine were going to be the same.

In other respects, I was taking after you. You were always a big man. You used to beat yourself up about it. You would berate fat people like your own parents, calling them "short, fat and round". You would tell me not to get fat – "don't get fat like me, once you're fat you can never lose it", you said.

I went into my teens. I was not slim like the other girls. I was bigger, but looking back now I wasn't huge. I loved to swim, cycle and play netball. I didn't pay much attention to food – I just ate then got on with my day. I liked sweets like everyone else my age, but I didn't gorge myself on them.

But you didn't like it. You didn't like me. I was developing my own personality and you didn't like it. You and Mum went into your 50s. I was 15. You both started to gain a little weight. It's entirely natural. You decided to go on diets. You decided that I was becoming fat and had to join in.

You thought you would help me, or maybe you were so wrapped up in your own pain you didn't think of the damage you were causing. You told me not to get fat, saying that if I were fat no-one would love me. You may as well have said you would withdraw your love. You made pig noises at me when I opened the fridge when hungry, and shouted out "not you again fatty". If you saw me with sweets you would say "oh Jennifer" with such reproach I felt my cheeks burn and my heart sink.

Eating around you became difficult, if not impossible. I began to buy food and hide it – I needed to eat in peace! Mealtimes with you both were awful – you would discuss your diets and how much weight you'd lost. Not every time, sure, but enough to make it unpalatable.

At the same time you both pointed out that I had been an accident, you hadn't meant to have any more children, and if you hadn't have had me you would have been free. I withdrew, hurt, and you blamed that on me too, calling me surly and difficult. I became the worst child of all three of us. All I wanted was to be left alone, to be loved and accepted for who I was instead of feeling forced to become something that YOU wanted. I was to be the clone of my mother, but my large body ruled that out.

You would comment on others – point out fat people in the street and tell me they looked disgusting. I put it all together:

Fat people are disgusting,

No-one loves fat people,

I am fat, therefore I am disgusting.

I am stopping you enjoying your lives – I am too big and I am in the way.

And I came to this conclusion: You didn't love me. Yet you would tell me constantly that you loved me very much and you were only criticising me for my own good. I learned that to love someone meant to criticise them. I could not cope with this.

The binges continued, and with them came the diets and the self-harm. To sink a knife into myself was the only way I could feel calm sometimes. I wanted to hack away at this disgusting body which had let me down. Perhaps if I had more control over food, I would be thinner then you'd love me. I remember eating a whole tub of ice cream with tears pouring down my cheeks, muttering over and over "eat it, you fat pig, eat it all, you're so useless this is the only thing you're good at". Those words had their roots with you.

I remember winning your approval once though. You were both so delighted when I returned back from a term at uni 2 dress sizes smaller, in just 10 weeks. What you didn't know was that I was only eating 3 or 4 times a week, then binging at weekends. I did this with the aid of amphetamines – 4 to 5 grams a week. I nearly went mad. I got help, got cleaned up and graduated.

The weight came on. Well, it would do, wouldn't it? Of course to you it was my fault, but this time I was smarter. By this time I had lived in Italy and learned to really value food. I didn't join you and Mum on another diet; I just upped my fruit and veg intake, drank plenty of water and cut back on meat. You laughed at me, mocked me, called me a "vegetarian". The funny thing is, a few years later you lost the weight that you had carried all the time I had known you by eating in exactly the same way.

I took up regular exercise as well, which you both advised me against. You were afraid I would "bulk up". You made me go to the doctor because you were afraid my cycling was making my legs fat. I had some water retention around my knees, I was fine, my doctors words were "don't stop cycling". We had a laugh about your ignorance. I cannot bulk up, I am female and do not have enough testosterone to do so, but actually getting the facts seemed to be beyond your capability.

And so on to today. I am 40, and I am fat. I stupidly did the thing you approved of - got myself an office job in a big company, and the weight came on. Once again, I was trying to make you love me, but it's so obvious I can never, ever be good enough. I'm too different, too radical for you. I have now quit my career to regain my health. I am living life on my terms these days. I wear outlandish clothes and I have my nose pierced.

I've worked hard to become a normal eater and to develop the mechanism to take care of myself. I am happy with how I look now. I stand tall and proud, yes even though I am fat, and I know I'm not disgusting. I love my big thighs, there's nothing better for cycling. I have a loving husband who accepts me and friends who don't want to change a thing about me.

I know you are ashamed of me. I noticed it recently – you don't introduce me to anyone as your daughter these days. I feel so rejected, but I can't put myself through an eating disorder in order to gain your love.

I wish you could love me for me. You're old now, one day you will be gone. I would so love for you to be my Daddy again. I would love to be held by you and called Toots, like you used to. But I fear your prejudice against my fat is never, ever going to let that happen. It breaks my heart, but I cannot go back to my eating disorder. I have to consider my health. I'm happy with myself, finally, after years of body hatred, and if you can't be part of that then so be it.

I want to end Body Hatred. It robbed me of my Daddy. If we lived in a world where people just accepted each other then maybe we would have found a way to be father and daughter. I don't know what you went through as a child, maybe you were on the end of some horrid fat talk too. But I choose to end this now. I won't give in to what is basically a form of bullying. I won't accept it from you or anyone else, and I will defend the rights of fat people to be left the heck alone until I die.

Jenny Jameson, 40

This Girl's World

I have three daughters and I despair at the world they are growing up in…

What a world to bring up girls
Freedom to choose
How big your tits
How full your lips
Have your fanny-redesigned
Step up to the mark to be maligned
Undermined
Humankind
Is misaligned
Out of whack
How can my daughters
Unravel the signals
The relentless images

103

Of Barbie-brained bimbos
Oh so slim-bo
Thinking through their quimbos
I shall arm them with self-esteem
Enable them to grasp their dreams
Expect respect
Whatever size their chest
I hold a thought of suffragettes
Starving themselves in prison cells
They did well for us
Now we must return the favour
And release our daughters
From the bling bling tyranny
Of perfection

Kate Tym, 40

My Daughter is Anorexic

My daughter is anorexic. My beautiful baby girl is starving herself to skin and bone.

I take off my clothes and look at myself in the mirror. I am a short, fat, 54 year old woman with cellulite on my thighs and bottom and with a floppy belly. I wonder "Is it my fault that my daughter will not eat – perhaps she looks at me and thinks I am disgusting?" I certainly do not look like any model in a magazine. How can I explain to her that it does not matter? That I am a real woman with curves and shape that are unique to me.

When I was young and slim and beautiful, I used to panic if I put on two pounds. I thought that nobody would love me if I wasn't perfect. I fell in love with a boy who loved me back. We went walking one day, my skirt caught on a twig and my thigh was accidentally exposed to his eyes. I was so ashamed that I could not look at him or even speak. I knew that he would not like me any more now he had seen how ugly I was.

I was wrong. A few months later, when we were closer, he told me that it was the most erotic thing that he had ever seen.

That boy loved me in every way and helped me to love myself. I grew up with him. I learned to accept that no bodies are perfect in the way that magazines like to portray them. Perfect bodies are healthy and come in liquorice allsorts shapes and sizes.

Some years after we had drifted apart I travelled with my backpack through strange lands filled with new experiences. Here I learned that age was not a barrier to beauty either. I met the wisest, the kindest and the gentlest of people and I loved them more than any false beauties from my world. The most beautiful woman I ever met was 83 and only had two teeth.

"Hello gorgeous girl" shouts my 56 year old husband. He comes homes from work and pours us a drink. You look great he says as he embraces me from behind, I feel him growing hard as he presses into the voluptuous roundness of my bottom. "You are the sexiest girl alive" he whispers as he slides his hand under my t shirt. He means it.

Two middle aged people frolic on the sofa, giggling like children as they peel off each other's clothes. "I love you" they cry as they devour each other. And they do. They love every little part of each other. He kisses her cellulite, she strokes his beer belly. Their hot, sweaty bodies take them to a place of ecstasy that no 24 year old version of themselves could ever do. Confident and happy because they have learned not to compare themselves to air brushed images and fakes, they have found true beauty in each other.

Please God, I can now teach this to my daughter.

Jo Molyneux, 54

Big Feet

Talk to her Bry, said my Mum.

Dad looked from Mum to me nervously.
Then his eyes drifted back to the flickering T.V.

But, just as Leonard Rossiter was about to tip his Cinzano down Joan Collins' top,
Mum stood up and switched the T.V. off.

I bet Joan Collins doesn't have big feet, I thought.

Bry? Mum insisted, are you listening?

Dad wasn't sure what was going on. He was scared of reading the females wrong.
He was starting to wish he'd stayed in the garden with his begonias.

His right hand took on a life of its own. It started to pat out a random rhythm on
the arm of the sofa. Then his eyes rolled up towards the ceiling as if all the
answers to life's mysteries were trapped like dying flies in the lamp shade.

Tell her said My Mum.
Tell her what? Asked My Dad.
She...
(My Mum waved at me when she said the word She).
She thinks she's got big feet.

There was a pause then, while we all looked at my feet.

Tick tock tick tock,
Nobody scoff nobody mock,
Tick tock tick tock.

And as we paused

I dreamed of being completely and utterly adored by everyone. Just like Purdy, in The New Avengers. Purdy had bobbed hair and nice white teeth.
And I suspected she didn't have size eight feet.

Tick tock tick tock.

I don't know exactly how long the pause lasted

PAUSE

Well? Said my Mum.

Well?

You see the thing about my Dad is, he just can't lie. And he isn't diplomatic so I have no idea why Mum got him started on my feet.

Did she expect him to have a sudden attack of The Bamboozles?

Big Feet, BIG FEET, is that all it is!
Dad took a deep breath and then let it out. Feet was a subject he knew about. The Hammetts have always had big feet. They keep us grounded you'll never get whipped away in a storm, girl, not with those feet, he said.

There was another awkward silence after that. Mum looked a bit gob smacked.

The thing is, I said in a small voice, they're not just big, they're flat!

And Dad was quite keen to talk about that too. He was on a run!

The Hammetts have always had flat feet! You see.

Shut up Brian! Said Mum.

And she turned the T.V. back on.

Tracey Hammet, 44

What Are We Protecting Our Children From?

For a while my local swimming pool had a sign up in the FEMALE ONLY shower area saying 'Please keep your costumes on as some people may find it offensive if you remove them', or words to that effect. I complained at reception and they said they thought it was a 'child protection' issue. I have three daughters and I would rather protect them from the relentless images of highly sexualized air-brushed women than from what they might see in the showers at the pool…hence the poem. The sign isn't up any more – hurrah!

<u>What are we protecting our children from?</u>

Big bums
Saggy tits
Old ladies wrinkly bits
Cellulite
Caesarean scars
What we look like out of bras
Wobbly thighs
Overgrown bushes
Knobbly knees
And skinny tushes
Bingo wings
Tampon strings
And other really scary things

Like growths and moles
And belly button holes
No two people are alike
Fluffy girly
Big butch dike
All of them have their place
In the fabulous human race
Yet the naked form is not the norm
Unless it's trimmed and tucked
The concept's fucked
My girls can see anorexic clones
Ribby chests jutting bones
Barbie dolls with blow-up knockers
Here's the shocker
Real breasts don't look like that
Some are deflated, sucked flat
From feeding babies
And d'you know what?
Maybe that's OK.

Kate Tym

And now to hear from the children themselves - we were lucky enough to receive these gems...

My Amazing Feet

My feet go through a lot while the day goes by. Wouldn't you like to give them a rest? Well if you want to know what I do through the day, here you go: I get out of bed and switch my little light off and go downstairs. We have a lot of stairs so it takes rather a long time to go down them.

When we have got down then we talk into the kitchen and get breakfast. After breakfast we go back upstairs into our rooms and get changed. I rummage around in a pile of clothes and search for a school dress.

After I find one I put it on. Then I put my socks on and go into the bathroom and brush my teeth.

When I have brushed them I go back downstairs again. If I'm early enough I watch TV if not I get my shoes, blazer, hat and folder and go with my sister. (We walk to school because it is only down the road.)

When we get there we go in the girl's cloakroom and take our blazer off and change our shoes. Then we walk to the classroom and do our homework diary.

While that lesson goes on, after we go to assembly.

While that goes on (I'm telling you about Thursday) after we do P.E. Our teacher tells us to go and get changed into our P.E. kit so we can do P.E.

When we are ready we go into the hall and do circuit training, so we have to set it up. Circuit training has a lot of running about included so it tires you out!

When the lesson's over we get changed into our school uniform and go upstairs to geography.

When it's lunch time we go outside and have lunch in the dining room.

When we have had lunch we go outside and play for half an hour.

Then we have history and maths and then it's the end of the day, so, we walk back home.

That's all you need to know about what me and my amazing feet do, so, goodbye, see you soon.

Charlotte (year 3)

It's Not Fair

It's not fair
I want long hair
My Mum says if I eat a pear
I can have long hair
But I don't like pears
So life isn't fair

It's not fair
I want long hair
Think of a bear
They have long hair
I'm sure they'd have some spare
But I'd be scared of a bear
So life isn't fair

It's not fair
I want long hair
Why doesn't Mum seem to care
On the other hand
Brushing it would be a nightmare

So maybe, just maybe
Life is not so unfair

Rosie age 9

Tummy

We all have a tummy
The things which go in it are yummy
Our tums have bad bugs
But when we wee they go down the plug
Wotsits are yummy
So they go in my tummy
Yum yum yum yum yum
Tum tum tum tum tum

Hannah (Year 5)

Sweety Delight

I was on the way to school one day
When I saw a sweet shop on the way
I saw a tray of Turkish delight
Then my face lit up in lights
I asked mum to stop the car

So I could eat from the sweetie jar
I chose a Smartie
That I had at my party
It went into my mouth
And down the oesophagus
Into my stomach
And then into the liver
Splat on the pancreas
And down to the small intestine
Through the large intestine
Ready for the anus
And I won't say any more!

Maya (Year 3)

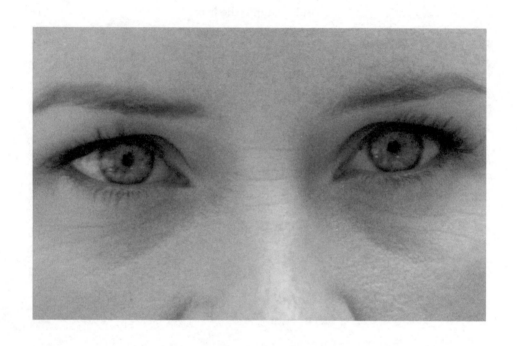

Chapter 6

THE MONSTER IN THE FRIDGE

Trigger Warning – The content of this chapter may be upsetting for those who are currently experiencing, or have previously experienced eating disorders.

A huge majority of the stories we receive at Body Gossip are about eating disorders. They reveal the shocking truth about these illnesses, which claim more and more victims each year.

We've learned that there is no 'fixed' way to have an eating disorder. The causes, symptoms, behaviours and mindsets differ hugely from person to person. This chapter contains some of the stories we've received and dips into the dark and occasionally terrifying world of the minds of British people with eating disorders (the number of which currently stands at around 1.6 million). They also reveal an overwhelming desire to conquer these illnesses and to reclaim body and mind...

My Anorexia Problem

Every day I wake up, I tell myself 'Don't eat anything today'. But the problem is, I just love food too much. As everyone else gets thinner, I seem to get fatter. Every time I eat something, I look at my last action in disgust. I've asked myself so many times, 'How do they do it?' Everyone around me is tiny compared to me. Once I thought about anorexic people and how they're so smart. It's obvious not eating anything is sensible. I look up to them. I idolise those people that can do what I can't. I can't restrain myself from eating my third piece of cake when I know they wouldn't eat the first. When I skip a meal I feel so proud of myself. I wish I could keep that feeling.

So that's my anorexia problem. The fact that I can't be anorexic.

Anonymous, 14

Once Upon a Time

And she lived happily ever after...

That is what I grew up to believe.
That is what I was expecting.
That, is what I thought would happen.

I didn't realise that life isn't quite like the fairytales I had been dreaming about.

It took time and some real hardships to learn that life isn't as simple as I would like it to be.

Nowhere in Cinderella did she get dragged down an alley and have things done to her that are beyond the decent imagination.

Nowhere, did I read about Little Red Riding Hood starving herself to near death, exercising herself literally into the ground...denying herself a life.

Nowhere is the chapter from Rapunzel in which she missed out on months of her life to a cycle of obsession and compulsion as the world just passed on by.

Maybe all these things were missed out to shorten stories. Censored so as not to scare children away from growing up and exploring the world. Simply hushed, avoided and ignored as is so often the case.

Or maybe it's up to us to write our own story. A true story, with the once upon a times, happily ever afters and all the real nitty gritty things in between.

The good times, the bad times, the unforgettable times and the 'I wish that never happened' times.

So that is what I am doing. I can't rewrite my past or delete any of the things I have been through, but I can help to shape my future and be the author of the rest of my life.

The next chapter has already begun.

No longer do the demons from the past dictate my every thought and action.

I am learning how to appreciate food and to eat when I am hungry, to stop depriving myself.

I can exercise because I want to, not because I 'have' to.

I know how to treat myself nicely and distract myself from negativity instead of etching self hatred into my delicate skin.

I have begun to discover what beauty the outside world holds and that there are people within it who are genuine and trustworthy.

Most importantly, I now know that I can just be me and enjoy it. I now know that that is okay!!!

I do still have to fight my struggles week by week. Life doesn't always treat me kindly no matter how much I try to be kind to myself. And I know that there are many more chapters of my life that are unwritten.

But one thing is certain.

I am now one step closer to my happily ever after.

Laura Tombs

My Declaration of Independence from my Eating Disorder

When in the course of her lifetime, it becomes necessary for one woman, Michelle, to break the ties between her and Ed, and to assume absolute and steadfast control of her life, the separate and equal station to which the Laws of Nature and God entitle her, a decent respect to the opinions of mankind requires that she should declare the causes which impel her to the separation.

Michelle holds these truths to be self-evident, that everyone is endowed with unalienable rights and among these are life, liberty, respect, and the pursuit of happiness. That whenever Ed becomes destructive and controlling of these ends, it is Michelle's right to eliminate Ed, to alter her life, and to institute recovery, laying the foundation of her life on such principles and organising her powers in her own way, so that she may achieve safety and happiness. The history of Ed is a history of repeated injuries and insults, all having taken away the rights stated above from Michelle. To prove this, let facts be submitted:

-Ed has cut off all emotions.

-Ed has damaged Michelle's health and sense of self.

-Ed has deprived Michelle of food and comfort.

-Ed has erected feelings of hatred, vulnerability, and worthlessness.

-Ed has hidden the truth from Michelle by telling her that she was not good enough.

-Ed has refused Michelle of self-love, confidence, and self-approval.

-Ed has silenced Michelle's cries of unhappiness and caused her to suffer in silence, often deserting her when she was at her worst.

-Ed has taken Michelle's morals, changed them, and made her act against them.

-Ed has united with perfectionism to make Michelle strive to ridiculously high standards, standards that are unattainable.

Michelle, therefore, solemnly publishes and declares that she is free and independent; that she has been absolved of all allegiance to Ed, that all connection between Ed and Michelle will be dissolved, and that as a free and independent individual, she has full power to eat, live in peace, express her feelings, and use the rights of life, liberty, respect, and the pursuit of happiness as she pleases.

Michelle Handy, 16

Dear Ana

You were there when I tossed and turned trying to sleep,
You were there when the weight on the scales made me weep.
You were there when they said I could no longer dance,
You were there as strangers shot a revolted glance.
Are you friend or foe because I never do know,
They say that you robbed me of my spirited glow.
They demanded I choose my favourite Fortisip,
Warning the consequences of another blip.
I ceased brushing my hair to stop more falling out,
Trailing the food aisle constantly left me in doubt.
I never knew where I ended and you began,

119

Scared as they sent me for a bone density scan.
I have gained weight now but you will always be there,
Obsessively guessing others weights to compare.
I am out of treatment so they think I am well,
But every meal time you voice still gives me hell.
Am I eating too slow? Am I eating too fast?
Five mouthfuls to go and I will be there at last.
You have dominated my life for far too long,
I have realised now that you will always be wrong.
I will miss you Ana when you finally go,
But you have to leave in order to let me grow.
This little girl's body must be a woman's now,
Ana the time has come to take your final bow.

Charlotte Gatherer, 22

Good Enough To Eat

So, there I was. Sitting down in the Kids' Corner at my mother's gym. I must've been, what…six… seven years old? I had my legs crossed… my dress pulled safely over my knees. And I'd sit there. I'd watch all of the mummies. Kind of observing them, I suppose. They'd wear silly leotard contraptions and lurch around on the floor. Getting all bony and no fun to sit on.

I looked at their bodies in the mirror. Twenty, thirty determined-looking ladies. And in my head I organised them. I lined them up in order of prettiness, hair colour, thinness. Thinness was important. I knew that already. All of my heroes were thin. My mother. Pocahontas. Hell, even Bridal Barbie. I guess I'd worked out that thin people were incredible. Thin people bagged Ken and John Smith. And, well… thin people were happy.

Maybe thinking that was what caused it all. If I'm totally honest, I don't really know why it all began. I guess I just sort of… fell for it. That age-old belief. If I just lost a few pounds, I'd suddenly be somebody new and totally brilliant. I would lose all of my freckles and get a fabulous new wardrobe and Kylie's bum. But it doesn't really work like that. I guess there's always going to be just a few more pounds. That little bit further to go. Then it'll be okay. Then things'll be alright. If only I was thinner, prettier… smarter. If only. Only it never ends.

It's crazy how losing weight can seem like the answer to everything. But you step onto the scales, watch the numbers go down and hey… you've finally found it. This one thing that you're really good at. Your clothes start to get baggy. Your thighs shy away from each other like they've never been properly introduced. You've become this Girl That Never Needs. My God you're in control. But then, there you have it. I guess that's it. Are you really in control at all?

It ends up being everything. It's like you stop one day, look around, and there you are. Right in the middle of it all. You're stuck with this silly obsession with weight. This encyclopaedic knowledge of calories. Eventually you find yourself bothered by the five calories that are in a stick of sugar-free gum. You're always exercising now. Always running. There's all this mad power-walking that frightens both children and small dogs. I suppose you sort of join an incredibly peculiar world. It's like going through the looking glass and everything's turned upside down… inside out. Your life becomes this big bundle of contradictions. This dangerous diet that makes you feel safe. A gesture of strength that makes you so weak. A big search for identity which'll eventually strip you of all sense of yourself. And you're stuck in this looking glass. Nothing really makes sense any more. You can bang on the glass, people'll see you…sure…they'll smile and they'll wave. But you're removed from them. Removed from everything that matters. You're left on your own now. It's a pretty lonely place.

You kind of lose a dimension.

You end up sort of, blank. Vacant.

Afterwards, people'll tell you how your eyes didn't sparkle. How you were, well, horribly thin. Sometimes I could see it, in a weird, disconnected kind of way. Like I'd sit somewhere outside of my body and I'd look across the room. My goodness, I'd think. What the hell were you thinking?

I honest-to-God wanted to eat and Make Everything Better. But to me, food seemed so scary. It was this little platoon of calories, all under strict orders to march to my thighs and set up camp. There was no logic in any of it. You forget how you used to feel alright. You end up forgetting what it means to feel alright 'cos you feel like shit all the time and you can't remember what it was like before.

It's a leap of faith, reverting to normality. I guess it's like leaving an abusive lover, who, in spite of everything, you're still not completely sure you can cope without. To start with, eating normally feels so indulgent, so wrong. It seems completely crazy that something that feels so strange to you could possibly be right. If you ask any therapist, they'll tell you, you just have to Think Differently. If you're anything like me, that'll sound like telling a blind person just to open their eyes a bit wider. But then, trust me, I guarantee it. It'll actually start to happen.

It was my sister who made me realise I wanted it all to end. She made me remember what life had been like before it all. How I used to have the energy to laugh about things. That one time we tried to make chocolate raisins. The way we thought the Lord's Prayer was "our father, who art in heaven, hello what's your name?" I think it was sitting in the kitchen on that crisp Sunday morning that I realised it. Everything had got to change.

Y'see, once you stop spending your time trying to be thin, you start to actually notice things. You notice lovely smiles from boys on buses. How the fruit seller wears a different hat every day. You notice that you've truly started to laugh. Laughter that's hard to contain, like hiccups in Church. You start making memories again, being yourself again. Actually living again.

I don't think you can ever really realise that you've essentially been dead until you really start to come alive again. Until you find yourself running your hands over silky shirts in department stores. Or laughing to yourself as you people-watch on a particularly windy day. I think it's only then that you can realise how tremendously lucky you've been. Lucky you've escaped something that so many people can never get away from. Lucky that, for you, it was all just a comma when it could've been a full stop.

It's hard because it has felt like such a part of you. And as much as you'd like to, you can't just put your fingers in your ears and sing Kumbaya and make the memories go away. But I think it's all like crossing monkey bars. If you ever want to really move forward, you just have to force yourself to let go. There is a sense of loss. I'd even say there's a strange sense of grief. But there's also, after a while, a time when it gets easier. And there is, in the end, a time when you are free.

Emily Holdsworth, 18

The Monster in My Fridge

There's a monster in my fridge you know,
It likes to scream and shout,
It tells me that I'm ugly, fat and like to lie about.
It wasn't there a week ago,
But I can't be truly sure,
And it only ever speaks to me,
When opening the door.

There's a monster in my fridge you know,
Eating all the food,
It's terribly ferocious, black, and really very rude.
My mother doesn't see it,
And my father thinks I'm strange,
Even when I tell them that,
I'll never eat again.

There's a monster in my fridge you know,
It's growing like a tree.
It's telling me that very soon it will take up all of me!
My tummy's getting hungry,

And my mind is getting blurred,
For all I ever think about,
Is eating like a bird.

There's a monster in my head you know,
It's moved out of the fridge,
It's making up these stories,
And it's stolen my porridge.
It dribbles and it swears a lot at people walking by,
My mum thinks that I'm being rude,
She thinks that I don't try.

There's a monster in my head you know,
It's eating up my life,
The monster is now huge and black, and tells me I'm in strife!
I try my very hardest still to tell my Mum about,
How the monster took the fridge and how it kicked me out!
The doctor isn't angry,
But my friends all think I'm sick,
And my Mum and Dad don't seem to think,
That cheese is like arsenic.

There's a monster in the world you know,
It tricks me to believe,
That feeling all the things I feel,
Will make me be diseased!
It tells me that I'm fat and ugly, that I am so wrong,
When all I ever want to do is eat,
And to belong.
It sits and tells me stories, about how my life should be
That I should disappear and then,
It will set me free.

There's a monster in the fridge you know,
It's in the world, and all,
In every piece of food, and drink and it's nearly ten feet tall.
It doesn't want to know you, and it thinks you are all fat,
And says that one day soon, it will be president, Pope and that!

It isn't very caring, yet it started off as a FRIEND,
It used to be called DIET but now it's called The END.

There's a monster in my ward you know,
Sucking up my life,
It's left me feeling empty too, and now I am in strife.
My body is all wrinkly, and it's bony, cold and grey.
The doctors and the nurses say I'm fading all away.
The monster thinks it's funny, saying that it is just no use.
There will be no escaping from the years of child abuse.
The monster says I'm tainted, and that I must go away.
That truth is that I am to blame, and now that I must pay.

There's a monster in my dreams you know,
He smells of beer and hair,
He runs and grabs my arms so tight, and says he doesn't care.
Another voice is screaming and I know it isn't me.
The monster is alive and hurting someone I can't see.
My feet they keep on running but I don't know where to go,
The monster says that if I tell then he'll be sure to blow!

There's a monster in the past, you know,
And now he's getting old.
His life is being sucked up from the lies and hurt he holds,
The monster cannot breathe, or eat, or run as fast as I,
The monster cannot live, and now no longer makes me cry.
His life is truly empty, and my fridge is getting full,
His feelings no one cares about and mine make me so cool.
There's no monster in my fridge you know,

I made it disappear,
And there isn't anything, food or drink or feelings that I fear.

Susie Hardgrave, 36

My Story

This is me. This is my story. It isn't perfect because, let's face it, I'm not perfect - nobody is. But there was a time when I thought I could be...

Lonely, lost, laughable. I was an outcast - at school, at home, in the world so it seemed to me. I was looking in on everyone else's lives - their fun, their friendships, their futures. But I wasn't a part of it. I worried. I worried about everything. The anxiety of life ate away at me. Literally. You see, I wanted perfection in my world. I didn't want arguments in my family. Arguments made me worry. I wanted ten out of ten for my essays. I wanted A* grades for my art work. Nothing less would be good enough. I had to be the best. But not just at one thing; at everything. Not because I had the intention of boasting to my friends - "I got 100% in that maths test" - but because failure was out of the question for me. It meant I hadn't pushed myself hard enough. But the trouble was my best was never enough. The goal-posts were constantly moving. I couldn't reach perfection, no matter how hard I tried.

I searched for perfection; I strove for perfection and little did I know I would ultimately starve in the name of perfection.

If I couldn't control what was outside my body, I would control what I put in it. I would look like the models that paraded down the catwalk. They looked poised and perfect. I would look like the celebrities emblazoned on the front covers of magazines. They looked poised and perfect. That would be me. I would carve out the perfect body. Cut away the fat that I had longed to take a knife to, as I stared repulsively at the lumps and bumps in my reflection. The fat that I had pinched as hard as I could, willing it to peel off into my palm, would melt away. I would melt away. Then I would have control, wouldn't I? Everything would be okay in my world. So, quite simply, I starved myself. And I was right: the fat dissolved, my bones protruded through a thin layer of skin. But along with the fat, I too faded from existence. I barely spoke a word - I didn't want to pass judgement in case I got it wrong and everyone laughed at me. I lived inside my head and drove myself to the edge.

My road to recovery began only when I realised that, actually, the world is not a perfect place. In fact, I am not perfect and I had to accept that.

So my question to you is: why, in this day, are men and women everywhere still trying to obtain perfection? Why is the media giving out the message that thin is perfection and perfection equals beauty? Why are children as young as 12 starving themselves? It is a problem. It is a huge problem and we need to face it.

We need to accept our bodies for what they are and focus on celebrating the individuals that make our world. Everyone is special. Everyone is unique. Everyone has a natural beauty and deserves to be happy with who they are. After all, it is what is in our hearts that makes us who we are; not what is in our reflections. To me, loving yourself is the most beautiful thing of all. This is my message and this is my story. This is me.

Sarah Wallace, 20

Bully

Her words taunt
As she stares at my body
The things that she's saying
Are punching and bruising,
My black and blue body.
Tired from all the abuse
Head hung in shame,
I am disgusting.
There's nothing to say
She's always up in my face
And she never stops yelling
At my body which just keeps on
Swelling, my distorted figure
In the circus mirror won't stop

Growing and groaning.
Her words they hurt
But there is no one to tell.
Can't tell mum or a teacher
They can't understand that all
Of her attacks are perfectly
Planned. I'm always alone
And she knows I won't tell.
I am repulsive.
Because who can you tell
When she's there everyday
Following me around, won't
Go away. Who can you tell
When the voice is in your head,
And the hatred lies behind
Your own eyes instead.
What can you do?
When the bully is you?

Elizabeth Heib, 22

Stream of Vomit

Brain all dried up. Like mushroom. Withered. Too much wine. How quickly alcohol absorbed? Dehydrated. Need water...no calories in water. But. Might make tummy stick out. What if all magazines are liars? What if want us all to be fat, guzzling water? Skinny journalists laughing, making people drink fat. Mum never drinks water, she's thin. Dehydration makes her...shrink. Why aren't I thin? Where did thin genes go? Ugly ugly ugly ugly... Anorexics drink water to fool doctors. Read it in Heat. 5 stone with water in tummy, water in pockets, doctor lets you go. Bloody water. Must make you fat...But. Ow. Head hurts. Need water. What if water leads to…What if can't stop? Water. Tea. Tea and biscuits. Biscuits and cake. Bread. Pizza. Melted cheese. Mmm all gooey. Comes out the same, but stuck together. Like cheese magnets.

What's in the cupboard? Nothing. Cuppa soup. Have to go to shop… First aisle…skip. Hate sicking fruit. All mushy. Like babies. Bitter. Seeds in bile. Urgh. Gross…stop thinking seeds in bile. Can't stop thinking 'seeds in bile' now… Is thought enough to make me sick?… Woob woob. Like film sick – what was that film with 'woob woob' sick noise? Why can't remember?... Why always have to use toothbrush? Why can't think of gross thing and vomit? Rowena could do it. Just bend over and be sick, she said… Crap even at being bulimic. Can't do anything right. Failure.

Want iced buns. Fourth aisle, by hot cross buns. All fat. Inviting. Why good for iced buns to be fat but not people?...£3.54 in purse. £10 in bank. Pizza £9.99…need wine…£3.99 x 2. 18 quid. Fuck… Nothing on credit card. Oh God. Breathe. Breathe. Letters. Red writing. Capitals. URGENT. Phone calls. Debt. Horrible word. Indebted Jeremy Kyle person… breathing in my neck. Argh… Is ok. Is ok. Heart hurts. This is it, this is it…oh. Better now… Money will be ok. Nothing for bailiffs to take, anyway. Bank shut now…1 hour till shop shuts.

Clean up face. Will scare children with panda eyes. Eurgh. What If bump into Stephen? Stephen… Mmm… Only likes thin girls. Not thin enough. Laughing at me. Who she think she is? With Emma bony shoulders all flirty. Sticky arms, flat tummy, thigh gap. I want a thigh gap. All sexy Shakira. Lithe. Twice her size. Fuck fuck. Fucking Stephen. No stretch marks…

Cringe. Throat closing up. One more. One more binge. Errr… binge. Heard word somewhere. Melodrama. Not bingeing. Just… Whatever. Once more. Start diet tomorrow. Diet: 200 calorie breakfast. 1 x slice wholegrain toast, no butter, plus piece fruit, 300 calorie lunch… soup. Salad or soup. Wait. Write down. Lock it in. Then have to do it. Write date on it. Only paper, though. Can tear it up. Maybe will get it laminated at the…laminating shop? New me. Skinny. Bony. Beautiful. Like… Need help. Doe eyes. Rescue. Stephen. Help me.

Anonymous

Thin is a Skill

Thin is a skill, didn't you know?
Who wants to look like a large heap of dough!
Exercise and diets is what I do best,
But they say I'm ill, not well and depressed.

"We're taking you away", my loved ones said
"Where the Dr can take a look at your head".
But didn't they get it? Empty is pure!
There's nothing wrong and nothing to cure.

The Dr examined my head and my weight,
And asked me when was the last time I ate.
I felt I'd been trapped, that I was on trial,
And finally admitted that it had been a while.

He looked at me, his face full of gloom,
And led me into mirrored room.
I looked at my reflection, what had I done?
Staring back was a flesh skeleton.

If I didn't start eating, I was going to die.
And when I told them the news my mother did cry.
From that point on, I promised to be good,
And to eat all the food that I possibly could.

Angharad John

I Wasn't Enough

I wasn't enough.

Not pretty enough, funny enough, clever enough, witty enough.

I could be healthy and fit, more than the others. I could maybe become as thin as the models on the guys walls. I could be the one who doesn't eat because I could be interesting.

Or I could fade away.

Now I eat enough. More than enough. I laugh more than enough. I shine more than enough.

There is no need to compare because I am more than enough and that is what matters.

I am enough.

Erin Barnett, 19

I Knew What to Say

I had every word analysed; every word ordered; every word arranged; into a direction of perfection.
Over, and over, and over again those words danced in my mind, reciting my lyrics until it was my turn to cry.
'Abby? Abby? Abby?'
I couldn't speak.
I couldn't, I wouldn't, yet I longed for the words to fall out from my presence.
The wall was too high, and the road was too long.

And you had built up that wall; brick by brick, stone by stone, in front of my mouth.

You had trapped me, contained me and seized me in your hands.

I was yours, and I did what you wanted.

Used, abused, hurt and silenced.

Until one day I decided that I was no longer yours.

You lied and broke me; cemented me to yourself but no longer was I willing to be your victim.

Day by day, brick by brick, stone by stone I removed your existence.

As you became smaller, I became stronger.

My words reached my mouth, and my mouth spoke the truth, of you and all you had done to me.

I was no longer your game; I was no longer your victim.

I was Abby and I had a voice.

That which you'd stolen for too long was no longer yours.

I'm human, I'm real, I'm alive, and I'm happy.

Most of all I know I have the power to achieve anything.

Abby Sian Baker

Curves are Sexy. Food is Sexy. I am...

…well, I'm working on that part!

Ten years ago, I wouldn't have been able to face my reflection in a mirror and hid my body with dull, baggy, boyish clothes out of shame. I was 14 years old, overweight, bulimic and had no self-confidence. I had become an empty shell who abused her body to extremes by constantly over-eating, not exercising and self-harming.

I was always very aware of the differences between my body and that of my peers, especially once puberty hit. I developed curves at the age of 11 and did not know what to do with them! My face changed too; my lips grew fuller, my cheekbones got higher and my dark eyes grew bigger. Other people started to notice me and the attention made me feel uncomfortable. Everyone seemed to have an opinion on my body, whether positive or negative, and it didn't feel like MY body anymore.

But ten years can bring many changes. How did I learn to love my body? I claimed it back.

The first step was to tackle my relationship with food. I absolutely LOVE food and I think about food all the time. I grew up in a traditional Italian family, where social gatherings revolve around big meals and eating large portions is the expected norm. Food provided my low self-esteem with the comfort I craved and I had to re-educate myself in order to break the negative cycle. I learnt to listen to my body; I ate when I was hungry and stopped when I was full, instead of eating out of boredom and stopping when I felt sick. I put an end to dieting, ignored any "tips" or "celebrity diets" magazines endorsed and allowed myself to eat the foods that my body craved. To this day I refuse to punish myself or feel guilty for devouring a big plate of pasta and enjoy nothing more than a proper cheeseburger!

I sought professional help to confront my inner demons. The guilt, shame and loss of control I felt caused me to spiral into depression. It was important for me to feel my emotions instead of using food to suppress them. For years, I was terrified of facing my fears and opening Pandora's Box, but in facing them I have been able to deal with them. It's still a work in progress and every day I have to make a conscious effort not to fall back into negative behaviour patterns.

I see my imperfections and I acknowledge them, but I won't let myself obsess over them and I don't compare myself to anyone else. So what if I have stretch mark scars? They don't define me. So what if I have cellulite? Everybody does these days. So what if I'll never be thin? I'm proud to say that I take after my Great-Grandmother. So what if my boobs wouldn't pass the pencil test? They're mine. So what if I have a big curvy backside? I'm part of the booty revolution. So what if I have big thighs? They help me hold myself upside down in pole-dancing class.

Real beauty comes from within. I take any compliments I get with a pinch of salt and remember that I look after my body for me because it is mine. The clothes I wear that flatter my figure, the make-up that complements my features, the various foods I eat that give me pleasure, the exercise I do to stay healthy and the people who love me as I am, all help to build my confidence.

Now, I can stand in front of a mirror, face my reflection and smile.

Christina Perrotta

To the Knight-in-Shining-Armour

Once upon a time, we got locked away, up on the highest floor
Of an ugly purple tower.
We were princesses, all of us.
Some of us were dragged there by loved ones.
Some of us went quietly.
Some of us shrieked and clawed.
(Some, I hear, were biters).
Some of us went of our own accord,
Because we had lost everything…
Because we wanted to feel human again…
Because we just didn't get it…
Because we had hurt ourselves as hard as we could…
Because we were tired of loneliness…

So many fables concentrate on what happens in the Tower.
Were there witches? Fairy godmothers? Angels? Ghosts? Poison apples?
Did princesses lose their hair? Meet a prince? Fall into a deep sleep for years and years? Get reprimanded for playing with their food?
Did they spin straw-into-gold, only to find themselves locked up and lonely?
(Again).

I am not concerned with what happened in the Tower.

No, I speak to the day we journeyed forth, into the spinning, fresh air of the Outside.

Once upon a time, we ventured Outside.

Into the forests, onto the cobbles, and towards the rocking sea.

We were princesses, all of us,

And what did we discover… Outside?

Well, we discovered that there were no princes or princesses or kings or queens or fairy godmothers…

Who would come - trumpets clanging - and rescue us from ourselves.

No, we would have to fight our own demons.

And we would fight them the rest of our lives -

Racing ahead on lilac steeds, turning to smack our pursuers with our magic staffs or swords

Or shoot them down, one by one, with a silver-tipped bow.

And, as hard as we fought, they would continue to hiss and sputter into existence.

(New devils too. Some tsetse-buzzing. Some huge and deafening.)

But that was alright.

Because we had found our Knights-in-Shining-Armour.

The warrior who would battle our demons.

Yes, we found her one day as we peered, too deeply, into a mirror.

And, for a fizzle of a moment, this enchanted mirror…

It showed us our true selves.

Princesses in Shining Armour.

Women who will save themselves.

I will save myself.

Zoë Eddy, 22

Body Gossip

There was once a skeleton woman who couldn't feel or touch so she doesn't do much. She got an ice cream but she dropped it you know why she's also a little shy. She got somebody to give her a drink she needed a bib it went right threw her spine and her ribs. She sings, which warms our hearts. She shows us great arts. She danced with a dog and found the way out of a fog. She had some eyes and caught a few flies. That's why she's the funniest skeleton alive. Get it? P.S she was me... Dead me.

Elysia, 7

The Mirror Never Lies... Or Does It?

When I look in the mirror, what do I see?
Who is that woman staring back at me?
Am I happy, content, a picture of health?
Or a pitiful shadow of my former self?
My body is ravaged, my bones jutting out,
For god's sake just feed me, my heart wants to shout,
My body lacks warmth, its cover has gone
Is that what I wanted, a walking skeleton?
I don't want it to hurt when I lay down at night,
I want to get better, continue my fight.
So I look in the Mirror and what do I see,
A fighter a winner, I'm beautiful...that's me. xx

Jackie Tanner, 43

Being Visible

Hello.

I've been asked to tell you my story, about how I feel about my body...

So, here goes.

Sometimes, when I hadn't eaten for a while, or when I hadn't eaten very much for a while, I'd think if I could just become that little bit thinner, I'd become invisible. Sometimes I'd think that was the whole point in coming off food – not to die, I was never that stupid. I didn't want to starve myself to death. If I'd wanted to die, I'd have just taken painkillers or jumped in front of a train. And, before you ask, I never believed I'd be talent spotted for being thin and then cast in a major Hollywood movie either. No, looking back, the reason for my not eating was simply to become thin enough so I could be invisible, to make invisibility my superpower. Sounds childish, I know.

But power often comes from pain, doesn't it? Or, in this case, hunger pangs.

Or, I'd sometimes think, if I couldn't become thin enough for that, if I couldn't cut out enough food to achieve invisibility, then at least I could still become as thin as an orphan from an old novel, maybe one by Charles Dickens. An orphan who could slip through black cast iron railings and run away from the round fat men in their black bowler hats; run, run away, free with the cold London air hitting my face – never getting bumped into, or trodden on by accident, but getting away with knowledge, with knowledge the fat people wanted and only I had because I was thin enough, thin enough to escape through cast iron railings with room to spare, and that, that I sometimes thought, meant I was special.

And we all want to be special, don't we? It doesn't matter if anyone knows about our special-ness or not, does it? Well, it didn't to me anyway. It can be empowering to have a secret.

It never goes away, not really. I still have to purposefully make myself do things other people wouldn't think twice about doing; but if I don't do them, then it might not be long before I start missing meals, running for hours in the rain, taking course after course of salsa lessons. For example, I make sure I always have milk in my tea, albeit skimmed; I have spread on my toast, though I choose Flora over butter, which pisses my boyfriend off a bit because he prefers butter but I tell him to be grateful for small mercies. I don't eat rice cakes for lunch; I have a large jacket potato instead topped with hard cheddar cheese. I can eat at my desk now too. I drink wine at least once a week – usually more now if I'm honest – and am a connoisseur of salad dressings from Waitrose. I try to maintain a high fibre diet so I don't need to use laxatives. On Sundays I give myself a treat, a cooked roast. The treat part? No gravy.

And it's through making myself do all this and making myself have three meals a day that I stay mentally composed enough to be well. I have to care for my body. I have to feed it and water it, but to be honest sometimes I'd rather not bother. I don't mean not bother eating. Don't worry, I'm not having a relapse. It's just, the other day, when I was preparing for this, I sat down and realised exactly what I do to my body as a matter of course. You ready?

I pluck it, wax it, shave it, exfoliate it, brush it, massage it; I straighten and curl my hair; on my face, I cleanse, tone, moisturise, put make-up on and take make-up off. I use face packs – oh and serum and moisture masks on my hair; hairspray and heat protection spray. I've been known to use Dead Sea mud on the rest of me. Would I bother this much with a tuba if I hated music?

Because I do still hate my body – maybe hate's too strong a word now. I've never liked it anyway. I like being alive, but I don't like what I live in.

The dodgy relationship with my body began when my pubic hair down below grew before all the other girls'. I remember three girls pointing at it and laughing when we changed for PE. I remember not understanding and saying 'it's natural though, you'll get it too' and one girl – Danielle I think her name was – had this look of complete incomprehension on her face. She knew it was natural, that wasn't the point; she couldn't understand why that meant she shouldn't laugh when it wasn't there for the rest of them yet.

I guess that sums up society really: the need to conform to the majority, even if we're perfectly fine as we are. And we all conform, don't we, if we can? Or we try to so we don't feel rejected or so we don't reject ourselves.

Like I did. Once.

Now I'm learning to like myself.

So can you. Like yourselves I mean, not like me. Though if you do like me, that's great, but I don't mind too much if you don't.

Lisa Parry

I'll Never Be Good Enough

I'll never be good enough. Try harder, try being thinner, trying sucking it in, or spitting it out, just try, try to make it fit…try fitting in, just for once…

The next twig that walks past me, I might just snap; clean in two…me or them, I don't mind which.

Every mannequin, every glossy paper pin-up Barbie, every channel, every magazine shot is like a drip feed. Chewing on their powdered bones and chiselled jaw lines leaves me with a bad taste in my mouth. Ironic, considering the only thing that passed their lips today would have been a glass of water.

Do you know that feeling when your stomach oozes over your jeans, thick and pale like curdling cream? It's impossible to contain or control… It's like I'm a saturated sponge, all soggy and overfilled.

I hate my body sometimes; I mean REALLY hate it.

It's like somebody left the tap on inside my skin and its rim is overflowing, blotting out the anorexic reflection I used to wear.

I feel like anorexia ate my body and recovery regurgitated it. And now I'm just this body on a clothing rail that feels 3 sizes too big. A big anorexic girl, try explaining that to someone, it's hard believe me.

I know I HAVE to eat today, I have to try, because my body can't be exactly what I want, or what the world tells me it needs to be.

And I WILL eat today, and I'll eat tomorrow too. And my body WILL get bigger, and it won't fit in your extra small t-shirts or skinny fit jeans. The little jiggle I have, all the squashy, wobbly, fuzzy mounds won't squeeze through the gaps in your clothing catalogues, or into the narrow spaces of those minds too small to see beyond this body I have now.

So here I am… I may hate my body, I need you to know that, how much I hate it, because god, I really do, but I also know hating it won't change it. This is who I am, and I'm stuck with it. So for better or worse, till death do us part, in a very literal sense, I'm gonna take my wobbly, flabby, bits and…well – maybe not honour, love and protect them, but I'm going to see if I can't at least say that they're MINE.

This is MY cellulite, MY belly, MY plumped up cheeks and overbearing roundness. MINE. If I'm ashamed today that's ok, today I'm ashamed, if I'm having an ugly moment I'll be ugly, if I'm in pain I'll be in pain. My body is not a fashion accessory.

I'm through. This is MY recovery, this is my life, this is MY body, and it is real.

And I won't have to try any harder, try being any thinner, suck it in or spit it up, throw it up or throw it out. Maybe I don't fit into your perfect sizes, maybe I don't fit into my own. I'm opting outside of labels, outside of playing this body image game.

So from here on in, whether you listen, or not…my body is the one that'll be doing the gossiping, volume turned up, dial tuned in, loud and clear.

Suz Hemming, 21

Tainted Mirror Image

For my dear friend (and anyone else out there who has suffered from the disease)

A mirror cannot see itself.
She only sees herself through others eyes,
why can everyone else get a glimpse of her beauty?
Is she not beautiful?
She feels invisible.
How can I help her see her beauty?
How can she not know the effect she has?
She is the most beautiful creature I ever set my eyes upon.
She is beauty.
She is natural beauty,
not the beauty make-up gives me.
If she does not realise her beauty soon she will disappear,
the beauty she possesses on the inside will fade.
I love her too much to see her vibrant colours dim.
Tell her! Show her!
Please let her know she is beautiful.

Anonymous

And I Will be Winning

Dragging myself along, weighed down by imperfection. Too wobbly, too fat, too wrong. All wrong. All wrong with no explanation. Tears without reason. Unexplained sobs. Change what you can. Cut out the crap. Just healthy. Seek perfection. Take control. Lunch time smells of pizza and chips. Resist. Just black coffee, diet coke and a cigarette.

And I will be slim, and I will be smiling, and I will be winning.

Not enough. Not yet. The scales say I'm smaller. Body still screaming. Crying out. Too big. Shouting in shame at its reflection. Sinking lower and lower into denial.

One apple, one cracker. 9 hours of dance. 'It's enough. I ate before. I'm not hungry. I'll eat tons later.' Keep going. Pain means its working. Surely. Enjoy the hunger, the growling sensation, the shakes, the dizziness. Drink it up, savour it. The clean, clear feeling of control.

And I will be light, and I will be numb, and I will be winning.

Stark lights scream fear. Medical terms manipulate the air. Needles. Drips. Glucose and fortisips. No control. Missing out. Missing life. Missing. Just a shell. No substance. No energy left for life. Losing.

Break it down, make it safe.

Observe. Calculate. How many calories? Round up not down. Be safe.

Add pepper. One sachet.

Breathe. 40 minute time limit.

Peas. 20 forks. Two peas on each. One on the end of each outer prong. One pea left. Odd numbers don't work. Let it 'slip' off your plate.

Sip the squash.

Potatoes. Boiled. 4. One at a time. Split into half, half the halves, split those again. 8 pieces. Times 4. 32 bites. One piece at a time. Chew slowly. Count the bites, 18, 19, 20, swallow.

Sip the squash.

Veggie sausages in onion gravy. Too many ingredients, don't panic. Think logic, structure. Structure makes it safer.

Separate the onions, one piece at a time. Eat the smallest first. Work your way up.

Sausages. 2. Cut off the ends. Split them in half. Slice right along. 5mm thick. Not too big, not too small. Eat the vegetables from each slice first. Then the rest.

Sip the squash.

Summer fruit crumble. With custard.

Custard first, get it out of the way. Clean it off the crumble. The tip of the spoon yellow. 32 yellow tipped spoons.

Fruits. Blackcurrants. 4. Raspberries. 5. Odd numbers don't work, break the last one in half. Make it 6. Apple. 2 pieces. Too big, cut them in half.

Crumble. 5 pence sized pieces. No more. Keep it slow. Notice. 18 mouthfuls. Keep control.

Sip the squash.

I will cry, I will shake, and I will panic. I will be terrified, hating every mouthful. I will keep going; forcing myself to continue though the tears because I refuse to let you win. I will be eating. I will be fighting. I will be winning.

Sarah Fullagar, 23

This One is for You

This one is for you.
For every day you owned and for every command I obeyed.
For the lies… the only food you allowed me.
For your constant screaming. In private, in public, and in sleep.
For taking every inch of my being… voice, strength and more, and leaving me with a hollow shell, a sharp edged skeleton.
For turning my young body into the ruins of a decaying ancient building.
For taking what was mine.

This one is for you.

For inviting me into your world... I hated every second.

For the life you claimed from behind my eyes... I'm claiming it back.

For the friends you said I didn't need. We are laughing at you right now.

For the cries of help you silenced.

For taking my womanhood and making me a child again.

For wrongly telling me that the rules of happiness manifested within appearance.

For the whispers you provided when I looked in *your* mirrors.

For making me believe that I should be eternally wrong, ugly and sorry.

This is to let you know...

That for what it is worth you can have your identity back.

To let you know how good it felt the day I realised the power to fight was in me.

To let you know that I ate breakfast today and I enjoyed it.

To let you know that every day is a struggle, but I will never give up.

This is to show you...

That I am not the brittle one you last saw. In fact you may hardly recognise me.

To show you that my body is changing and however hard it may be to adjust, being healthy is incredible.

To show you my posture now as I look down upon you with my head held high.

So this is to tell you...

That I never want to hear your voice again.

To tell you, that you are not welcome, in fact, you never were.

To tell you and everyone, that I am beginning to like myself inside and out.

To tell you that your company is not required at the meal I enjoy with my loved ones tomorrow.

To tell you that I am winning.

This moment is for you... For you to hear me when I say that the only thing that was ever ugly about me was you.

Laura Nation, 21

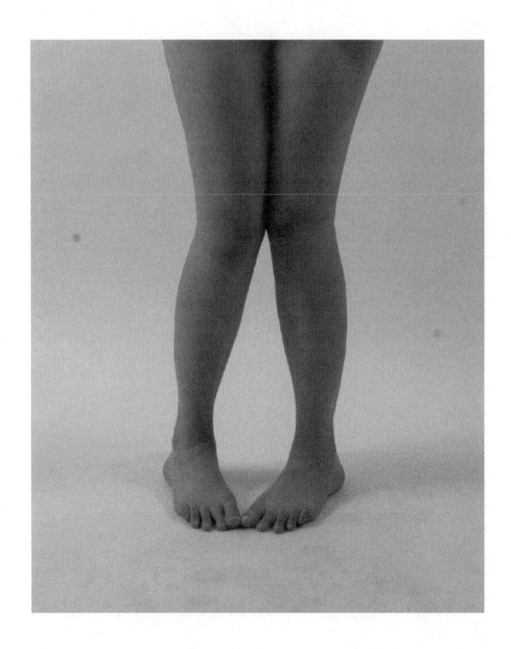

146

Chapter 7

THE HANG-UPS

You know 'that' girl in the changing rooms in Top Shop? The one who parades around in just a g-string and has the thighs of a recently shaved gazelle? Well, it turns out she has body insecurities too. Everyone does.

Don't believe us? Then this is the chapter for you. We're lifting the lid on the Nation's body hang-ups. If you could see the people who have contributed to this chapter, you'd realise that the thing they hate about their body, the thing their eyes are irresistibly drawn to when they look in the mirror, is the last thing you'd notice about them.

It comes with the Body Gossip territory. People reveal their 'sordid' body secrets to us. "My thighs are huge!" they say or "LOOK AT THIS MOLE ON MY FACE!", when we were busy admiring their quirky dress sense or beautiful eyes.

So, this chapter is here to reassure you that you're not alone in having the odd insecurity and to inspire you to focus on what you DO love about your body, instead.

Psoriasis

An incurable skin condition.

"It's not what's on my skin, it's what's under it..."
Anyway...
Things aren't so bad...
I've still got a cracking pair of tits.

Sarah Kingdom

Hello...

My name is... oh I am not allowed to.

Well let's get on with the important stuff.

Ever since I was in about year 5, one of the horrible boys said to me that I have really big eyebrows.

And the worst thing is that he was a boy I had a crush on. I had liked him for ages but then he HAD to go and say that to me. One of my worst things about me. My body.

I always knew my eyebrows were big, black and bushy like. But I didn't know it would cause trouble and make me upset for weeks.

I decided I had to do something about it before I arrived at Secondary school. So instead of just keeping it all to myself and making myself all worked up about it I asked my Best friend. She said I shouldn't do anything. I asked her if it would be better if I didn't have ANY eyebrows than big horrible black ones.

I was tempted to do it WHATEVER my friends said but then I realised that I was silly to think of it. So one day I was outside on a summer day playing a game with all my friends that I lived near, when a girl came down the block. Oh yes, I was scared that she would say the same things that boy said. She walked over with her nose in the air and one of her best friends trailing behind her trying to keep up with her!

I was so silly, and I didn't think about confidence, so I didn't put up my hair because I thought that she would laugh if she saw my eyebrows showing. So in the end I went in and walked up to my room and thought about myself. I was thinking, why am I so ugly? Why does it have to be me that has these HORRIBLE eyebrows? I started to cry.

Even at secondary school, I still get picked on. At least once a day I get an insult thrown at me.

I have been called fat a number of times now as well. I just don't know what to do. All I can think about is my eyebrows...

My best friends are going on photo shoots too. And they have booked me one as well so we can hang out a bit more. What am I going to do? This was one of my birthday presents. I told her I don't know if I wanted to go. And all that was going through my head was excuses of what I shall tell her on the day... 'I am ill.' 'I am going out on that day'...

That's how bad I feel. I don't want to spend time on a birthday present my best friend got me. How horrible is that? I also haven't had a boyfriend in donkey's years! And I have to go and get my eyebrows waxed sometimes too. This is how far I have been pushed. They will push me more and more.

People are always' saying that I have BEAUTIFUL EYES! And I find that amazing. But they get shielded by these horrible things that lurk on my forehead.

Anonymous

Long Jeans and Ugg Boots

I have a condition with my leg that makes it noticeably skinnier than the other and my foot is deformed (I don't like using that word but it's the only word to describe it). I've been skitted an tormented all my life. I don't wear skirts or shorts because I'm scared of what people think and what they will say and, on top of getting called names for that, I also get skitted for being fat. My friends try and tell me I am not but everything they say isn't going to change the reflection in the mirror. I even get it 24/7 from my brother. Most nights I cry myself to sleep wondering why I can't be normal. I try and hide my figure but I can't. It's hard for me to see other girls in little miniskirts or shorts and sandals in summer when I have long jeans and Ugg boots on to hide my leg and foot and baggy tops to hide my fat.

Jenny Coughlin, 14

The Stretch Marks' Hiss

I think I was eight when you gave birth on my skin
You were a snake supposedly passing through my body
Until you crawled in between the cracks
Installing yourself upon me
Rapidly darkening with time
That's when your presence began to alarm me
So I tried to bury you underneath layers of clothes
I wanted to imprison you with the bruises, burns and birth marks
But you were a free spirit, couldn't stay hidden for long
Bathing costumes brought attention to your hisses and your turning head
Then the whispers began

About how the rest of your family invited themselves on my arm, breasts, legs, shoulder blades and a big gathering around my stomach
You were an overnight sensation
With a woman asking if I was expecting
I was twelve years old
Then I learned your name: Stretch Marks
You have made my body your home
And I still hear your hisses telling me: That I am an undiscovered canvas which cannot see its own beauty

Anonymous

Who Am I to Judge?

Everyone has things about their bodies that they hate. Its just human nature I suppose. It's always the same thing; "I'm too fat" or "My boobs are too small." The worst one I hear all the time is "I'm ugly." No one is ugly. Well, I don't think anyone is ugly but then again, who am I to judge?

Nonetheless, I could pick out a million things I hate about my body. I'm so freakishly tall that I tower above my friends and my hips don't look child-bearing; they're more monster truck-bearing. But I've learnt to live with these things because I know deep down (and I mean way deep down) that they don't really matter. But there is one thing that gets me upset every time. Every single time.

I've had eczema since I was born. I kind of just accepted it as a fact of life but as I've gotten older it's become harder and harder to live with. It breaks out all over my neck and people glower at me all the time, thinking I have a love bite. As if! I try to hide it as best as I can but I can feel everyone staring. Or maybe I just think they're staring. I always try to cover it just in case.

I'm the girl that sheepishly goes into the toilet when getting changed for P.E. I'm the girl that refuses to take her jacket off in case people ask about my arms. I'm the girl that has to stop herself from manically scratching her leg during classes.

But you know what? It doesn't even matter. I might not have flawless skin (the opposite if anything!) but it doesn't bother me as much anymore. Being self conscious isn't going to get me anywhere so I look at the positive parts of my body. I'm fairly slim with long legs and really brown eyes. Maybe if I'm confident enough about these things then people won't notice my flaws. That's if they're not too busy worrying about their own problems...

Gemma, 15

This Scar

This piece is not a blemish.
Not an imperfection.
It's a piece in my puzzle.
It's part of my body's tapestry.
The patch of lighter coloured flesh marks a thread in my memory.
However,
It was not intentional needlework in my body
like my piercings.
It was an accident
- like many unexpected wonderful things in life.
I would not unpick this scar from my skin,
like I would not unstitch the memory of my exotic holiday.
Skin, unlike most things, mends itself with little effort.
When it mends, it does not always return to the way it was.
But a damaged section of material does not mean the same on my skin,

a loose thread will not unravel the whole masterpiece.

This scar serves a purpose like no other imperfection.

Merely a glance refreshes in my mind a picture; an emotion, a story.

A memory of clear aquamarine waters;

white sand,

the quickness of my breath following the advancing jellyfish,

the pain I felt as the side of my boat cut my leg.

The stupidity I felt after my dash,

learning the breed of animal would not have harmed me unless I had meant it harm.

The lesson I learned of haste and fear.

This scar is no imperfection.

This scar will always be sewn into the tapestry of my skin.

A memory.

Alice Bodenham

I am, In Fact, Ginger

For many years as a young child I suffered with a stress related illness which resulted in my legs breaking out in blood popping scabs every month, but they never went away. I was also a very chubby kid, not fat....just ate a lot......I was in women's size ten at the age of 10....I was also left to deal with my hair colour....I am, in fact, ginger and growing up in tower hamlets in the east end of London was particularly difficult, when people didn't like things different.

Jodie Ward

Hairy Tale

"Lift up your arms! Go on, show us!" – Master V, Year 6, 1999.

For me, puberty started when I was 9. Breasts seemed to have appeared overnight and suddenly I was plunged into a world where my Marks and Sparks training bra would come undone after the slightest movement (doing it back up again discreetly under a summer dress in a full classroom was not an easy task I can assure you!) Next, was the smell. Why did my armpits suddenly start producing 'B.O.' and why did Impulse not stop it? It was at this point that I properly observed my mum's morning washing ritual. This was going to make getting ready for school so much longer! And then there was the hair. Hair. The bane of my life. Not content with being everywhere, it had to go and be black as well. No hiding that! I think that I can always remember having one single, solitary pubic hair and not really understanding why it was there, then suddenly, BAM! A fanny full of 'em. Not the worst part of course, I think they came just after the dreaded armpit hair. They decided to spring up at 10, which is when Master V caught sight of them at the class swimming lessons. His fun was soon ruined when I told the teacher that he'd asked if my period had started (which it hadn't, and would in fact wait a further 3 years to do so) so that showed him. I danced a lot then too which made certain costumes very embarrassing. I remember watching rehearsals for a show once and wondering why all the 19-year-old girls had no hair and I had loads. That's when the concept of shaving was explained to me and, whilst I was brimming with excitement at the prospect of having no hair again, my mum – in all her wisdom – decided that it may be too early to start. "Don't want to ruin your body. No-one can really see it anyway". Seriously. This was 1999 not 1960 when going au naturale was acceptable. So thus I stuck out the rest of Primary school wearing t-shirts and keeping my arms tightly pulled down when in swimming lessons (telling myself that the water covered my pits when I had to actually swim). Then of course there was the embarrassing 'asking for advice' moment, which may have been ok had it not have been my Mum asking every female person I came into contact with whether it was too early to start, and if a lady-shave was better than a razor. Shrinking away from the conversation, I still managed to glean that shavers were the way to go, so off we went to buy one. Well, they all lied. A shaver simply takes off the top layer. What good is that to someone with pitch-black hair?! I want to look like a 5 year old again, not a 40-

year-old woman! Sadly, the shaver disappeared after sometime, I honestly have no clue where it went, but I wasn't sorry to see the back of it! Finally, I was able to use dad's razors (obviously after mum asked my aunt if it was safe first!) Well what a discovery! My legs were smooth as silk and my arms, well they still weren't perfect, but they were so much better! Until the next day. Body hair really is quite persistent. And thus began the daily shaving of the arms, which in hindsight was probably a mistake as a nice shadow is almost always present. Thankfully now I've discovered waxing, but only rarely, for special occasions and suchlike.

As I grew older, other areas started to affect me more. My stomach for example. Why the hell have I got hair on my stomach?! Though it's not black so I may have got off lightly there. A lady once told me that she waxed hers about four times and then it didn't grow back. Thank god my friend is a good waxer because going to a salon and asking for a stomach wax sounds far too embarrassing. And nipple hair, what the hell is that about?! Got to keep an eye on those, don't ever want anybody to see them! Do be careful when shaving around the nipple however as it's a very dangerous procedure. Now my bikini line, less of a line more of a wall. No matter how many times you get rid of it, it just keeps coming back, longer, stronger and so much more of it! Holidays and swimming are always quite embarrassing. Whilst I love my body when it's slim and trim, there's always the slight fear that when I bend over or do a handstand in the pool, a cheeky few hairs will escape. But there's just so much of it, removal becomes quite the task, which I have neither the time nor the patience to do properly. Fingers crossed a few more waxes will sort that right out!

The thing I got the biggest complex about was my eyebrows. When I was younger they were very thick, in fact I was mistaken for a boy on three occasions, which I still remember all too well. So my mum's friend waxed them for me when I was 15 and they were great, really sleek and sophisticated. But I didn't want them to come back; I didn't want to be teased anymore. That's when the plucking began. Relentless, constant, and a release. Pulling out my hair made me feel good. I'd sit in class, in exams and at home and pull at my eyebrows, eyelashes and even my pubic hair. When one stuck out I'd pull and pull until it came out. Itching meant a hair was ready to come out, usually from my eyelashes, which once were commented on because they were thick and black and needed little mascara, but were now starting to have gaps. Thankfully the eyelashes just seemed to be a one or two-year phase and they're ok now, if still a little thin on the ground. But my eyebrows are a different story. Sometimes I still wax them if I can bear to not pluck for a while, and they look much better when I don't, but little gaps appear where I still pick at them if I'm tired or stressed. Even if I'm not aware of something consciously, I can usually tell my state of mind from how thin my eyebrows get. I wish I had normal brows. Some of my friends have the most beautifully shaped, thin haired brows whilst I'm stuck with coarse black 'things'. When looking at old photos, my friend once jokingly said "That's when your eyebrows went from caterpillars to commas". I'm not entirely sure she realises just how much of an effect that statement had on me, even now, 2 years later.

The one bit of hair I have always loved, though, is my head hair. Thin, light brown, lots of things to do with it! I've just had it cut short for the first time and I love it! But even that's starting to hate me. White hairs, at 23, I ask you! And thanks to my height I'm always very aware that people can probably see it. Still, you can't have everything. I've got a six-pack so I just look at that when I get down!

Emma, 22

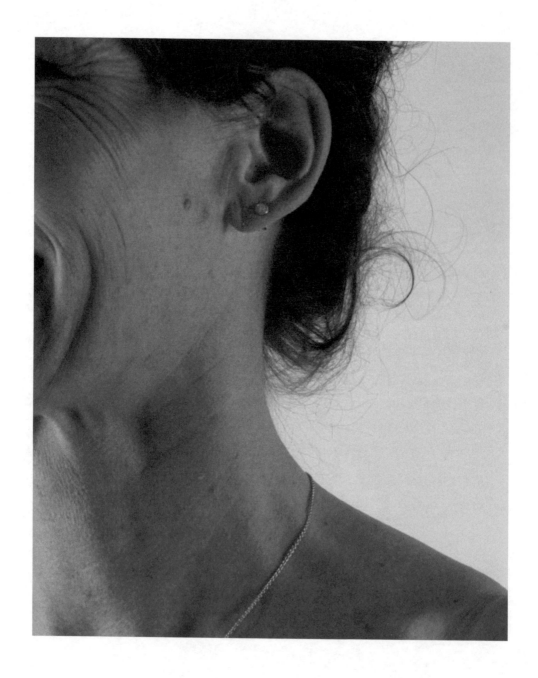

Chapter 8

AGEING GRACEFULLY

We live in a culture where age is seen as the enemy of beauty. We spend our teens trying to look older and then, as soon as we hit 30, the process is reversed and we're suddenly overwhelmed with a desire to look like a teenager again.

"You look so young!" is the ultimate compliment. Why? We're not sure.

There's nothing more heartening and inspiring than someone with wrinkles proudly proclaiming to the world "I am old and I am FABULOUS!" Forget botox, this chapter is all about people who realise that with age comes experience, wisdom, maturity, humility, perspective and other sexy things.

But it'll also show the other side of the coin. What's it like to get older in Britain, in a society obsessed with youth? You're about to find out...

Ageing Gracefully

Have you bought a moisturiser recently? I was trawling the skincare aisle in my local supermarket the other day in search of something to put on my face in the morning and was appalled to discover that over 90% of the lotions and potions on offer were of the anti-ageing variety. The choice was mind boggling: anti-ageing radiance serums, wrinkle reduction creams, ultimate lift lotions for mature skins, firming day creams to reduce the appearance of fine lines, energising fluids for tired skin, re-plumping night creams, wrinkle de-crease collagen re-plumpers, double lifting dermo pumps, regenerating oils, deep wrinkle fillers, age spot correctors, brightening balms, pro-contouring systems...and on...and on...

Tucked away in the corner of a bottom shelf I found a few lonely 'bog standard' moisturisers which didn't exhort me to look younger, smoother, plumper and less wrinkled - just more moisturised.

I'm going to be 40 next year and I like my face. It tells a story. The story of a woman who has laughed and cried and spent a little too much time in the sun. My face shows wisdom and strength, vulnerability and experience and a few scars from a life lived fully. I don't want to look younger - why would I? Why would I want to look 10 or 20 years younger than I really am?

When we spend all our time and money wishing we looked younger, or thinner or different, we miss out on now. We are constantly striving to look like we did, or like we wished we had, or like we hope we will one day. We ignore what we have and lose touch with who we are.

Of course there's nothing wrong with looking after yourself and doing what we can to look and feel more beautiful, but what's wrong with looking like a beautiful 39 and a half year old? Is it not allowed? I will still be a 39 and half year old, however much I plump, firm, lift, smooth and de-crease.

Own your body: be beautiful and wrinkly, be beautiful and have laughter lines, be beautiful with age spots, blemishes and uneven skin tone.

Because I am worth it – 39 and half times over.

Audrey Boss, 39

Fat Old Woman

This morning I looked in the mirror again and saw a 69 year old 20 stone woman looking back. Who is she? Please don't say I am that Fat Old Woman. Of course it's me, it was me yesterday, and the day before. Worse than that, it will be me tomorrow.

As a child, I was skinny, 'Skinny Liz' was actually my nickname. I was a tall and thin teenager. My father used to tell me he could hang his hat on my hipbone. My older sister was shorter and more shapely, so was my best friend, and I envied them so much. I felt like the runt of the pack. That was possibly the start of my poor self image. Then it was not fashionable to be thin. Curvaceous was the theme of the day and Marilyn Monroe the screen idol. Years later I saw a television programme which said the public didn't appreciate how very slim she was. But the curves and how she used them was the thing. I was a yard of tap water, and ungainly with it.

My mother and grandmother, thin in earlier years, put on weight as they aged but they didn't use to diet then, just accepted that they were older and larger. I remember grandma's partiality to sweets and cakes – but she lived to 96 so defied current scientific thinking.

Back to the mirror. Problems don't come in ones, that's for sure. First, there is the age. It shouldn't be a problem because it is a natural occurrence and happens to us all. Nevertheless, ageism is rife. It was a shock to discover the reality of 'becoming invisible' at 50. You just wait and see, it seems to happen overnight. It seems that one day I was being told that I may be an older woman but I was an *attractive* older woman, and the next day they were serving the person in front and behind me at the deli counter as if I were Casper's aunt. Inside you don't feel any different, that's why it is such a shock.

Liking who I am has never been an easy ride. Leaving out a few traumatic life experiences (everyone has a story) I spent most of my twenties in hopeless relationships. Thirties and forties saw a problematic marriage which ended in a total life change. Now I look back I realise that I was quite personable with a good figure but, with no money to buy nice clothes or cosmetics and no-one to tell me I was attractive, the time just passed and I somehow never knew until it was gone.

After that age your appearance seems to change rapidly – the face looks a tad grumpy, the shoulders droop, the boobs droop. The eyes get hooded, lips and eyebrows disappear, the teeth start to go bad or go missing, the hair becomes thin, grey or both. Eyes lose their spark and the skin its colour. It creeps up on you, the ruthless silent enemy. I still remember the first time I saw a chubby old lady struggling towards me on the high street and realised it was my reflection in the shop window.

If you are up for it, you have a fight on your hands. Creams, lotions, oils, routines; make up tricks fit for the Magic Circle. It's a law of diminishing returns, but at least you feel you are doing something even if it is spitting against the wind.

Then there are the ailments. Apart from the deterioration in looks, nothing seems to work properly any more. Arthritis is the bag I am into. This also seems to be gifted from the bloodline. The stride becomes short and faltering, getting up and down painful, standing for long is worse. Exercise, any exercise, becomes difficult, full of effort and often pain. So I sit for longer, have stopped walking far, can't run. Plan trips upstairs, down the garden, and to the internet shop.

The weight piled on, big time. So dieting started in earnest, big time. You name it I have done it, been there, got the T shirt. Diet groups, diet books, diet pills, acupuncture, hypnotism, internet clubs, TV specials, slimming drinks, meal replacement bars, meal replacement powders. Every diet has resulted in a subsequent increasing weight gain. I recently tried for surgery but am above the age to have it done.

I am now 8 stone heavier than I was when I first started dieting 'seriously' about 12 years ago. My knee joints are both at a severe and painful stage of arthritic deterioration, but I cannot be put forward for a replacement operation as it is too much of a risk with the extra weight I carry, apart from the fact that the pressure on the new joint would be too excessive. I have apparently wrecked my metabolism with 'see-saw' weight control and dieting alone cannot get the weight shifted. Exercise could be an answer, but… Catch 22 situation or what?

So here I am again, in front of the mirror. How or why did I let this happen to my body? I just can't believe what I see, although I see it every day. My body is ugly in clothes and uglier undressed.

A few weeks ago I was walking to the local surgery and passed a young mother sitting on a low wall watching her children play in the garden. After I passed I heard her call out after me, 'porky!" and then they all laughed. I walked on thinking it was a sad way to bring children up, but it has stayed with me.

Sizeism, as ageism, seems also to be socially acceptable. Janet Street Porter was scathing about overweight women the other day – said she had no patience with people that let themselves get fat – she nearly asked an overweight women in the supermarket why she didn't eat sensibly and lose weight! I wonder why Janet Street Porter doesn't get her teeth fixed or perhaps have speech training? Perhaps I will meet her in a supermarket one day and ask her.

But in the meantime I will stay optimistic and look towards something that will interrupt the Daily Carousel Without Joy of too much weight and pain, too little mobility and self worth.

Perhaps I could have one more try, find a new eating plan. Starting on Monday…

No more Fat Old Woman? Watch this space.

Delyse Phillips, 69

Who Cares What the Papers Say?

At 63 I have the problem of everything heading south. My breasts are long and thin instead of puffy and full and I hate them. I have never had a lovely figure because I wasn't born to have one. It is difficult to get clothes when your top half is a different size from the bottom. Added to all this I have short legs and arms. My teeth are falling out as well, hee hee! So you could say I am a bit of a physical wreck. But growing old is hard enough without the disappearance of any look you might have had years ago. I am feeling sorry for myself now and am looking for a partner which I don't think I'll ever get. Women of certain age have a problem meeting men of their own age without the worry of stripping naked in front of them. So girls, keep hold of your figure as long as you can, for nature can be cruel to the human body. Diets come and go but our bodies don't and we have to learn to live with imperfection. The media drives me crazy with their comments about people in the news. I think the latest batch of skinny minnies in our newspapers are a bad example, they all look either bulimic or anorexic – in other words: drastic. Most men love their love handles with enough beef on to hold, so who cares what the papers say? I'll eat what I want and live another day.

Pat Plunkett

BodyShock

I am finding bits of my body
Starting to crumple
I can see crepey skin on my arm
If I twist it in a certain way - in a certain light
At night my hip hurts
And I can't lie the way I used to
My shoulder is seized
The result of an injured wrist
The wrist is a memory
But the shoulder remains
The pain of a body
Not supple and youthful

But used
I pluck the odd white hair from my head
And my chin sprouts tough little wires
Armed with tweezers
I take them on
My skin no longer glows
And liver spots - Liver Spots!
Smudge across my cheek
Back in the day
I was cute, blonde, lithe
Men looked at me
With that look in their eyes
And I sparkled, twinkled, fluttered
I knew which side my bread was buttered.
Where has she gone
That kitten?
When did she become a fat cat
With flat breasts
And caesarean scars?
When did *she*
Become me?
But I'd tell her it's OK
In my head I'm the happiest ever
Forty's fine
In my mind
And my body?
My body is doing what bodies do
And that's OK too
It's a slow path towards death
And with every breath
I shall enjoy living

Kate Tym, 40

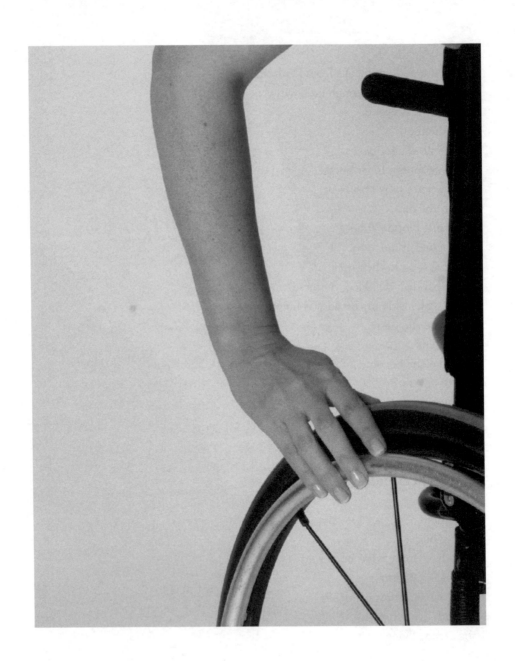

Chapter 9

CHALLENGING BODIES

There's nothing like suffering an illness or injury to make you realise that your body is there to do a job first, and to look good second.

When our bodies malfunction it has a profound effect on our lives. And all that time we spent worrying about how far our stomachs protrude or why our hair JUST WON'T GO HOW WE WANT IT pales into insignificance. Ruth discovered this when she damaged her back in 2011. Whilst laid up on her sofa, she wrote her first ever Body Gossip story (five years after founding the campaign!) and you'll find it within this chapter.

These stories document the realities of living with an illness, an injury or a disability. They reinforce the truth that our health is the most valuable commodity we own, a truth we can all too easily forget.

Middle Aged Spread

Old, fat and frumpy; how I hated my body, all twelve stones plus of it. Over the years the weight gain was gradual, 'middle aged spread' everyone called it. Too true!! My husband was part of the problem. He liked my full pendulous breasts and never complained about the 'love handles' and large bottom that went with the 'package'. On our wedding day, forty years earlier, I weighed only seven stone but he was 'skinny' too. Unfortunately, we both adored cakes and pies and I could never resist those fudge donuts in our favourite coffee shops. There's a photograph of the pair of us frolicking in the sea off Queensland Australia, looking like a couple of playful whales! I longed to get back to the ten and a half stone I weighed at my younger daughter's wedding in 1990.

And then IT happened, just a routine operation to remove a small precancerous polyp in my large bowel. I was told it was nothing to worry about and just wanted to 'get it over with'. I had just retired at sixty and we were both looking forward to lots more fun and travel. I seemed to recover well from the operation but somehow things were not quite 'right' afterwards in hospital. I was fevered and had little appetite but they kept giving me huge trays of food which went back mostly uneaten. They didn't notice!! I was 'melting' before their eyes. Clostridium difficile is a VERY nasty superbug which produces two toxins which destroy the bowel lining. I incubated it for six days before being discharged from hospital.

At home my willing husband took care of me, doing all the food preparation. He bought me lots of tempting little treats to encourage my appetite; but now even the thought of a donut made me feel sick. I still can't manage any foods with a high fat content. I was so unwell that it was some weeks before I even cared to mount the scales, although I was aware that all of my size eighteen clothes just 'hung' on me. I now weigh just over ten stone and my dress sizes are a twelve on my bottom half and a fourteen on my top half (I have broad shoulders). My new body has been toned up by regular trips to the gym. I threw out all of my clothes and bought tight jeans and fashionable tops and dresses. It is weird to find that some men now make passes at me. I am nearly 63!!

There is an old Chinese proverb and it goes like this: 'Be very careful what you wish for because you might get it'!! My lovely new body has been given to me at the expense of my health. I wish I was fat and frumpy and HEALTHY and HAPPY again!!!

Jennifer Allan, 62

Dawn

He traced the pink line
of her absent breast and
wept at her beauty

Julie Bainbridge, 51

The Eviction of Roger the Lodger

Sat alone in a sterile room,

contemplating impending doom,

I pick at ancient mental scabs and chew on their crusted pus.

I realise my morbid reverie is doing me no favours. But...can objects of memory ever really be forgotten?

Can we lose our minds but keep our senses, or does it all just rot? The MRI's sinister blob only showed that it was doing its job so the surgeon could locate the dense mass, which was "Benign" – Thank God! I counted my blessings, nodded and gave a smile and sighed with relief, glad that I hadn't soiled myself.

I wanted to give him a kiss but it seemed inappropriate,

so with a straight face, totally deadpan, I said, "Will it require a drill

or is a Black and Decker not quite the thing?

Sure it's nothing a hole in the head won't fix, is it?" As I continued to grin his expression said 'frontal lobotomy' and I asked rather casually, "When you go in can you take out the trash? I assure you, I'm not mad but it needs a good clear out of stuff making me sad."

"Let's hope it goes well and you keep all your faculties. With this type of surgery, I don't see any difficulties." "But you will do a clear out - evict Roger the Lodger - that's my pet name for my meningioma." He looked aghast at my dark sense of humour, you're not supposed to make jokes about a diagnosed brain tumour. "I can't guarantee anything else will come out but the surgery will be successful, of that I've no doubt." So they bored holes in my head and removed some bone, my hairdresser couldn't style my newly tonsured dome and Roger the Lodger was ousted from his squat and I fooled the physio into thinking I could walk. Then I was discharged and didn't need to have a funeral, though I'd organised and planned it and it would've been a good'un. The horseshoe scar had thirty six staples and my parting now sits like the leaf of a maple, but who cares about vanity when you're lucky to be alive, trifling and petty, I suspect, were also excised. So when you hear people say 'what doesn't kill you makes you stronger' it's true - even though you might not live longer - at least you'll have perspective and a positive frame of mind and can face life's unpredictability and remember to be kind.

Please don't mock those dancers with two left feet,

It's hard, with the damage, to maintain a beat.

If you'd my left foot, you'd be a heap on the floor.

It can't dance at all and won't any more.

Siobhan McKinney, 52

As Good as Anyone Else

'Spazzy, spastic, hop-along, teacher's pet...come here, we want to talk to you!'

They always caught up with me and I would inevitably end up, head first, in one of the wire rubbish bins in the playground. My two legs would stick out the top, the plastic leg brace taped to my left leg waving about for all to see. When I was 7, going on 8, most days at school went on like this (unless a teacher or friend stepped in at the right moment) and, while being scared at the time, I also remember being mad...really mad! (I have always had a bit of a temper!) Until one day, before they could lift me into one of the bins, I lost it completely and shoved the ring leader so hard that she fell back, hit her head on the ground and started crying. Then I felt guilty. Bullies are just cowards and I wasn't the only one being bullied, that was for sure!

I always knew I didn't deserve to be treated badly because of my cerebral palsy...I just was.

From a very young age my parents had instilled in me that I was no different from anyone else. Yes, there were certain things I could not do, like ride a bike, go roller skating or kick a ball, but it wasn't a big loss and they always made sure that I had a go at everything. When the doctors wanted to put me in a 'special' school, my parents refused and, looking back, I am so grateful they did. Body confidence (which mustn't be confused with being conceited or arrogant) comes from believing that you are OK...just the way you are. Not better than anyone else, just 'as good as' everyone else, regardless of your personal circumstances. My mother was always very comfortable in her own skin and never felt the need to 'dress up' for other people. She would only do it for herself. To this day I still believe she honestly didn't care what other people thought (one of the many qualities my father loved in her) and was always just herself. When you have a role model like that, no matter how young you are, it definitely has an impact.

Most of the time I don't feel different from everyone else.

Don't get me wrong, I still went through the same teenage angst as everyone else and boys definitely didn't want to go out with me because I was 'different'. And sure there were days when I really hated my cerebral palsy and my body. I used to look at my left arm and leg and think 'WHY won't you work properly?...WHY?' But there was always something, or someone, to pull me out of my 'blue funks' as my father called them. I was always allowed to vent my frustration/upset but then I was picked back up again, told I was loved no matter what and told to get on with it and because I was stronger than most... I did. As I hit my twenties I found I didn't have the same insecurities as many of my female friends. Things that bothered them didn't even register with me. I didn't seek approval in the same way they did. I remember saying to one friend, 'when there are things about your body you cannot change, no matter what, the rest of it becomes slightly insignificant.' You can either learn to live with it and accept it, or you can spend your life being utterly miserable. Most of us choose the former, of course. I also don't for one minute want to underestimate, or belittle the problems and insecurities that my friends went through, we all have our own journey.

The occasional bigot actually helps me like myself more.

Now I'm in my late 30's and slowing down a bit, inevitably. My left hip and leg hurt more often, my arm seems to be tighter. This is no doubt the dreaded 'middle-age' slowly creeping up on me. I do need to lose a few pounds (well OK…more than a few!) but I've lived with cerebral palsy for 38 years. To me this life is normal. A well-meaning friend of my father's once suggested that if I meditated in a certain way I could 'cure' myself. I looked him straight in the eye and said, "But there is nothing WRONG with me, I don't need fixing, I'm not imperfect, this is just the way I am and I'm fine with it. If I could walk 'normally' tomorrow I would probably fall flat on my face. That to me would be a problem!" When what I am seems to make other people feel uncomfortable, I like putting them at ease and opening their minds a bit. I have to say I have the most wonderful family and friends. They have accepted me EXACTLY as I am and that to me makes them pretty incredible.

There are plenty of people out there who don't accept people who are 'different'...at all. People like them actually help me to like myself more. Sure, I still have down days, it's only natural, but on average my state of mind about myself is positive. I live a good life. I have a degree (something some people still find amazing because they assume that if you have CP your intellect is impaired as well). I hold down a full time job and live in a lovely flat, on my own, in London. I have a great social life and have had quite a few boyfriends over the years. To be honest, the odd time someone says something bigoted towards me, I still feel affronted (that old temper again!) but I don't CARE what they think. I guess I really am my mother's daughter after all.

Lisa Jenkins, 38

BodyGossipRuth's Bad Back

"I've had an accident". So says the waggy-tailed, squeeky-voiced underdog.

This month, that's me (woof). Lying on my back recovering from an operation on my spine.

I went to hospital, which was pretty awesome actually - morphine, codeine and ice cream. Yum. My mates came to visit, I read all the shit celebrity magazines which I usually despise (Kate Middleton was getting too skinny, Posh Spice was getting too pregnant) and really did have a lovely old time.

Then I came home to the Tyrant Cat aka Leon, my beautiful ginger feline, and settled in for a month of old fashioned R&R.

You know those days when all you want to do is lie on the sofa, watching your Grey's Anatomy season 5 DVD and eating Easter eggs? And you think "wow, how lush would that be, snuggling up with my blanket, maybe with a cheeky glass (OK, bottle) of Sauvignon Blanc. Heaven!"

But it isn't heaven. It's pretty dull really. And today, I feel sad.

BodyGossipTash thinks therefore it's probably not the best time to write my first ever Body Gossip story (I know, I've been running this campaign for 5 years and never written a story *slaps own wrist*) but darn it, I feel inspired!

Because I'm frustrated!

And bored!

And I think I'm putting on weight. The stomach that has always wrinkled my brow with a mixture of concern and contempt is definitely squidging over my jeans more than usual.

And all the things that define ME - cycling everywhere, my incredibly physical job, even co-piloting Body Gossip - I can't do any of them. Because my body doesn't work, and my mind seems to be joining it.

And I know I'll be better soon, and I know I should be so grateful for that, but right now, on 1st May 2011, because I'm sick of the pain, because my legs are itching to be exercised, my heart wants to pump and my skin needs to sweat, and my mind is numb and I'm running out of positivity.

Because of all that.

I want my body back please.

Ruth Rogers, 30

A Flawed Reflection

I stand on the scales and hate myself. Ashamed, I step off and shove them quickly under the bed in case my husband sees. Over half my body is fat. I am morbidly obese.

I haven't always been big. When we met in 1980 I was barely seven and a half stone, petite and sexy, confident in my firm young body. He could hardly keep his hands off me then.

Now I stand before the bedroom mirror and look at a stranger. A fat, ugly stranger. Stretch marks from two and a half pregnancies and years of ballooning weight mar the once perfect skin. Breasts sag, stomach bulges, hips and thighs erupt with fat. I can't see my hipbones or my ribs. My double chin has a double chin.

I can pinpoint the exact moment when I lost control of my body. It was in 1991. My annus horribilis. You don't have to be royalty to have a crap year.

I lost my best friend to cancer, was made redundant the day after her funeral, then had a miscarriage. To cheer me up, my mother-in-law brought me the biggest bar of chocolate known to man. I ate it all, and I haven't stopped eating since.

Life did get better. A year later I had a beautiful daughter. I've had some fantastic jobs that have been much more interesting and fulfilling than the one I lost. I still miss my friend, but have others who are loving and caring and fantastic fun. But I can't stop eating. It was a trigger, you see. The chocolate was a comfort when I was vulnerable from multiple traumas. Without a job, mourning my friend and my lost child, I sat at home and ate. By the time I gave birth, I had put on almost six stones.

What none of us realised at the time was that my annus horribilis had awoken a deeper trauma from my childhood. My father had killed my mother and then himself when I was ten years old. The scandal meant that no one would talk about my parents or what had happened. I had buried it deep in order to cope and now it all came bubbling back to the surface in confusing, distressing ways.

It was another four years before I was diagnosed with post traumatic stress disorder (PTSD). In the meantime, food had become my refuge, my friend, my comforter.

During months of therapy, I put on more weight. The memories being exposed for the first time were painful, frightening and far stronger than I thought possible. After a session I would buy cakes, sandwiches, chocolate, and wine. I would eat all the food on the way home, and the wine was a soothing anaesthetic which allowed me to sleep dreamlessly.

My therapist assured me that I would lose the excess weight, that I was a strong woman who had successfully kept PTSD at bay for almost 30 years, so a few years' worth of overeating would be easy to deal with. He pointed out that I had chosen the 'healthiest' addiction – others chose drugs or alcohol. Then he discharged me. I kept on eating. I sometimes wish I had become addicted to drugs or alcohol because then I'd get help to stop. I have to learn to control my addiction on my own.

I asked my doctor for help. He told me I needed a bit of willpower. I told him willpower has kept me sane for decades, so don't tell me I need some willpower. He was a bit more sympathetic after that but couldn't help.

I went to slimming clubs, bought books on changing your life. I tried numerous diets, spent a fortune on hypnotherapy but nothing stops me eating. I joined a gym; completed a 5,000 metre swimathon, trekked along the Great Wall of China, and in Jesus' footsteps through the Holy Land. I am the fittest fatty you'll ever meet. But the fat remains.

Even after 18 years of fighting this demon, it still takes me by surprise when I look in mirror. I see a stranger. In my mind I am still that petite, sexy young woman. The hideous creature that looks back at me from the mirror frightens me, saddens me.

My daughter is a teenager now. She's slim and beautiful. I am so proud of her. But I'm also deeply envious of her. I wonder, with a sense of despair, whether I will ever be content with this flawed, damaged body that has become both my refuge and my prison.

Alison Knight

Beauty Unsuspected

I wear the top button of my jeans unbuttoned at all times. For most women, this would make me a slut, but in my case it just makes me pathetic. Today, I have funky red hair, I'm 5' 2", seven and a half stone, a 30-F, Banana Republic size zero. I have blue eyes, eyelashes so long I can't wear sunglasses, lovely skin, and a smile that never stops. I've been schooled in classics, theology, philosophy, Spanish, Arabic, Attic Greek, ballet, athletics, kinesiology, theatre, karate, and politics. I've travelled to 16 countries, broken 5 international track and field records, and taught school in Mexico.

Like what you're hearing? I'll go on. I've got a cute butt, an absurdly long tongue for cocktail party tricks, a set of wheels custom made for me, and a great sense of humour. I'm an hour glass figure, a la Marilyn Monroe, very flexible, and ready to embrace the true meaning of freedom.

All of this and I've never been asked out on a date.

After nearly twenty four years of living with a disability, I am still constantly amazed by how sexually frustrated young disabled women are. I've seen girls with all types of disabilities burst into tears and held them time and time again as they sobbed, "But I'll never have a boyfriend. Just look at me. Who would want to date me?" Often it seems as if perceived asexuality is the greatest disappointment from disability. I watch young women yearn to feel beautiful, desire a man's touch, wish to have the freedom and confidence to invite him back to their room for the night.

Just like all women, we too crave to feel cherished. We want to open a magazine and see someone who looks like us. Most people think that body image issues revolve around a size or a reflection. But it doesn't stop there.

It is particularly difficult to watch idealized images of love, even though my mind knows that these ideals will falter, fall flat on their faces, and cause more heartache that I can ever imagine. I remember coming home after a bridal shower for both of my best friends last year and sobbing in the bathtub, "I want to be loved like that. I want to be held like he holds her. I want to be someone's sexual dream. I want so badly to be given dishtowels by my best friend and be excited about them."

Perceived asexuality does have a wonderful advantage though. I may cry every time I see Cyrano de Bergerac, but I am able to take the time many girls primp and throw themselves ruthlessly at guys to truly excel at everything I wish to do. And I know I have given desire that only certain guys are man enough to fill. True, pure, hunger is made to be satisfied.

It's amazing how guys who do not know about the disability will give me compliments without hesitation. On the way back from work today, I looked out the car window to see a car full of guys whooping and yelling at my eye contact and wagging their tongues at me. In Switzerland this summer, during a particularly hot evening, I opened my third story window and stood alone on the balcony to watch the sunset. Within a few moments, a Swissman walked by, stopping to stare at me. He yelled up, first in French, then in Italian, and then in German. After all attempts failed, he tried English. "You are the most beautiful vision I have even seen. I wish I had a camera to make your picture. May I come up to see you?"

Unaccustomed to such attention I always smile and back away, knowing that mystery is more romantic than exposure.

I am beautiful. I am sexy. I am built perfectly. I will be cherished by a man someday. I don't need to waste my time with false lovers, for I know I have these characteristics, even if no one else suspects it.

Athena Stevens

Different to Other Mums

No-one would know by looking at me and my three year old twins that I'm different to any other mum. But I am.

To be told I needed a hysterectomy wasn't ever going to be welcome news. But to be 33 and have dedicated the last three years of my life to getting pregnant meant it was a big blow. There was a big plus side, the years of my life being restricted by pain and heavy bleeding caused by uterine fibroids was about to end. No more would my bag be stuffed full of changes of underwear and enough sanitary products to plug an oil leak. I should have been overjoyed to get my body back and I would have been if I only I could have had my family first. But after my second largely unsuccessful operation to have the fibroids removed, the doctors told me they didn't like the rate the cells were dividing. I was told I definitely wasn't to have any more IVF and I needed a hysterectomy as quickly as I could bring myself to go through with it. I think I surprised the consultant and myself when I asked for some dates then and there. I was teary of course but I felt if that was my fate I just wanted to get it over with and move on.

Coming to terms with losing my womb was a like a grieving process. I felt an aching loss for not being able to carrying my own baby, feel them kick and to breastfeed. People like to tell me I'm lucky to never have to experience a pregnancy and birth and I'm sure it isn't a bundle of laughs from start to finish, but I never got to choose. For a time I resented my body, I felt sorry for it too, for never fulfilling its biological potential.

My husband and I were lucky, we had a second chance. It always helped me to have a plan and keep looking forwards and six weeks after my operation (doctors orders or it would have been sooner!) I was back on the case. I had kept my ovaries and so with the help of an amazing gestational surrogate we could still have our own family. Soon after finding the right lady for us she fell pregnant and as if things couldn't get any better it was twins! Surrogacy, as we found, is not something everyone agrees with and it wasn't our first choice but, well, without that choice the exhausting but joyous family life we have now just wouldn't be.

The surrogacy pregnancy threw up lots of body issues itself. Some we'd expected, like the feeling of a loss of control, although we were so lucky to have a surrogate we could trust. And then the unexpected heartbreak I felt when I watched our surrogate drive away after the 12 week scan with my babies in her tummy, I so wanted them with me. There was guilt too at seeing her after a c-section looking so tired and drained and knowing it was all because of me. She never complained, quite the opposite, she thanked me for giving her the opportunity to carry twins. As I said before, amazing people both her and her husband, and without my hysterectomy I would never have believed they could exist!

I wasn't prepared for how much people see a new mum coming down the street and check out her size. I also wasn't ready for how they don't keep those thoughts to themselves! It was summer time when the twins were born so no big baggy jumpers to cover me up but I decided I wasn't going to try and pretend I'd been pregnant and I wore my normal clothes. The first time someone commented on what great shape I was in it took me off guard and I blurted out the surrogacy story. But in the end I got wise and just took the nice comments graciously!

I may have beaten my body and had a family but I only managed two years away from the operating table. I developed a tumour on an ovary, so the whole thing had to be removed. Whilst operating they found parasitic fibroids that had continued to grow even without a womb. Another operation closely followed that one to remove yet more fibroids. As I write, I have an ultrasound scan booked to check out another lump I have found in my abdomen. I am thankful that my problems haven't been life threatening, but it doesn't stop me wishing that it would just all go away.

All of this has left my stomach in a bit of a mess! I said when I began this story that no-one would be able to tell that I'm different from other mums from the outside. Well if they saw me in a bikini they would! As well as lots of small scars around my ovaries I have a large vertical scar that starts above my belly button and divides my tummy in two. Privately I've embraced my scars and accepted them as a part of my story but when I'm on holiday I cover them up and would feel too embarrassed to expose them.

My children now have begun to understand that babies grow in tummies. And so of course the questions have started. It is true to tell them that they came from my tummy because they did but, whilst I don't want to lie to them, I also don't want to tell them something they are too young to understand yet. So for now I tell them that they are extra special because mummy's tummy is broken.

Alison Burnside, 37

Topless on the Beach

The first time I really cried over my breast cancer was when my baby, albeit 22 at the time, gave me a bath when I came out of hospital following my mastectomy. When I stood up for Sarah to help me out and dry me, I caught sight in the mirror of a bloodied mess where my breast used to be. It didn't seem fair that Sarah had to help her mum. It should be the other way around.

I was diagnosed with early stage breast cancer in October 2005. Two lumpectomies and a course of radiotherapy later, my left breast was already pretty disfigured. When my surgeon told me the cancer had spread into a blood vessel and recommended a mastectomy, I accepted his decision and went ahead in August 2006 with an immediate reconstruction. I didn't think back then that I could live without a breast. Although only small breasted, I actually liked my boobs. They had served my two children well through their early years and, at the age of 55, I still went topless on the beach.

The reconstruction was unsightly from the start and the initial attempt was followed by 15 pretty miserable months with many hospital visits to get it right. It eventually ended up failing completely in December 2007. So, two years after my original diagnosis, I finally had to face up to life without my left breast. And, do you know what? It's really not that bad.

There are many companies out there that cater for ladies with mastectomies and my style of dress has only altered slightly. I can look in the mirror without feeling appalled at what I see. My husband has been amazing throughout and his support has no doubt helped tremendously.

I am awaiting a final revision of scar operation in April to tidy up my left breast where the reconstruction failed. I will then try a contact prosthesis which actually sticks to your body, enabling you to wear normal underwear and strappy tops. Marks and Spencer here I come!

And who knows, once the area is not quite so unsightly, I may even go topless on the beach. I don't want to hide my body away and now I can see there is no need to.

Audrey Bullock, 60

Born to Survive

Diagnosis: December 2010.
Hodgkin's Lymphoma.
Status: June 2011.
I was born to survive.
And I have.

Jan Kingdom

Chapter 10

MEN

We'll let you into a secret. We didn't want to have to include this chapter. We're so careful not to exclude anyone from the debate here at Body Gossip, we wanted to be inundated with stories from blokes and to be able to include them throughout the book.

Although the stories in this chapter reveal that body image is very much an issue which affects both genders, it seems that there is still a reluctance for men to talk about it.

So, boys, this is a call to arms! We hope the stories on the following pages will reassure, inspire and galvanize you into action! You have bodies too and it's time you got talking about them. Here are the men who were brave enough to lead the way...

Shakespearian Sonnet: Amateur Chef Forsakes a Treadmill

To run and run on a conveyor belt
and make a body a commodity
re make oneself into what mirror felt
re shape oneself out of an oddity
physique is best a suit that never suits
in retrospect, I thought I would impress
women, as one of many gym recruits
mind tricks the naked body to un-dress
(another masculinity turns ripe)
but, to women, I happily confess
I love food – food, I would have, through a pipe,
even! A woman I would love no less.
so tell me if love for food can be shared,
I want to impress you with meals prepared.

Kyle Inducil

Every Day I Fight a War Against the Mirror

In the words of a famous song "Every day I fight a war against the mirror"…

That phrase used to be very true of me and in the space of a few years here I am now bounding around in front of audiences, shouting on the radio and even sometimes seen having the occasional rant on television!

I suppose I should go back to the beginning where this whole story started and detail the experience, without which I would not be bounding around in front of people talking about what I do.

A far cry from the happy, bubbly, outgoing person I am now my teenage years were not particularly fun. You can imagine the usual, you are different, you don't quite fit in and others pick up on that and in turn pick on you. How does this leave you feeling? Deflated, self-conscious and wishing you would just disappear?

Believe me I tried to disappear, I almost let them win. The people dictated that I was different, therefore I should be punished. It was a lot to do with appearance, how I carried myself, how I dressed and how I acted. I kept thinking, "well maybe they are right, maybe I should just be the same", but that wasn't enough for me.

As the time went on, the bullying got worse and the other things piled on top, I can safely say I finally lost it. Food became my way of escape and the result was far from emotional eating, I simply stopped. I decided one day I shouldn't eat and instead I would deprive myself of it.

This may have started as a way of coping but in the end it became about how I looked, how skinny I could become, not for anyone else, but for me, to show myself the willpower I had and the strength I had to abstain from food. I slowly became paranoid about my body, how I would look and how I would appear to others, spending ages getting ready then deciding I couldn't go out because this wasn't right or that wasn't right. It literally took over every waking moment of every single day.

Hours in front of a mirror, scrutinising every single part of my body, and picking at faults that, looking back, simply were not there. I hated what stared back at me. I wanted it to go, I wanted to just disappear. It sounds weird, but it was almost like it wasn't me staring back but my worst enemy, never before have I despised someone so much; my own reflection!

So that was it, I had an eating disorder. Congratulations, was this what I wanted to achieve?

I had a real problem coming to terms with it, trying to deal with the incredible self-loathing I felt and finally I gave in and accepted it, broke down in tears and said to myself, "I really need help".

From that point on I spent years trying to help myself with professionals trying to help me at the same time. With many ups but far too many downs, not much changed, but strangely enough it took just one phrase to change it all.

One night I ended up in hospital for what must have been the umpteenth time, oh the glamorous world I lived in!

My friend came when he heard I was there and he simply said to me, "You're being a silly dick, ain't ya?".

While that phrase wasn't the one thing that cured me, I will admit it had a massive impact. What had I done to myself, my mind, my body? Why did I put myself through this?

From that point I was determined to make a change, I was better than this!

And so my four year recovery begun, learning many things along the way about respect for what you have, respect for the one body I will ever get and respect for the one mind I lost and found again. I found my body again and I was happy with it. I could even go as far to say I love it now, it's not perfect, but what is?!

I now work with a leading charity which works with eating disorders, talk at events and help others with my experience, something I never thought I would have the confidence to do and frankly something I could never see from where I was those few years ago.

I can now leave the house smiling, unashamed and proud of what I have achieved. So maybe it wasn't the best way to learn a valuable lesson, to be broken down and shattered, but I got there in the end and came out the other side a better person, a happy one, even a successful one.

What was the one lesson I learnt?

This is who I am, I won't change for anyone, so accept me for me, and most importantly no more wars against that mirror.

I suppose that was the quick tour through my life so far but I left one major thing out of this whole story and I did it on purpose. The one fact about me that if I said it at the beginning would change your whole perception of this story...

I'm a 25 year old man.

Nick Watts, 25

That's it, I Think...

I know that this is a bit of a rant but I was really happy about my body and I thought I was well built-ish. I know I do next to no exercise and eat chocolate as much as I can, but I was ok. Recently, however, I have started really going out with people and they have commented on my body and said things like "ohhh, I thought you were more muscly than that" and stuff. Also, I know this is a little bit personal, but I have also found out a few things about my dick. I'm not really sure if you want to hear this, but I'll tell u anyway – it's "broken" as it slants slightly to the left. Mmmmm...that's it, I think.

Anonymous

My Body Hair, a Metrosexual Account

I love my hair. I have lots of it.

I grew up in the 1990s, when I was little I thought that a guy with long hair was incredibly sexy and glamorous. The thought of flowing hair in the wind, while a man did manly things like wield a sword or charm women was very appealing. There's no doubt a bit of that rubbed off on me as an adult. When I was at school, it was an all-boys Jesuit Catholic school, where the rules about hair were strict, nothing reaching the collar, basically, and if you had longer hair you were suspended until you had a haircut (is that legal? Ah who knows...).

I wasn't much of a teenage rebel, I did okay in school, I was nice to my parents and had nice geeky friends. Then something just washed over me at sixth form. I saw these pictures of 18th Century people, such as Newton and Kant, and I saw these pictures of them with long hair and a glorious ponytail respectively (now I realise they were probably wigs!). I thought that it was an amazing sign of being an intellectual during that time that they were allowed to have such hair. Combine that historically inaccurate thought with how the Jesuits liked teaching about Kant and Newton, and I had an intellectual justification: I definitely wanted to be a long-hair guy so I started growing it in sixth form. At school in my last year, because I was such a good pupil and a prefect, the teachers gave me a bit of leniency about my hair, but my head of year did say to make it look like you made an effort to get it a little bit shorter to not make any issue with the headmaster, like a centimetre. Most of my other non-prefect friends got suspended with the same kind of hair that I had.

My parents weren't too happy about having a son with long hair. Guys with long hair get all sorts of stick, they are seen as either some kind of 'Conan the Barbarian' muscleman (but I don't have any muscles), or they are seen as some 90s Goth culture leftover, or heavy metal fan (but I don't like the makeup or the moshing, though the music is okay). I love my hair and I don't care for fitting into any boxes, although people seem to think I fit in their box on many occasions. My worry sometimes is whether they put me in a box that I don't fit in.

Being a bit of a nerd, I like to talk about things most people don't understand. I've had a bizarre thing happen to me in recent years, lots of new-agey, hippy type women find me irresistible! Because I have an MA in Philosophy and I know about 18th Century Metaphysics and because of the hair, I seem to look like some exotic guru to them. I'm not really a guru, but I do like the attention. I'm very shy with women and apparently that's endearing too! I love my long hair, sometimes I have 'long hair dreams' where I wake up and my hair is short. I have a little scream when I wake up about that.

Another nice thing about my hair is that I can blend in to all sorts of environments. Tied up, I can be indiscrete and just like anyone else, sometimes I use my thick black glasses to add to my geek chic. I then have a guilty pleasure of removing my glasses and pulling off my hair band to have some Clark

Kent/Superman transformation. I am a little vain but I also can relate to a lot of women about hair. Having long hair makes it easier to talk to women about their hair, or men for that matter. I'd like to think of myself as a modern day metrosexual: I get hair care advice from my girlfriends; I seemingly have girlfriends in that non sexual way women have girlfriends; and I wax.

I suppose it's an odd thing for a man to admit but my parents' genetic heritage is as follows: My mother's side of the genes have given me nice thick hair; my father's side has given me nice wavy hair, the kind that many would go for a hundred pound treatment to make; oh, and another thing, I've also got my dad's hairy shoulders (thus the wax). Waxing is a horrible sensation, at least at first, then some strange masochistic drive goes over me and I want to see more hair on the next strip. I think the one awkward part of waxing other than the waxing itself is going to the store and buying it. Why is it that so many of the products I like are marketed to women? When I buy some wax strips, they are in a pink box. That feels very embarrassing indeed at the counter, especially when the old women in Boots are looking at me carrying a box with a woman's bare legs on the cover.

I am a strange man. In many respects I'm a nerd, I use Linux and I read Sophocles and Aristotle. But I also like weightlifting and going to the gym. I love my long hair and am always looking for the perfect conditioner and I'm asking for hair removal advice from many girl friends. I am a man who likes to take care of his appearance and maybe some people might see these things as effeminate. I don't know to be honest, I don't care for labels, if you want to give me a label, call me Michael.

Michael Pereira, 24

A Race for Life

Where to begin in my race for life?
One that is littered with trouble and strife.

We'll begin at the start, on the blocks, get set go,
A new talent was born and waiting to grow.
At school I excelled, 'A' grades there were plenty
And my sporting diary was never empty.
Things were 'just great', the future looked bright
The world was my oyster to do what I liked,
But then, without warning I hit a hurdle and fell.
And so commenced my journey through hell.
I loved my Nan and it hurt when she died
Of course I was sad and obviously cried.
But the world didn't notice and lives just went on
It was business as usual for everyone.
It felt wrong and unjustified
For me to be happy when someone had died.
Soon guilt took over and with it great pain,
And the eating disorder started to reign.
With no fight inside and little resistance
I embarked on a regime of punishing existence.
I denied myself food, pleasure and fun,
I withdrew, lost friends and soon there were none.
Yet still I ran, I ran and I ran
Pushing harder than any man.
Always cold, sad, tired and drawn,
I kept up the punishment, from daybreak till dawn.
The gnawing inside, my body simply dying,
Pleading parents and endless crying.
Day after month after year went by,
And all this time I kept asking 'Why?'.
A chest infection, I was too weak to fight,
Gripped hold of my body and held me there tight.
Pneumonia now and a collapsed lung too,
Hospitalised, alone and scared what to do.
'Will I die? Please Lord no', life's just too dear,
I love my family and wish they were here.
This can't end now; I'm not ready to go,

I've got to fight back; I've got something to show.
Mum and Dad I'll make you proud,
And once again I'll stand out from the crowd.
I'm going to bounce back; once again I will run,
The formidable challenge - a full marathon.
I'll run for Macmillan, their work is inspiring,
Their support for others just never tiring.
So the journey began on the road back to health,
Life's what's important, not money or wealth.
A tough journey for sure, a mountain to climb,
But the view from the summit was simply divine.
I conquered my dream in April 08
The Paris marathon – Wow! Wasn't that great.
But, don't stop me now I'm on a roll.
The London marathon my ultimate goal.
That was completed in 2009,
Knocking 30 minutes off my previous time.
I'm finally living, my dreams coming true,
And Mum & Dad, it's all down to you.
When the chips were down, when I seemed beaten and done,
You never gave up on your youngest son.
You gave me the chance, the spark that I needed,
Your endless love is why I succeeded.
2011 – Well what a year!
One to remember and one I'll hold dear.
Marathon three, for Macmillan once more,
My adopted charity and yet so much more.
Fuelled with excitement, determination and drive,
Another PB 3:13:55
And so I'll go on, it's my turn to inspire,
Others, who are lost, whose lives seem dire.
However sad your world, however dark the place,
You can beat your demons, you can win the race.
And after the victory, when your troubles are beat,
You'll soon understand that life is just sweet.

Living is fun and life's just a ball,
And that's my message to one and all.

Ian Sockett

Does My Bum Look Small in This?

My name's Chris, I'm thirty years old, I play the piano for a living and I have no bum.

To be honest, I'm not really sure how long I've been this way. Possibly even all my life. I still remember the taunts in the playground. Celery-arse, the other children would call me. The Bumless Wonder.

I've carried this stigma around for as long as I can remember. Years of unrelenting heartache, the weight of a thousand sleepless nights piercing my chest like a freezing ice pick. And will they give me a disabled badge for my car? Will they heck.

Okay, yes - technically I do possess two rather sad little slops of muscle that connect my posterior superior iliac spine to my greater trochanters. Technically they are there. But try comforting a virtually blind man with 'it's alright, at least you can still occasionally make out homogenous brown blurs during daylight hours'. He may as well not have any eyes. It's just insulting.

On the rare occasion that I'm able to summon enough self-confidence to approach a member of the opposite sex - and the even rarer instance in which I sufficiently overcome my crippling arse-paranoia to remove my clothes with the lights on - the reaction is always the same.

'You're a freak!' she cries.

'You're not normal!' she wails.

'Your bum's SMALLER THAN MINE', she laments. 'It's just not right.'

I've tried everything I can think of to remedy this terrible affliction. All the usual tricks pulled by sufferers of this disease - walking at a right-angle to accentuate my curves, expensive home-pumping kits, wedging a couple of rump steaks down my pants before leaving the house. Nothing works. In Korea they sell underwear with ready-made bum implants sewn into them. Which would be great. BUT THEY DON'T DO THEM IN MY SIZE.

There is, of course, one final option staring me in the face.

Well, arse.

Surgery. Medically-licensed mutilation of my precious human body, carried out at massive emotional and financial cost to myself and my family, simply so that I can blend in with 'mainstream' society. And then the taunting would stop. The persecution would cease. I would walk amongst you all, head held high (well, arse held high), basking in the bumglorious ecstasy of the possession of a superior posterior.

But I refuse to lower myself. I just won't go there.

And do you know why?

Because every time I sat down, I'd hear, 'You're a fake'. 'You're a human Barbie doll'. Well, Bumbie doll.

And that's not me. I, like the millions of other people across the globe in possession of so-called 'imperfect' bodies, intend to stand tall in the face of oppression and shout loud and proud to the world:

"My name's Chris, I'm thirty years old, I play the piano for a living…and I have no bum."

Chris Russell, 30

A Vasectomy is for Life, Not Just for Xmas

I have two wonderful sons, a beautiful (if feisty) wife, a house in a market town outside of London, so what more could I need...? What I really need is the answer to the ultimate question – am I firing blanks now?!!!

About three years ago I kept getting 'the nudge' about having the dreaded snip. I must admit I didn't need all the angled reasoning or the clever devices that women conspire to utilise to get what they want, I actually was happy to stop spawning and once again have unprotected sex without my wife being on the god-awful Pill with all of its side effects.

I went in, got drugged, had a 'doomed man cigarette' and dropped my boxers. The doctor was great and apart from an awkward moment when he commented "nice shave" it all went swimmingly. A few weeks later and after a bit if a scare when the stitches dissolved too quickly and I thought my nuts would drop out, it all settled down. Unfortunately, things in my own world went a bit weird and I needed to pay attention to my marriage and then my own sanity. I then ended up in bereavement counselling for the loss of my father some seven years previously and the next thought I gave my vasectomy was about seven or eight months later.

Then I was faced with the awkward bit of having to call them up and say "sorry what's the procedure for getting the "all clear" again?" – I had vague memories of 'give two specimens four weeks apart' and the letter that said you had to produce the specimen at home into a jar and then keep it warm (preferably under an armpit), drive it to a hospital that is only open to "deposits" on week days for a few hours, all within 20 minutes! Oh and I nearly forgot you had to phone them and pre-warn them you were about to drop 'It' off!!!

It all seemed not only a bit embarrassing but a logistical nightmare – I'd worked out a timetable of getting up, waving the kids off to school, the wife off to work, masturbating into a pot, sticking the pot under my armpit (I'd also worked out an appropriate sweater that would accommodate the sperm vessel), driving like a 'w@nker out of hell' down the A41 and then hot-footing it into a hospital to say here's my sp*nk sample. Only to have to do it all again a few weeks later.

Like any true man, I stuck my head in the sand whilst I got on with real life until I got a crappy email saying they'd destroyed my base sample (which I never knew they took). I wrote to the Doctor to say "sorry, what next?" - he ignored it and that's where I'm at. I've had the operation but still don't know if I'm infertile or not so can't have unprotected sex.

Why can't they make the whole submission process just a tad more dignified???

Chris Bryan, 43

I am a Man! Hear me Whine!

I used to believe what I read about myself in the papers and magazines. They're always talking about me, what I should be wearing, what job I should be doing and even what women I like! It's absolutely amazing what information these people have on me! Except, of course, it's all bollocks! This is the adult conclusion I have come to, no other word can adequately summarise it in quite the same way. Psychologists, geneticists, physicists, neurologists and even florists have all got something to say, about my taste in women especially. Funny thing is, I actually know what I like thank you very much and I don't need to be told and have it rammed down my throat everyday!

Here are some things you really need to know about me and my fellow man when it comes to our likes and loathes.

1) We cannot tell the difference between a £30 pair of shoes and a £500 pair of shoes. Apparently there are these ones with red soles that are expensive, white shoes do not mean you are from Essex but clear ones mean you're a wannabe stripper/ho (or in fact are) - just what I heard… Oh and bloody well take the labels off the soles of your shoes! Looks horrendous.

2) In any normal day you may be admired from afar dozens of times. If you are going to show any amount of cleavage or leg, this will quadruple. Please

understand the effect bared or nearly bared flesh has on men. I cannot explain, nor will I attempt to, needless to say I will probably be one of those admirers of you flesh bearing ladies… Funny thing is, age, size doesn't really come into it, when it comes to looking, us men are totally inclusive (unless we're with our partners then no other women exist, honest).

3) It's much appreciated that women spend a potential fortune and hours beautifying yourselves for that date you've been waiting weeks/months to be asked out on. I am actually ashamed that some of my fellow men do not put in the same effort. I hope we make up for this in some quarter with our wit and charm. Failing that whipping out the Gold card to settle the bill! I actually believe this is as it should be for a first date and possibly a second date. Third date depends on how plunging the neck line is…kidding, actually no I'm not! Although we are generally happy to pay, please recognise that man cannot live by bread alone, which he will be if he's shelling out for dates where actually the target of affection is just out for a free feed. I know you know what I mean ladies!

4) If all women looked the same, the slightest blemish would make you an outcast, let alone being tall short, curvy or skinny! So if all women did look like, say, Kelly Brook this would be a very bad thing (maybe), as all guys would have to look like those hunky rugby players or ripped actor types to stand a chance of ever pulling! We guys wish women would embrace their looks and not worry over what Marie Claire has to say. I mean, when was the last time you met a guy who fretted over an Esquire article?! If I surveyed my friends we'd all agree on a woman that we all thought was great looking. However, you'd find their actual partners are very different to the 'ideal' woman discussed. There's far more to it. The best weapon a woman has for me personally is confidence and a great smile. Now that's sexy to me!

Derek Mensah-Kane, 37

The Scarlet Boy

OK, who knew that it was still possible to get Scarlet Fever? This is not the 1900s?!

Well that's what I get from 2 years of bulimia. My immune system took a metaphorical tumble down the stairs and I ended up weak enough to catch a disease that should be pretty much extinct.

I didn't think anything of it at first. I woke up one morning before university and my throat felt like it had been covered in carpet. Then again after pulling another late shift at the bar where I worked, and only subsisting on a steady diet of McDonald's and cigarettes, my fuel tank was pretty much running on fumes. I guessed I must have been coming down with a cold but I decided to brave the day ahead and get myself ready for my afternoon lectures.

It was only when I got out of the shower that I realised something was up. I had to double take my own reflection when I saw the marks. Bright red blotches that were all up and down my arms and legs. I didn't know what to think and I was just staring at myself in the mirror trying to think clearly. I looked like a flesh coloured Dalmatian.

I actually did still try and go to my lectures, trying to cover up the splotches with an extra fluffy jumper. Sadly it wasn't enough and after about 30 minutes in the lecture hall I felt someone tap my arm and point at the nasty ones that had just begun to show on my neck and my face. It was about that time that I had really begun to panic.

The doctor made the diagnosis of scarlet fever after I wandered to the hospital and nearly passed out in A&E. I had heard of it but I always thought it was one of those diseases that was wiped out years ago. Turns out immigration brought it back, or so the doctor seemed to think. Still, he packed me off with a prescription of some nasty but powerful antibiotics, I remember the side effects listed showed a possibility of developing a black furry tongue.

Cut to me being told to take two weeks off of work and university and then being bullied by my mother to go home and stay in bed while she tried her best to 'feed me up' as she delicately put it.

The scary thing is that I didn't need to be bulimic to lose the weight, the infection was more than enough to take me from a relatively healthy 10 and a half stone, to 7 in the space of 2 weeks flat. Eating three times a day and drinking my mother's tea with 4 sugars did nothing to stop the wasting effect the sickness had on me.

My mother would only tell me many years later how frightening the transformation was. She used words like 'skeletal' and phrases like 'death warmed up'. I could see it too, though, and I did not like what I saw.

I thought my luck was changing when I began to get some colour back in my cheeks and decided to go back to university and try and catch up. That is until I started to feel sick again. I was prodded and poked by another doctor and told that I needed to take another course of antibiotics, one which was much stronger. I was tempted to ask him if this meant the black furry tongue would be any bushier, but I resisted.

Another two weeks off of work later and I decided it was time to get out of bed and go to the shops. I felt sick to my stomach and all the way to the high street I had to stop to pull my jeans up which were slowly trying to fall down every 10 or 20 paces. When I got back all I wanted to do was go back to bed and when I did I slept all night and most of the day afterwards as well.

Suddenly I was back at the surgery and being poked and prodded by yet another doctor. The amount of men who were asking me to strip and feeling me up, you would think I would be having a good time. A new diagnosis this time, it had a very long and complicated name, one of those conditions that leaves you feeling weak and tired because your immune system is officially shot to oblivion.

The real embarrassment came just a few weeks later. The side effects finally began to kick in. If you thought I would develop the black furry tongue, I have to leave you disappointed. What did happen was the perpetual pain in my joints and my hands never stopped shaking. The dramatic loss in weight meant I was cold all the time and had to sit near a radiator to stop myself from shaking. The final straw was the embarrassing state of my digestive system, which seemed to go into shock when anything with more calories than a Pringle passed by my lips. The doctor said the problem was because I had let myself get into such a bad situation in the first place.

I was angry with myself, so very angry that I didn't take better care of myself. I was angry that I had thought that throwing up to look good would have made me so ill in the future even though I had been recovering. I was angry at the bar for the late nights and smoky conditions that probably contributed to the worsening state of my condition. My recovery took well over six months, and in that time I couldn't work, go to university, or have much of a social life. I became a nonentity in my own existence. Why did I think that being as thin as possible was a good idea? All it did was cost me my health and stole half a year of my life away.

If I had my chance again, I would do it all differently. If I had my chance again, I would take care of my health properly. There is that saying, the one for when you lose everything. You are meant to say 'At least I still have my health.' I know now just how true it is, because once your health goes... you have nothing.

Scott McMullon

Miracle Day

I went to the swimming pool
With my friend
And her boyfriend
(slash my brother)
And after a fully fun
And psychologically exhilarating
Experience
We all split off to the baths
She to the ladies'
We to the men's

Quick shower and head over to grab my stuff
And passing this guy
He turns to his friend
"They shouldn't let people like that take their clothes off in here!"

Laughter
Even as I look up at my brother
And as he mouths "Don't"
I'm halfway there

"Excuse me."
Head turn
"Was that me you were on about just then?"
"What?"
(expression of a gormless fish)
"You know, "they shouldn't let people in who look like that" or whatever?"
"um"
"Coz I just wanted to ask you, what makes your body so special?"
"Sorry?"

(rage building)

"Because unless yours can produce organs that are available to every person on the planet, regardless of blood or tissue type, then I don't see the big deal.

"Oh no, wait. You're the answer to the AIDS crisis aren't you? We should get you to the hospital quickly so we can start replicating your DNA on a scale that is going to be able to help all those people in Africa!"

"What are you on about?"

"Well, granted, you have a higher muscle mass in your upper torso, but I can see that, by the veins popping out on either side of both your arms, that you take more chemicals than is available in both yours, mine, and half the country's kitchen and bathroom combined.

"And you should probably know that the little voice inside your head that is screaming "Kill him" and "Run AWAY!" simultaneously is called the fight/flight response, and that you should probably use some of the adrenaline coursing through you before you accidentally have a heart attack."

"What?"

"But even if you don't and your noradrenaline doesn't build to the levels that it seems to be attaining already, then you should probably be aware of the inherent risks to your bollocks due to increasing the amount of testosterone in your body chemically, because it also raises the levels of oestrogen due to bio stasis, and if you stop the testosterone, you'll grow boobs".

"Mate don't."

"But, if you want help with the reason you're doing this, which is ultimately lack of confidence in yourself and your body, maybe you should check out our website."

I walked back to grab a pen

"My name is Jake Basford and I work for a charity called Body Gossip" as I wrote the address on his arm "we can help you with your self-confidence issues". I finish and dead-eye stare him "because this kind of gym-worship technically constitutes an eating disorder called Bulimia".

I walked away, my brother grabbing my stuff.

"Excuse me?"

I turn, he's walking toward me.

"Can I get your number, so you can explain that again over coffee?"
I smiled and grabbed my pen and wrote it on his arm
"What's your name, sorry?"
"Andy"
"Lovely to meet you Andy. Gimme a call later"

I walked out of the changing rooms, slamming the door behind me. Oops, I'm still naked.

Fuck.

Jake Basford, 23

Going Topless

I was just eight years old when a punch in my back broke my spleen. I was rushed to hospital and my spleen was removed, leaving me with a large scar stretching from just below my navel up to my breast-bone. Perhaps, as an eight year-old, I wasn't as careful as I should have been whilst the scar healed or perhaps I was operated on by the junior doctor who was not as skilled at stitching as a more experienced surgeon might have been, I will never know. Suffice to say I grew to feel that my scar was anything but neat; quite gross, in fact.

Fast forward to aged nineteen or twenty; I am running a public address company in my spare time from being a student. I am setting up all the speakers on poles for a carnival on a very hot summer's day. There are other men all around me doing various jobs without their shirts on, but not me; no, I'm keeping mine on. No-one wants to see that nasty scar and women manage without going topless don't they?

Well, women have my sympathy and I really think we should break down this discrimination; breasts are not sexual organs, they are for feeding babies, so we should stop sexualising them and let mothers feed their babies in public. Women being free to go topless on hot days would help to normalise or 'de-sexualise' breasts and I'm sure society would be all the better for that.

But I digress. The thought that occurred to me that day was; did I really want to spend the rest of my life hating my body that much? There and then I decided I had to do something about it, but what?

I had always had Naturist tendencies, although I didn't know that was what it was called and, given my shyness about that scar, I had only ever enjoyed the freedom and comfort of nakedness when alone. Never one to do things by half, I decided that to overcome my issues I should go all-out and get naked in public. After some (pre-internet) research, I found there was a beach in Wales where I could do this, so off I went.

With some trepidation, after I had determined by the presence of other naked people that I had definitely found the right place, I found myself a quiet corner and stripped off. I still remember the courage it took to do this.

The world did not end, no-one shouted at me, indeed it was a hour or so before someone wondered over to even say hello. How often do other beach users on 'textile' beaches go out of their way to say hello? It was not long before I was chatting to all and sundry, joining in beach games and being invited to a (bring your own steak) barbeque, back at the local camping field.

And not one person mentioned that scar. They didn't even seem to have noticed it.

That was over thirty years ago and I have never hesitated to take my shirt off on a hot day ever since.

Brian Taylor, 57

A Part of Me

The human body... Hmmm...it's a rather interesting piece of work - if you ask me. We all get worried about things to do with our bodies. May it be small things or things out of the blue.

But your body is what you make of it, everyone is different, we all feel in different ways.

I have a special condition called Sherman's disease (or if you're really posh Scheuermann's disease). I developed the condition playing rugby. It was the constant bending down all the time and playing hockey made it worse. It caused my spine to slip out of place and then form a curve in the spine. This left me with an unsightly curve on the top of my back. 'Hunchback' is what they call me. I've been living with Sherman's disease for nine years now – I've learned to accept it as a part of me.

I'm small for my age, but I'm very athletic. I got all depressed 'cause I was small with his horrid 'hunchback'. I put on lots of weight, became large in a short period of time. This lead to me being rather ill but I've been working my ass off for the past six months, been through two foot operations (had the final one today), trying to get my old body back because I felt soooo good when I was younger and more attractive. But it turns out there is nothing they can do really to sort my back... I was really upset when the doctor told me that he cannot do anything to help me.

January 14th 2006 is when I found out I had it, the doctor told me I've had it all my life but it mostly starts during puberty. It can happen to either sex but is most common in males. He explained to me that it was very rare and I'm lucky it hasn't got worse.

The condition is the root of all my depression because I just can't do anything about it and my friends don't seem to understand how hard it is to live with this condition. A simple pat on the back can feel like a knife being shoved into my spine.

No-one has really been there for me. So I think I held back all my emotions. Which are just building up and up and one day I'm just going to let go and it will be a terrible sight.

Well that will do it for me.

Thanks very much Craig.

Craig Bisset, 16

Driven

I go to see my doctor and she basically tells me I'm dying and I'm totally cool with that. I've lifted weights my whole adult life and I was taking steroids before I even knew how to take them, so I'm going to have a few problems. I've got injuries on top of injuries. Ask any weightlifter and he'll tell you. It's just part of the sport.

There are three types of harm you can do to yourself; hurt, injured and fucked up. Hurt is a temporary thing and, if you're afraid of hurt, you're playing the wrong game. You should be riding a bike or reading a book. Injured is a little more serious. It means your dick is in the dirt and you're damaged in some way, but you'll be back in the gym. Dislocated shoulder, broken arm, whatever. Fucked up, though, means you're shut down. Fucked up means you've been retired. And although my doctor may be the one with the qualifications, she doesn't know shit about my body. Weightlifting isn't her world. She doesn't belong here and she knows it. She leans over to me and asks, "Why the hell are you doing this to yourself?"

I'll tell you why I'm fucking doing this to myself. I do it because everybody talks but words are cheap. I have no respect for words. Fuck opinions, too. People love to talk about their beliefs and the bullshit they believe in but I can guarantee you that ninety percent of these fuckers have no idea what it takes to truly believe in something. It's a journey you can't explain with words. You have to go there to come back and sometimes you don't come back at all. It is about dreams and hope, but it's about nightmares too, and being afraid and risking it all for the one second when you might earn the right to call your soul your own.

Believing isn't about being pretty or being famous or being loved or being clever or living to reach a hundred. It's not about approval or acceptance. It's about giving until there is nothing left to give. Until you've given it all. Until you've burnt the fucking house down and laughed at the rubble. It's not about looking for answers or wanting to be saved. It's lying on the floor, broken and breathless, because broken and breathless are the only way you can breathe.

This is where the magic is for me, in the sacrifice and the commitment. You ever see that movie *Shogun Assassin*? It's about a ninja named Ogami who is the Shogun's chief decapitator. Well, the Shogun grows paranoid and tries to murder Ogami but kills his wife instead. Ogami offers his infant son, Daigoro, a choice. He lays in front of him a brightly coloured ball and a sword. If he chooses the ball, he joins his mother in death, and if he chooses the sword, he embarks with his father onto a journey into hell to get revenge. And that's exactly what all this is, a journey into hell, for as many years as you can take it. There is self-abuse here, and suffering, and pain, and anger that people nurture like the calluses on their hands that they never want to heal, because these calluses are what they need so they can look at their faces in the mirror and respect themselves for the rest of their lives.

A lot of people ask me how I got started at the gym, but I don't have an answer to give them. When I was twenty years old I hated the world and everybody in it. I hated everything I had and everything I didn't have. I hated the people who had the balls to hold a stare with me, and the faggots who turned away. But the only person I hated more than you was me. I wanted to burn up so badly that I could feel the fire. I was probably doing about a gram of coke a day and a boatload of other shit. I was never talented. I never had a pretty little girlfriend to fuck or a proper job, and if you've got nothing to live for then you've got to die of something.

I mean, I was in trouble. I could be in the middle of a three day coke binge but I still couldn't escape the emptiness. I could drink and bar fight every night of the week, but it wouldn't do shit. There were warrants out for my arrest and I was still out drinking. I was answering my bail in court with black eyes. It's like I was waiting for a phone call I was never going to get. I needed to hear somebody's voice through the darkness to save me from myself, but there was nobody to come back for me. And what fucking good could they do anyway? I thought about praying, but I'm not that kind of guy. I was too weak to stand up but too strong to fall on my knees.

I can't remember exactly how I found the gym but it made sense to me like nothing else ever has. It was like I was lost and found. At the bottom of all those repetitions and sets I found a peace that a thousand prayers couldn't provide. The more I hurt and the more I burned, the happier I was. I was happier than the devil in hell. The sweat that pissed out of me was like tears that I couldn't cry anywhere else – couldn't let myself cry anywhere else. It was like I could hold the whole world in my hand and the only thing I was doing was looking inside my heart.

The gym is an unhappy place. I mean, you have to be fucked up to lift those weights day in and day out. To lift weights so heavy that they tear tendons away from muscles and wear your bones to dust. And to pick up those needles and stab yourself and pump that shit in, you have to be fucked up. But it's a beautiful place, too, because it's the only place where you can throw everything you hate and love into the air and make something of it. It's a church where you can really heal your hurts, if only for a little while. What else do you need? It's like writing without words. It's like singing when you haven't been given a voice.

I'm sitting here writing this, but I'm never going to be your fucking hero. I'm a nasty piece of shit and you have to be to have the tenacity to lift heavy weights. I have what you might call an aggressive personality. When I'm there, in that moment, I don't care if my body crumbles and the world caves in around me so long as the weight comes up. The way I figure it is, if I haven't made a name for myself by the time I'm thirty, I've failed. I'm not going to be fucking around in the gym when I'm thirty. I'm going to burn out and disappear.

I've got the same attitude to shooting steroids. If you want to be a name, you have to be on. And everybody and his sister is on something. I've run shit at ludicrous dosages for years at a time. I was sprinkling Dianabol on my cereal in the mornings. I thought it was funnier than hell! I don't respect anybody going into this half-cocked. If you're going to do it, do it all the way. Load up the pin, get in and keep on going till you're gone.

Steroids are completely different from other drugs. When you do a line of coke or drop a pill, you can ride the high. With steroids, you don't know where the high is. And it differs depending on what you're shooting. I mean, the harder anabolics like test and Anadrol can make you into a mean bastard. But the lighter androgenics like Primobolan and Masteron can turn you into an emotional bitch. They just fucking swing off of your emotions. Either way, whatever you're taking your sex drive will go to shit. Your girlfriend will be curled up on the other side of the bed wondering why the hell you can't stick it to her, you limp-dick bastard. The roid-rage thing is a non-issue with me. I always hear some son of a bitch talking about it, but I was a prick long before I ever took a shot in the ass.

The thing with running the shit this hot is, it ages you. Severe bone deterioration and tendon strains. Your hair will start falling out and that's the reason everyone in power lifting is bald. You stay on the juice long enough and you will eventually stop your body's ability to naturally produce testosterone, meaning you're going to have to stay on shit for the rest of your life. You also have to be careful of abscesses and infections. I mean, if you're dropping that shit into yourself regularly you're going to get infected eventually. That's when you get complications, Septicaemia, blood poisoning. So if you ever see a big guy with a piece of his leg cut out, you know that's from where his buddies have carried him into the emergency room with his leg turning black, out of his mind with fever, screaming to the nearest doctor "What can you do for this?"

This is the dark side of hardcore weightlifting. And you will be afraid, but it's okay to be afraid because everybody gets afraid. That's where the magic is, because that's how you know what you're doing is real. It makes everything else seem like conversation. You don't come to the gym to be saved; you come to pay your dues. One of my friends watched me drop a gram of test into each leg and had to fucking turn away. He said I had to be in hell to do something like that to myself. And I was in hell, but some people are more comfortable in hell than in heaven.

Jack Woodward

Bald by 21

My hair has long since gone, though it seemed I was doomed from day one.

I was born with a head of hair, which is great in all respect, but being ginger leaves an ever-lasting effect.

Why not brown, blonde or even pea green, but no I was cursed with the evil ginger gene.

School was approaching with a fear of dread, how would they feel in the presence of a red head.

School didn't seem to be all that bad, for I was not the only ginger lad.

School passed by in the blink of an eye and my ginger friend sadly said goodbye.

I stood outside the gates of Heath Park High, kids were laughing as they passed by.

Secondary school was not that simple, to top it off I got a pimple.

Kids could not accept my ginger mop, I thought they were going to give me the chop.

Work had arrived but I did not care, for I was more concerned about my bright ginger hair.

I looked in the mirror with an image of fright, for my hair looked different, it wasn't as bright.

Strand by strand my hair disappeared, my friends and family looked and sneered.

I cannot bare it I love my ginger hair, there had to be a cure so I looked here and there.

Like the common cold a cure could not be found, my hair continued to fall to the ground.

A year has passed my hair had gone, at the ripe young age of twenty one.

I wanted to be a model and go out with Kate Moss, but having hair like Phil Mitchell she wouldn't give a toss.

I have now got a girlfriend who washes, cleans and cooks, she loves me, but not for my good looks.

Ginger at birth, bald by twenty one, my hair has been and gone.

It went in the blink of an eye without even the chance to say goodbye.

So waxing, gelling, styling that will never be me.

But hey it could be worse, I have got over my bald ginger curse.

Craig Bryce, 23

Things Will Never Be the Same Again

CHARLIE: Today's the day. Today is actually the day. I wake up at 5 o clock, plenty of time to catch my train. I jump in the shower, give myself a good clean and think: 'This will never be the same ever again'. I dry myself up, pack my bag: Comfortable underwear x 4, check, loose fitting clothes, check, jogging bottoms, check.

I then jump on a train and I'm racing towards Paddington. A bit too quickly. I need more time. At Paddington. I am starving. It is 8 o clock. And the letter said I'm not allowed to eat after 7. Bugger it… Bugger it, I'm going to eat anyway. Something simple, I'm the one going through the ordeal of this and I'll have some breakfast if I fancy… Something simple, something simple… Ooh, but a breakfast bagel would be nice. That would make me feel a lot calmer, a lot better. £3.95? No problem. Bought, scoffed, done… I hope I don't regret that. The letter said to not eat after 7… what have I done? What if this screws everything up and has massive consequences… I could die, DEATH BY BAGEL…

I calm down, I'm sure everything will be fine. I jump on the next train. The letter said I'm not allowed to drink after 10am. I neck the rest of my water. Then I really need a wee. I pop to the loo. Whip it out, I have a wee. Have a look down, put it away. Look into mirror, still nervous: 'Things will never be the same ever again'. I arrive. Taxi waiting for me. Taxi man starts patter: 'You came here for a course or something?' 'No' I reply. I hope he stops digging at that, I struggled enough to tell family and friends; I'm sure as hell not telling the bloody taxi driver! 'You visiting someone then?' 'No'. He looks puzzled. I mumble: 'I'm checking in… just for today… just for a quick…' 'Oh' he says, sort of aghast, and mumbles something else. He is now blissfully quiet, just concentrating on driving the car which means I can concentrate on how things will never be the same again.

We arrive. I am entering the hospital. I go up to the day unit. Tell the nurses who I am, they look at a clipboard and its all friendly smiles from there on in. 'Oh, you're early love' they say. Well, that's because I was so petrified that if I was late they might send me home without it done and I may have to go through this whole ordeal again. They send me to the waiting room. I sit surrounded by lots of people in silly dressing gowns and slippers, a huge fishbowl with either hiding or little to no fish and a TV blaring in the corner. The Olympic parade is on. All our successful athletes jumping up and down on buses as they grind central London to a stand still, on lookers frantically waving their hands in pride and delirium. I bet those athletes haven't had to worry about what I'm worrying about. Their prime, supple powerful physiques wrapped up from the cold; the symbol of the best Great British bodies. I bet they have never had to have anything like this done.

I look across at a couple sitting across from me. The woman is holding the hand of this chap, this late twenties - early thirties chap who looks ABSOLUTELY PETRIFIED. I wonder if he is getting the same thing as me done?... I BET he is getting the same thing as me done. I wonder when he last ate?... He looks terrible… This makes me feel much better. A friendly smiling nurse pops in and calls: 'Charlie Whitworth?' I smile, get up and follow her into the room. 'Hi Charlie, are you okay?' she asks… She prattles on for a bit.

I'm then left with friendly smiling nurse number two. She says: 'I'm just going to take your blood pressure and oxygen levels, love for this that and the other'. Or something along those lines. She smacks on a black wrappy thing on the right arm and a black little finger glove on the left arm index. Perfectly healthy she deduces. 'Now have you got any fillings at all Charlie?' 'Nope'. 'Any metal pins or nails in your body at all?' 'Not that I'm aware of!' I jest… How many times must this poor friendly smiling nurse have had some plonker joke about if they have any metal in their body from previous operations etc. Why oh why couldn't I have responded differently, maybe asked her 'no I don't, have you?'

We move on: 'have you got any medical conditions we should be aware of?' I give a no to that one. 'Have you ever been under a general anaesthetic before?' No to that as well. 'Alright that's all fine, Charlie. Now, have you eaten anything since seven this morning?' Ah, I think. Oh blimey, is that bagel going to kill me after all, I think again. I suppress the thought. 'Er, yes I'm sorry I did. I read the letter but I was feeling a bit faint and er…' 'What time did you eat last?' It was 8 o'clock. 'Er, about half seven'. 'Okay' she mumbles. She checks her watch, does some maths in her head. 'That should be fine as you are second up in surgery today, what was it you ate?' 'A bagel' I say. 'A bagel!?' she echoes in surprised shock. 'Oh okay, that should still be fine though'. Crumbs, I won't tell her that sausage egg and bacon was crammed into this bagel then! Why did I let my stomach get the better of me! At least if it does do me in it should just be a case of me not waking up.

'Okay Charlie, if you want to head back to the waiting room the anaesthetist should call you shortly'. I head back to the waiting room and Terrified Chap is returning at the same time as me, clearly having just gone through the same questioning. He still looks petrified and he is still making me feel a lot better. I am finally calm and I just decide what will be will be. Time passes and then

Anaesthetist chap calls me. He asks exactly the same questions as friendly smiling nurse number two: 'fillings, nails and gen anaesthetic?' No, no and no. He then goes on to explain the procedure. Prattle, prattle, prattle. Who really knows what was said as I'm a bit numb by the fact that things will never be the same again. Then anaesthetist chap says: 'I will also be injecting an anaesthetic into your willy just to help with the pain'… Willy. My anaesthetist just said willy. Can that be considered professional? He wouldn't even look me in the eye when he said it! How many times has he done this? If he can't even speak confidently about IT how on earth can he be trusted to INJECT something into IT?!

Next, I'm whipped into another little room with friendly smiling nurse two. 'Have you bought a dressing gown and slippers with you?' she asks. Bugger. 'Um, no sorry. I don't own any!' 'Okay, no problem'. She deduces that my shoes are clean enough and I can wear another surgical robe over top. Next, Terrified Chap and I are whisked to a ward. Friendly smiling nurse one starts to pull curtains to separate compartments. 'You two get changed in here, take everything off including your knickers… you two can feel sympathy for each other as you are both getting the same thing done!' Is that entirely professional to tell patients what the other is getting done? Does she believe that either of us wears actual knickers? Oh well, I think she meant well and at least it confirms my suspicions about Terrified Chap! I got changed into the robes they provide… and might I say how ridiculous said robes are?! They have Velcro all down the back but there is no way you can reach round to stick it, if it stuck anyway, meaning your buttocks are available for the whole world to see! I put another one on the wrong way round to hide some pre-operation dignity (which is silly really as nurses, surgeons and anaesthetists alike are going to be viewing and accessing everything once I'm under, anyway!)

The curtains are drawn back and there is Terrified Chap, looking very nervous. Despite our shared destinies we don't say a word to each other (I should also say he had a hideous red and green dressing gown with matching slippers). He gets taken away and I'm left looking out the window. 'Things will never be the same again'. I accept my fate; what will be will be, and I wait. Friendly smiling nurse two arrives. It's time. I'm lead to another small ward, on my way to which each buttock is exposed by a sudden gust of wind.

In the ward. Two nurses are there, surgeon is smiling and joking and anaesthetist is reassuringly looking like he's in his element. Everyone is cooing and encouraging me, as they get ready to make my bottom half starkers. They pop a needle in my arm, which is fine, never had a problem with needles. They put an oxygen mask on my face. 'Just breath normally, you will be out soon'. I think back to watching some American surgery drama; I'm expecting to have to count or something. I also think of the episode where someone doesn't go under properly and they experience the whole operation in searing pain. Please don't let that be me. And please don't cause me grief, breakfast bagel. Anaesthetist starts telling a joke, I'm wide awake and can hear it and...

Then bang. That's it. I'm sat up, in a hospital bed, back in the ward I got changed in. Friendly smiling nurse two: 'Are you okay love?'... 'Is that it? Have you done it?' I ask: 'Yep, it's all done love, you're all fine'. She pops away, I look under the covers. They have actually done it; never to be the same again. They've wopped my foreskin off.

Charlie Whitworth, 23

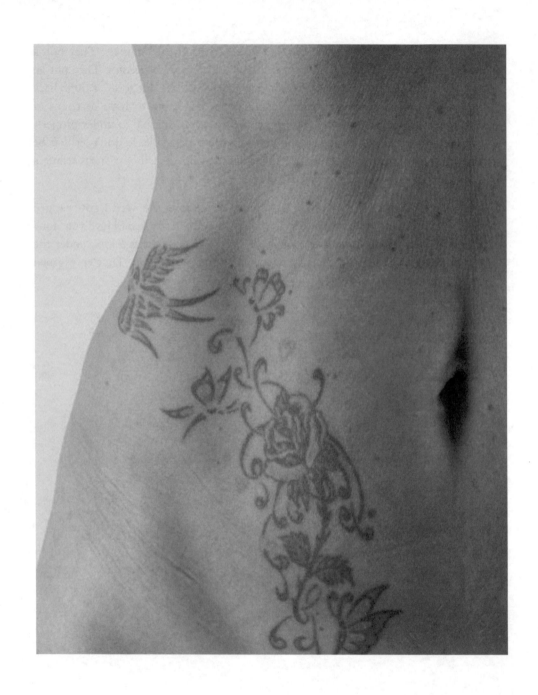

Chapter 11

REBEL REBELS

Remember when we said body image doesn't fit into neat little boxes, right back in Chapter 1? Well, here is the proof.

These stories just didn't fit into a category, but we felt they still needed to be told. You'll find BodyGossipTash's story nestled amongst these treasures. It's about her left arm. There's nothing particularly special about her left arm, as you'll discover. That just about sums this chapter up; these are the nebulous thoughts of the body non-conformists – the sorts of thoughts that might assault you at 2am on a balmy summers' night.

We've called it 'Rebel Rebels' in tribute to BodyGossipTash's bordering-on-clinically-insane adoration for David Bowie.

Enjoy!

Questions

Am I the only person whose tummy sticks out more than her boobs?

Am I the only person who is convinced they've got a brain tumour after talking for ages on her mobile phone?

Am I the only person who thinks that penetrative sex is less intimate than oral sex?

Am I the only person who has to sleep in her pyjamas but has to masturbate naked?

(Am I alone in finding the word 'masturbate' kind of cringey?)

Am I the only one who hates people touching her feet? And her stomach?

Am I the only one who thinks she's getting sexier with age?

Am I the only girl who, even though she's definitely old enough to be called a woman, still prefers to be called a girl?

Am I the only girl who wants her body to be really, really old before she dies?

And if I'm not, I hope it's helped you to realise you're not alone.

Anonymous

War Horse

My body is really amazing. Ok, so I'm not totally happy with that. My ears are a little bit wonky and my stomach isn't totally flat. But it can do brilliant things every day when I run round a stage with a horse on my back. Penguins have little round tummies and they're cute in every way. So I'm not disappointed that I am not perfect, so I am quite happy with that.

Everyone has an issue...but if we all looked the same wouldn't life be boring.

Emily Cooper, 29

The Art Tart

I am a size 16...more like an 18. I perform all over the world doing comedy characters, from being a man in a brown coat to being a leopard skin tart. I also am my own character called Rose Popay. I rarely put makeup on as me. I try to eat healthy food but over do it on the beer. I have a big gut, my boyfriend loves cuddling me. I wear slightly unusual clothes. I'm glad I don't have to weekly shop at Primark to get my celeb lookalike fix, I am proud I am different. I am proud that I have never seen anyone like me. I have hairs growing on my chubby tummy, my fanny bush isn't that impressive and I have scatty pubes growing either side. I've just bought an epilator to control the growth. My armpit hairs are like little afros when I leave them be. My boobs are massive, when I dress as the art tart it's a different story. I drape myself head to toe in leopard print, squeeze into corset, drip diamante necklace on my heaving bosom and top it off with a Marilyn wig - as well as deep make up false eye lashes and heels. Normally, as me, I wear flats, Birkenstocks or flip-flops - just been told I have flat feet hence my knee problems. When I'm the tart everyone sees me and admires me. Skinny girls drool at my big bosoms...so does everyone. Sometimes I wonder what would happen if I got breast cancer. If I'm dressed as me or as the tart I am happy knowing who I am. I can play at something...I don't have to be so desperate or too serious about being someone else. I often feel huge despair going in to the centre of town seeing fake tan hair straightened clones shopping and strutting what is basically somebody else's stuff. In some ways its fine if that's what they want to do...but I wish they would be more comfortable with themselves...to realise we are animals...hairy mother fooking animals. Most girls have hair sprouting on their boobs, on their upper thighs, the back of the thigh, the chin, the upper lip. My boobs are an asset...and a hassle. They are odd sized. One defiantly bigger than the other, tricky in certain symmetrical dress.

My nails grow...that's cool, sometimes they flake on the ends so I cut them all, but my fingers are long and slender...unlike my chicken thighs legs... My face is pretty, especially as I smile so much. I love food and live with a vegan chap so we often fart...with delight! I was single for 12 years, I had loads of flings, some wildly exciting, some rank. I loved learning to love my self...an ongoing thing which we must all do...and I can flick my bean to perfection within minutes!

Rose Popay, 32

A Rant about PMT

Can anyone please explain to me WHY, after all the scientific advances in recent years and all the wonderful results of the clinical endeavours of people far cleverer than myself, women throughout the globe still have to endure the undignified nightmare that is Pre. Menstrual. Tension?

I always know when my period's due, because it's usually around the time when I have the irrational desire to shout at total strangers for the most spurious of reasons. The other day I said 'for fucks sake!' OUT LOUD when an old lady of about 80 in the queue in front of me in Starbucks said "can I have a coffee, please?" She's an OLD LADY. Coffee probably wasn't even invented when she was young. She wouldn't know a de-caf skinny mocha latte with extra foam if it bit her on her wrinkly backside. It wasn't her fault. Several of my carefully collected karma points were deducted on that day, I think.

Then there's the unattractiveness. You're sailing along, quite confident in your own curvy fabulousness and then one day, for no fathomable reason, staring back at you from any reflective surface is the most hideous, bloated, lumpy, swollen, hippo-like image of grossness you've ever laid eyes upon.

Despite this, you cannot stop eating. Your hunger knows no bounds. And it's not like you can crave something nutritious and wholesome like, I don't know, avocado or cottage cheese. Oh no, suddenly there is only one aisle in the supermarket you are frequenting and it's the one up the far end by the booze that harbours the crisps, nuts, chocolate and LARD.

Your chin erupts into spots the like of which you haven't had to deal with since adolescence, you find yourself being one of those intolerable examples of womanhood who cries at crap made-for-TV movies with terrible acting and, to top it all off, YOU SMELL. I don't know why PMT makes you more prone to BO, I just know I suddenly find myself having to make twice as many visits to the shower every day. Which is annoying because it detracts from precious ranting-at-strangers productivity.

And has anyone else got one evil ovary? One month period pains are bearable, the next you're hopping around going "OWEYOWEYOWEYOWEYOOOOW!" and frantically trying to remember where you stashed the hot water bottle and Anadin from two months' hence.

Why oh WHY do I have to spend three days being an irritable, bloated, spotty, smelly, weepy nightmare? I have to lock myself away and not speak to people. I become a hermit. I don't even want babies. The whole thing is utterly futile and pointless.

Please can scientists work on this, or forever have to endure the irrational wrath of premenstrual women everywhere?

Cheers.

Anonymous

Mirrors Are Evil

Have you ever looked in a mirror before going out, done a double take and gone back up to your room because it's embarrassing just to be seen with yourself? Or got out of the shower and checked the mirror to see if it was still cracked from when you checked before you got in? Or even just avoided them? I'm fourteen and I really shouldn't care but I just do.

The day Natasha Devon came to my school was the day I realised two things. Mirrors were evil and I hated them for showing me, me. Natasha told us all about her story and how she overcame her fears with the help of David Bowie. And when I asked her about the tattoos, I got exactly the opposite response I expected. She had not got her tattoos because she thought they made her look better or because they're awesome (which they are), but instead she got them because they reminded her of who she is. She'd found something close to her and it helped guide her. I think.

So I get home and go to the mirror and think. Look, you may not be the nicest person to live with. Definitely not the sharpest knife in that place where you keep the knives, or the best looking but I'm kind of stuck to you so I'll try to get along. And so I think, who am I? And I think and think and think when suddenly it hits me. From nowhere. I'm me. And before you throw the book down thinking that was a complete waste of time, just remember: It was probably the most wisely spent time I've ever spent. So go spend some quality time with the only person that will really understand you for who you are. You.

Sam Reeder, 14

What Mrs Collins Taught Me

It is 2009.

THE LIST MAKER:

If I were to begin anywhere then it would be with a list.

I like lists after all. Not just regular shopping or packing lists (though I like those too), or even lists of resolutions or of pros and cons (it is, I am sure you can tell, a riot in my house on New Year's Eve), but lists like five albums I would smuggle in my belongings come a nuclear meltdown or my top ten train stations without barriers in the South of London (shush, you know we all do it) or fifteen reasons why I should never date actors (ignoring the alternate list, fifteen reasons why I always will). So given my adoration of lists it's unsurprising that this particular one is in existence.

For want of a better title - like five best soap deaths ever or five greatest singles by Steps - we'll call it: My Least Favourite Body Parts Ever.

Every list has a beginning and this particular one is clearer than most:

1. "What's your least favourite part of your body?"

It is 1994, a red roofed school standing on the fault line where this Northern City meets the untamed fields beyond. In a classroom with blue tac marks on the walls and scuffed footprints on the floors I sit on a crimson carpet, its too-short fibres scratching my bare legs.

Mrs Collins, meanwhile, looks expectantly –

The question snakes its way around those gathered on the floor. The answers that come out have long been lost to the black holes of memory but I can still feel the dilemma buzzing around my own head. For though I had never thought to acknowledge this question the answer I would give if I were being entirely truthful is there the moment Mrs Collins finishes speaking. An answer just below the surface of my 11 year old self.

For my two front teeth are too large. They sit, rather uncomfortably, on my lower lip, protruding whenever I lose myself in something else. And - I am already aware - I lose myself a lot.

But I cannot possibly mention my two front teeth. I do not want to share this weakness with the group in case it is noted. So I play with the piece of rubber which is coming off of the bottom of one of my plimsolls and when it is my turn I say the first thing that comes into my head.

"My feet".

"Your feet?"

I hear the slight surprise, but I just nod.

"They're too small".

I feel sorry for my feet which, even with their little toes that bend slightly the wrong way causing them to sit under the toes next to them, have done nothing to place themselves on this particular list.

But Mrs Collins has already moved on, not knowing the crime just committed against my feet, and I return to pulling the rubber off of the blameless plimsoll.

And that was that - a new list in my life.

For my teeth, they were just the first...

2. Around the time that I found myself sandwiched between buying Blur's "Country House" and Take That's "Never Forget" my sebaceous glands decided it was time to get in on the (Take That and) party. Suddenly my otherwise pale face (and I should write that too – my pale skin) became dotted with red eruptions that made me run with tea-tree oil in one hand and an increasingly expensive concealer in the other. Though what no one ever tells you at the time is that the concealer, at least in the hands of a thirteen year old, does the opposite of conceal and instead announces to the world: SPOT here.

3. By the time I was playing The Verve's "Urban Hymns" on repeat and professing that I could not love anyone who didn't love that album (and if you're still interested even after having seen my complete list, please note that this album remains a deal breaker) I'd noticed that I hadn't actually grown from the age of 13. And where I had once been the tallest in my class I was now one of the girls

who couldn't reach the top shelf and most likely never would now. So – on went my height.

4. Around the same time I became obsessed with if I'd inherited – as my mother observed in a casual moment – my father's large forehead. Mr Johnson – our pony-tailed art teacher with a side-line in quick put-downs – informed us confidently that symmetry in portraiture is everything. And the forehead should be the same size as the chin. I didn't need to get a ruler out to know that my forehead had missed this marker by some distance. Not Nick Cave proportions, mind you, but enough not be part of perfect symmetry. And as I took my pencil out to begin the sketch I knew I needed this to add to the list as well.

5. To the noise of the soundtrack to Dawson's Creek I added my thighs, where they have stayed ever since with a rather sinister power. Why? Because they are too large and wobbly of skin and (did I write this down before?) pale. If you have seen my thighs – and there are a few of you out there – then please know: you are in a very exclusive group. My thighs are – at the very least – the Groucho Club of the thigh world.

6. Soon after thighs it seemed as well that I added my bottom. Adding your bottom is more problematical just for the fact that physics and general lack of bendiness have conspired to mean that I have never actually seen it other than in photos or by craning my neck at a ridiculous angle. But what I have seen is enough to know that it needs to go on the list. There was even a foray into the world of scary-bottom-and-stomach-holding in pants, something that I thought went rather well. Until, that is, the night I forgot to take them off (something which Bridget Jones seems to nicely side-step). And – as a word for the wise – it would seem all that holding in technology actually holds your organs in such a position that it makes like things like digesting your food impossible. After a morning spent with a new-found intimacy with my then-work toilet, it is safe to say that they have lost favour with me since.

7. At 21, on my way to see the latest Boy with Guitar who was masquerading around my life, I found my first grey hair and gained what was, for at least the next twelve months, a new obsession. I wasn't exactly a stranger to hair dye by this point but there is something distinctly sobering about having to read the labels for percentage of grey coverage.

8. There would be other words I should write down. That my skin bruises if someone so much as blows on me.

9. That all too often I have fat-arm syndrome on photos.

10. That my Dulux Pale Skin goes bright red at the first sign of any sun.

So this could go on. It could be my list. Or your list. I'm sure you've sat there thinking - yes I agree, or no I quite like my bottom thank you, or my list would begin with... If I were doing this right, we'd band together and end with some supposedly cathartic moment where we'd all chant about our thighs and then, with great flourish and fanfare, I'd rip down this list of mine and we'd get the matches out and burn it. And then I'd flick my hair and go forward and that would be that for my list.

But that wouldn't be right. Because that isn't how this story ends. I don't get to meet Mrs Collins and question her as to why she asked a class of 11 year olds about their least favourite parts of their body. I've got no idea where Mrs Collins is – she could be sunning herself in a deck chair on the sea front at Whitby (Ten Favourite Places in the World), ice cream in one hand, fried mars bar in the other, for all I know. And even when, years later, I sat in a bar in the same Northern City where all this began and the boy who is reason number three on the list as to Why I Should Never Date Actors (and reason number 2 on Why I Always Will) brushed back my hair and assured me that I didn't have an abnormally large forehead it didn't really change anything. Because I've still written this for you to see. And chances are that I would write it again tomorrow as well.

So where does this story end? Well, here. This is me. I'm pale. My thighs are too big. My arms wobble more than they should. But also - I still cry at the Muppets Christmas Carol (Films That Cause Me Embarrassment), I can give CPR (10 Things You Never Knew About Me) and, let me not display false modesty, I play a mean version of 'Wonderwall' on the recorder (10 Songs I Can Play Without Sheet Music). So the story ends with me folding up this list and saying that whist I will always be a list maker that doesn't mean that every list I write is important.

And sometimes - just sometimes - I need to remember that the ability to play the greatest hits of the Britpop era on the recorder says more about me than the circumference of my thighs ever will.

But then - that would be another list altogether.

Corine Furness, 26

Body Image

'So, who wants to go first?' Dan looked round hopefully.

Claire surveyed her colleagues, too. Weren't medical students supposed to be intelligent, eager...? Instead, Holly giggled, Neil scowled and Emma seemed to be studying her finger nails. 'OK. I will,' Claire offered.

There was a collective sigh of relief.

'Scalpel!' she demanded, grinning and opening her palm in readiness. 'I've always wanted to say that!' Deliberately, painstakingly, she made the first incision. The skin was dry and old, but still elastic.

What an efficient, flexible, waterproof covering. Better than lycra, better than PVC.

Dan supervised while Claire drew the scalpel downwards. 'That's right, Claire. Don't go too deep at this stage. What's that muscle?'

'Trapezius?' Neil suggested, his voice a bit squeaky. Claire looked up.

Poor old Neil. His face is as white as his lab coat. I bet it's only peer pressure that's keeping him vertical.

'This cadaver didn't have much muscle.' Dan paused to look at the notes. 'Cadaver Fifteen. Eighty-nine years old. Any muscle she may have developed as a younger woman would have wasted away. She was probably quite fit when she was younger.'

Bet you respected your body, Mrs Whoever-you-are. Were. Bet it served you well. Thank you. What a fantastic gift to humankind to donate your body to medical research. You deserve a medal, but of course you've got nothing left to hang it on now.

Claire was glad they had Dan as their supervisor. She'd have felt on edge if they'd had the Prof. 'Oh! Is that the spinal cord, Dan?' she asked.

'Let's see.' Holly leaned in, wrinkling her nose at the formaldehyde.

'No chance,' Dan replied. 'We won't reach the spinal cord for several weeks. There are all sorts of fibres and bones to get through first.'

'Ah. I've always wanted to see a spinal cord. What's it look like?' Holly asked.

'They say it looks like a cheese string,' Claire commented. 'It frays at the bottom if you pull it apart. My mum used to put them in my packed lunch box.' With an ominous hiccup, Emma turned and bolted, hand clapped over her mouth.

'Maybe it's time to take a break,' Dan said kindly. 'See you back here at eleven.'

Outside in the courtyard Neil said, 'You done good, Claire. Cool as ice.' He turned to Emma. 'You OK?' In the fresh air her colour had returned.

'Yeah, thanks. But what we're doing is awful. That poor woman…it's revolting.'

No it's not. It's amazing. Beautiful. The human body is an incredible demonstration of design and engineering!

In the weeks that followed they took turns. Holly was just as fascinated as Claire. Neil seemed to gain confidence and approached dissection with academic precision. Emma remained reluctant. 'This is a person, not just a…a piece of meat. We ought to show some respect.'

'We *are* showing respect,' Neil remonstrated. 'Cadaver Fifteen is an excellent specimen. Let's call her CF. Bet she was hot when she was young.'

Trust you to think of that, Neil. Still, you can't help it. You're merely a bloke, after all. But what did she accomplish in those eighty-nine years? Who did she love?

Who loved her? She must have been born during the first world war. Did her dad survive the trenches? Did she have a job? Was she discriminated against because she was a woman? Did she ever think about job satisfaction? Was she happy? Did she have any idea what we would do to her body?

'We'll never know.' Claire glanced at the bag that covered CF's head. For the dental students.

'It all seems so heartless!' Emma complained. 'Aren't we allowed to have any feelings?'

'Course we are!' Claire objected. 'Gratitude is a feeling. I'm very grateful to this woman. So is admiration. And ambition. No good becoming a doctor if you don't like flesh and blood.' She knew her voice contained a measure of scorn, and immediately regretted her harshness.

As the weeks went by, CF began to look more like a butcher's shop.

OK. Stomach today. Last session before the holidays. Wonder if I'd make a good surgeon? Wouldn't like to wear scrubs all day. They don't do anything for my figure. Reckon I look efficient in a lab coat, though. Quite the part, really.

Claire turned sideways to catch a glimpse of her reflection in the window, then began to pull on her gloves and follow the others into the lab. Wait a minute! Something was different, not right. 'The bag! They've forgotten to put the bag back over the head!' Claire's knees were threatening to give way. Shakily, she took a step nearer. 'She's got no eyes,' she whispered.

Emma moved to stand next to Claire. 'You can't preserve eyes. They're ninety per cent water,' she explained gently.

'Yuk. Looks like something out of a horror movie,' Holly grunted.

Claire wanted to look away, but her own eyes were riveted to CF's face, the high cheek bones, the small, neatly defined nose. Her grey hair had been cut short, but it was still thick, with the hint of a wave and no scalp showing. Her chin was strong, determined.

'What's the matter, Claire? You don't usually…'

Emma, how can you be so nice to me when I was so horrid to you?

'Nothing. Really. Only – she looks like my Great-Gran.' She lied because she couldn't put into words the sudden desperate longing that her life should count for something before she succumbed to the fate of humanity. They'd all think she'd lost the plot. Maybe she had.

Neil replaced the bag. Claire wiped her face on her sleeve and forced a smile. 'You lot will be a credit to the medical profession one day,' she declared with an attempt at lightness.

Neil smiled. Somehow he looked older than his nineteen years. 'That's a long way off. First, we gotta find out how six metres of bowel can fit into such a small space. Gloves on, everyone.'

Helen Parker

BodyGossipTash's Story – My Left Arm

The other day, a friend of mine was beside himself with delight to discover that a beer he had previously believed to be available in Europe only was on sale in an obscure little East London bar we'd happened to stumble upon. He demonstrated this delight by taking a picture of his pint for posterity (as you do). The resulting photo found its way onto Facebook (as utterly inane pictures significant only to the photographer concerned tend to).

Directly opposite my friend's prestigious pint there was an arm. The disproportionately slender and yet bafflingly muscular arm of an Amazonian gym-o-phobe… My left arm, in fact.

It took me a while to identify my own arm. Weirdly, I recognised the pint first. Then the table. Then the limited edition David Bowie collector's pin on the sleeve of my jacket. "Oooh! That must be my arm!" I thought. Then came the inevitable well-rehearsed ritual of close scrutiny. I reflected that, all things considered, I have a perfectly respectable left arm. I'm rather fond of my arms, it turns out. "How refreshing!" you're thinking "hurrah for arm-specific body confidence!"

…Can you be confident in something you feel only a minimal connection to, though? I'm not particularly proud of my arm. It doesn't feel like an integral part of me. After all, I haven't contributed anything to it (accidental shopping bag related work-outs, sporadic application of nail varnish and adornment in Bowie badges aside).

You see: My left arm, my entire body, in fact, or my image in a photograph, feels oddly distanced from my perception of myself. Actually, I've realised, I see myself as a mind, trapped within a vessel of no real consequence, floating around, experiencing life. I'm actively proud of my mind. It's been moulded by my experiences, shaped by my education and honed by my desires and whims. But my body's just there, with all its imperfections and glorious bits and foibles, existing organically, perpetuating its own existence, free from any conscious will.

In more lucid moments, I'm able to accept that, of course, my body is as much a part of who I am as my mind. Just as my mind has been sculpted by the life I choose to live, so my body has been too. And therein lays the moral of my little left arm memory. You see, it wasn't just my arm in that photo - It was me.

Natasha Devon, 31

Chapter 12

TALES FROM THE MEDIA FRONTLINE

Contrary to popular belief, most models would not wish us all to stop eating, with immediate effect. Most celebrities would baulk in horror if they thought a young person was comparing themselves to their airbrushed pictures. The people who make radio and television are not sat in gigantic leather armchairs cackling evilly to themselves as they imagine all the fervent body insecurity their programmes will spawn.

Our problems with our bodies are the results of attitudes, of prejudices, of ignorance, of capitalism, of scientific advances - Great big Goliaths which we wrestle with daily. But 'media people', well, they're just people. They have bodies too and they, too, have days where they really don't like them. They're subject to the same pressures as us and for some of them, having a certain type of body is their livelihood.

So, in this chapter, we've given them their say. You'll find presenters, actors, models, musicians and politicians on these pages, giving us a glimpse of what life is like on the other side of the media divide...

Dying to be Thin

Another day of tears and pain,
Lying here I'm going insane.
Fighting hard not to be fed,
Trapped in my body lost in my head.

Feeling fat and looking thin
Rejecting life my gravest sin,
Leave me here upon my bed
Trapped in my body lost in my head.

I want to be free and seal my fate
Why is my life all about weight?
Hope is gone though its never said,
Trapped in my body lost in my head.

x Nikki x

Nikki Grahame, TV Personality (From her book 'Fragile')

Celebrating Individuality

In the last decade the focus on being young and thin has become relentlessly sharp – the desire to be thinner now starts earlier and continues later than ever before. And it really irks me that this obsession exerts such power even though it doesn't bear any relation to a body which has given birth to one or more children and seen many summers come and go. We are way too tough on ourselves about our shape. It's not necessarily about celebrating individuality for me – that matters, but it can sound trite. It's more about being kinder to ourselves. And more realistic. And less uptight about it all. And the older I get (I'm happy to announce I'm in my 48th year) the more convinced I am about this, especially because when I think about the women I have admired most in life it is never because of their size-related 'achievements'. Actually, quite the reverse. Beauty products shouldn't just be about making you young or thin. They should give you confidence by enhancing your natural form and beauty – helping you feel as good as you can on every level. There is a fine line between making someone feel positively challenged and punished, and only a few insightful beauty companies understand the subtle nuances of that these days.

Kate Shapland, Beauty Columnist

Acceptance is a Beautiful Place

Is a woman ever happy with her body? Many bottles of wine and girlie chats later, me and most of my friends think not! I've been every weight possible over the years and always wanted to be slimmer. After 2 children I consider my battle scars - no my stomach isn't what it use to be and after breast feeding 2 children I could probably tuck them both into a bra (if they were big enough!) But I have 2 beautiful children and a healthy body which needs looking after. Acceptance is a peaceful place to be!

Terri Dwyer, TV Presenter

I am What I am

Everyone has some sort of body issues right? It's strange, now I'm older I realise we all feel the same, everyone of us has something they don't like or wish they could change. I just wish I could go back to the teenage version of myself and let her know what I know now. I wish I could tell her to not worry about it and that everything works out fine…

I was brought up by two loving parents and although we didn't always have much money or material things we certainly weren't lacking in love. I grew up feeling very safe and secure so I was a very lucky girl in many ways. I was always brought up to be content and happy being "me" and I was until I was about 13.

But then one simple thing changed everything….boys!! My teenage hormones must have kicked in! Me and my mates would sit around gossiping about who fancied who, it was a full time job discussing the latest crush. I'd write boys names on my school books and we'd talk about the fit lads 24/7.

But the problem was all the other girls looked so much more grown up than me. Now, I was never deluded. I'd always known I was smaller than my peers and my nicknames in school were Titch and Tiny T, so it gave me some indication of my diminutive size! But it'd never been an issue before. I liked being different but now I hated it!!!!

All the boys liked the womanly looking girls and my straight up and down, no hips, no boobs, no bum body was way out of fashion. Then one day the boy I'd had a major crush on for ages sauntered up to me and put his arm around me, wow my heart skipped a beat! He looked down into my eyes and I looked longingly into his and he then said to me "aww Titch I could never go out with you, people would think I was getting it on with my little sister, I could fit you in my pocket". Oh no, my 13 year old heart was broken, but one day I thought I will grow into a womanly curvy body…

That one day never came and here I am aged 27, 5 foot 1 and still no curves to speak of, however one big thing has changed in me and that is the way I choose to look at myself. Instead of looking at what I don't have I embrace what I do have! I now love being me and surprisingly I've grown to like being small. Ok sometimes I still see curvaceous woman in magazines and think ah that would be nice, but the difference is I never beat myself up or put myself down. Why would I choose to hate on myself when I can be content and hugely grateful for what I do have?

And what I do have is a very positive loving self image. I am happy in my own skin and big or small, curvy or beanpole we are all perfectly individual and the uniqueness is what makes us great.

My daughter is nearly 3 and in my eyes she is and will always be perfect inside and out. She isn't like anyone else and why should she be, her uniqueness is what makes her perfect. As she grows up (or like in mummy's case doesn't grow that much), I hope to teach her to respect and like the person she is on the inside and be content and accepting and loving of the body she has.

And as for boys the number one thing I will let her know is if the boy is good enough then he will think you are perfect just as you are!

Tina O'Brien, Actress

Two Scary Episodes

My body has always just been that thing that hangs from my head. It gets me around, sometimes faster than others, sometimes slower, it gets fidgety and likes exercise then gets tired and needs sleep. It's of average height, width and attractiveness and looks better dressed than not. It has dimples where it shouldn't and is wider round the middle than I would like. But it's my body and, until now, it's always worked and has pretty much done as it was asked. Until now. After two large pregnancies and subsequent emergency C-sections my stomach was left with a large hole, through which pesky bits of intestine kept making bids for freedom. A hernia repair did little to help, they just wriggled past and popped out elsewhere. After four years of thinking "I really must do something about this bulge, constant pain and irritating people asking 'when are you due?'" So I did, and last week I went into hospital to have my abdominal muscles sewn back together, meaning no hole, no escaping intestine and no pregnancy congratulations. Since then, my body, that ordinarily most compliant of things, has not been happy. I have had two scary episodes; the first while in hospital when I suddenly couldn't breathe, something I'd found pretty easy to do up til then. Last night I was carried limp and helpless from our car by my strong but terrified husband into hospital once again; car and flip flops abandoned by the front door. My body had decided to shut down, I was juddering and shaking in pain, hyperventilating myself into senselessness. A few hours later, when scans and monitors showed my jumbled brain that my body was doing fine, I calmed down. My body, this thing under my head, is fighting back. It does not like being cut open and prodded and just wants to get back the business in hand: doing the school run, catching the train to work, making love to my husband. I have been sent home and told to lie still for two weeks, which my body would love if it involved a beach and a few cocktails. Instead it means back to the spare room, where the children thunder in after school to tell me about their day and I panic silently that they may hug me too tightly and burst something. My head wants it's body back. My battle-scarred 41 year-old body that is too busy to be laying here in a druggy sleep. It's buggered, this body, but it's mine.

Andrea McLean, TV Presenter

Fillets

Fillets, and no I'm not talking succulent chicken breasts, I'm talking cold rubber objects that sat in my bra for the majority of my teenage years.

I was given an amazing opportunity growing up and attended a theatre school for the whole of my secondary years. Which meant I had to dance in a leotard in front of my friends, male and female, every day. For the first year no one took any notice of each others bodies, back then our main concern was getting our steps right. But as time went on and hormones kicked in my favourite jazz lesson started to become my worst nightmare. At the age of 12 I hit puberty, hips widened, the mood swings were in town!! I thought I was on my way to becoming a young lady.

My only concern was the fact that my breasts didn't seem to be developing like everyone else's. For the first few years I covered the 'problem' by wearing two bras, which was rather uncomfortable and probably didn't even make any visible difference but it made me feel a tad more confident whilst taking my t-shirt off in classes.

As time passed and I started shopping in underwear stores with friends looking for the newest colour french knickers (was all the rage when you hit your teens in our group of friends, not sure my parents were best pleased) I came across what I thought at the time to be the 'best invention' ever. Chicken fillets or Breast Enhancers.

We had great, but mostly embarrassing, times me and my fillets, from poking out of my tops, moving around in my bra making me look like I had three breasts in a leotard, and a situation that still makes me cringe to this day, getting thrown in the swimming pool on holiday and floating to the surface with my two fillets either side of my head. Everybody saw. I couldn't step foot by those sun loungers all week.

I used to talk about boob jobs 24/7. I became obsessed with researching surgery and clinics. I remember thinking the moment I leave school and get a job this is the first thing I'm going to invest in. Before I'd even left school I was lucky to land a roll in Eastenders, the biggest confidence boost I could ever have received. It helped me grow as a person and learn to believe in myself in more ways than one.

At just 17 years old I won an award for being the sexiest female on soap. Me, flat chested Lytton, sexy? I actually laughed out loud when they told me. That's right FLAT CHESTED and still, as they called it, sexy. 'Being sexy or attractive isn't about having big boobs or a tiny waist its about being confident and happy!' I was told. I wouldn't say that's the sole reason why I changed my mind but I think it helped an awful lot and from that day my new found confidence grew!

If someone told me at the tender age of 12 one day you will wear clothes without a bra or non padded bikinis in a few years I would have raised an eyebrow but I can't think of anything more liberating than wearing a top that shows off the fact that my top half is smaller than my bottom half as that's what makes me different, that's what makes me ME.

So to all my 'flat chested' sisters whip out those fillets and just enjoy what you have!! Because being 'small' really can be sexy!!

Louisa Lytton, Actress

Identity

Secondary school was the most fun I've ever had. But being a teenager there is always something, right??! Well mine was just being me!

I lived in Brixton and went to a theatre arts school in Barbican. Worlds apart some might say, but in my mind it was only a tube ride. To the boys of Brixton who didn't know me I was seen as a hip hop honey and "wifey material" to those who did but in school I was practically invisible.

I didn't have a dancers body and my hair didn't fly out of a hair bobble when I danced in a sexy Brittany Spears era way. Nope, it was slicked down with a bristle brush and had fifty hair bobbles keeping it in. The slightest drop of sweat meant it frizzed out like Tina Turner. Not cool when everyone else has long flowing swinging pony tails.

One time, I remember sitting against a studio mirror and leaving a huge grease patch where my head had been! My Beyonce bum came in handy though as I discretely slid up the mirror smudging it away. I was so embarrassed and ashamed. I didn't know who I was quite suppose to be, but some things I thought I wanted to change were frankly clinically impossible and not being understood by my peers in either postcode made it even more difficult.

As a young girl my father use to take my sister and I WINDOW shopping every weekend. Notting hill, Whitelys, Portobello Market, Oxford Circus, Piccadilly

Circus, Bond Street, Park lane, Green Park, Harrods! By six years old I knew the tube map zone 1-3! And at the time I use to think "what's the point in going shopping if we don't ever buy anything!"

But now it couldn't be any clearer why he did it. He did it to show me another world just five stops away on the Victoria line. He did it to show me that nothing is out of my reach and so that I would never be intimidated by anything or anyone and that knowledge is power.

Once I remembered that, I began to embrace being different and use all that I was learning about all different kinds of things to grow and flourish as a person.

I realised I was pretty awesome!

Zaraah Abrahams, Actress

Strictly Craig

When I lived in Melbourne, my obsession with losing fat left me with serious food issues. Many people think that this is more of a woman's problem, but a lot of men battle with their weight too, and I've struggled with it all my life. I was always prone to chubbiness as a child. At ten, I was slightly porky and had little, fat boy boobs. My Auntie Mavis used to call me Tits, which I hated. I got bigger at twelve and even fatter at thirteen, much to the disgust of my unsympathetic PE teacher. It wasn't until my overnight growth spurt that the plumpness left me. When I started dancing, I began building muscle. I was still developing physically, which was a good thing because it enabled me to get a decent bone structure for a dance body.

In the six weeks I was away with Mr X, I didn't do any exercise or dancing at all. Walking up Sturt Street in Ballarat one day, after my return, I happened to glance at my reflection in a shop window. The sun was shining, making the likeness crystal clear, and I received quite a shock. 'My arse has dropped!' I thought. It had fallen, literally, by about an inch. Due to sheer lack of exercise, my whole body had sagged. I couldn't get back to the dance class quick enough. By the time I took up aerobics alongside the dance, I was really just bones, but I still thought I had all this body fat, because I wasn't toned enough. I used the gym instructor job to try to create my perfect shape, but it soon became an unhealthy fixation. I was actually really thin, and had lost far too much weight, but I always thought I was tubby. When I looked at myself in the mirror, I saw my skin and anything that wasn't rock-solid muscle as fat. Looking back, I now know that I was suffering from a severe eating disorder. I would starve myself and eat only lettuce for lunch and dinner for two weeks at a time. I was paranoid about every ounce of fat on my body, but I wasn't helping myself because I wasn't eating protein, so my energy levels were plummeting too.

There were times when I would go on a drink binge, and then pig out on ridiculous food like pizzas and burgers. I had no energy for dancing because I was either drinking and gorging on rubbish, or eating nothing at all. It was an awful time. I was performing in one of my favourite shows of all time. Sugar Babies is a revue-style musical comedy, a tribute to the old burlesque era. I was in the barbershop quartet, which sang, tap-danced and acted in the comedy skits. I also understudied the MC, who was compere for the evening, played the straight man and sang a few songs to link the acts. During the run, I was laid off work with suspected glandular fever. I'd been dieting again and had lost loads of weight, which lowered my immune system. My glands were really swollen and as one of the boys in the production had already been diagnosed with the illness, I was signed off from performing until I learned the outcome of my blood tests, in order to protect the rest of the cast. Fortunately, the results came back negative; I was just severely run down. Then I hit another problem. While I was laid up, I ate and ate and did no exercise. Suddenly, I'd ballooned in size.

The weight issue really has plagued me for my entire life. It's horrific. At my heaviest, I have been 106 kg (16 stone 10 lb). The lightest was 72 kg (11 stone 5 lb). I tried to keep my dance weight at 75 kg (11 stone 11 lb), but I remember, on one occasion, standing on the scales and watching the needle go to 83 kg (13 stone 11 lb). I nearly had a heart attack. I couldn't believe how heavy I was. I'd gone up to a 34-inch waist and I thought that was an absolute disgrace. I really beat myself up about it.

Just after Sugar Babies, I was cast in a show called Starkers, in which I had to strip completely naked. After landing the role, I went home and took off my clothes in front of the mirror. I scrutinized every inch of my body. I still wasn't happy with what I saw. The diet had worked and I was thinner, but I looked way too puny. So, I started going to the gym; I knew I had to build my muscle tone. That's when I began to achieve my healthiest weight. I was eating an enormous amount of food, to maintain the bulk, but it was the right kind. I would eat a whole chicken for dinner, snack on nuts, and eat some dairy products too. By the time the show opened, I was at the peak of physical fitness and happy with my body for the first time.

Craig Revel Horwood, Dancer and Performer

Glee

I am a big fan of Glee for this reason: Glee celebrates individuality and encourages kindness and for each of those kids to be the best that they can be, and to revel in each other's respective talents whether they are large, small, with big noses or challenged in some respect.

I believe in people being themselves, and I also believe in making the best of one's self. Not in the sense of looking like someone else, or aspiring to have someone else's body, but instead to be the best that each of us as individuals can be.

We all have something different to offer, and even though I find this hard to believe all of the time, in my brighter and more optimistic moments, I really do believe this to be true.

I wasn't raised around any beauty magazines, and one day in my late teens I bought a few to see what all of the fuss was about. There was one article that promoted you to be comfortable in your own skin, and the next article was promoting 10 things that you can do to lose weight, reduce lines, be younger etc etc.

The truth is that age is the great equaliser. We all grow old inside and out but as The Sunscreen song says, your body is the "greatest instrument that you will ever own". I abandoned all of those magazines, which I believe are designed, for the most part, to make us feel bad about ourselves.

I decided to eat well, exercise, drink water, have fun, and to wear sunscreen... We are the consumers. We control the market. We can choose to keep the cycle of impossibly airbrushed magazines alive, or we can turn the tide by changing our buying habits.

Think big and start small. Then we can have our dreams, but start from a realistic point, rather than an impossible goal. As Gandhi said, "be the change you wish to see in the world".

Paris Jefferson, Actress and Photographer

Body Gossip Rap

I used to be that shy guy in the club at the side,
You know the one, who spends most the evening blending in, trying to hide,
You see, I was really skinny and they used to call me lanky,
Now I look back, I was kinda marga, even made skinny jeans look baggy.
People used to tease me, I'd get taunted daily,
I used to look in the mirror and really really hate me,
Wished I could be him, coz he looked much better,
He looked all swaggered out in his G Star jeans and Polo sweater.

Still, I'm a nice person, at least that's what my friends said,

I shouldn't let looks and material things get to my head,

It's easy for you to say coz you look like America's next top model,

And he looks like the guy on the Fitness supplement bottle,

I know what I'll do, I'll join the gym,

So I too can be toned and chiselled and look just like him.

Four days a week, each time, two hours at least,

Then home to eat tuna pasta, egg whites, a real gym bods feast.

Transformed me into a 17stone muscle bound man,

Now my friends joke, say my arms are a car and my legs are a van.

I'm getting noticed now, and it feels great,

Hold on, but wait...

I'm the same person I was, same goals, same desire,

I think and feel the same way, and love life with the same burning fire,

Ok, I'm a little more confident, out spoken and lively,

But I realise that deep down it's the same skinny, lanky boy that's inside me.

Hearts still the same, breathe the same breath,

I guess all the muscles are a jacket made out of flesh,

So to all of you I say, be who you are, put ya self first,

And no matter what people say, realise your self worth,

No one's perfect and we can all wear a coat,

But it's what's under the coat, deep inside that counts and what shows your worth,

And on that note, I'll steal one of my girlfriend's quotes,

She says "When you die it won't say how many cars, houses you have or how your body looked on the grave stone",

Real friends remember you for you and the things you do,

Not how you look, your big car, gold chains, or expensive shoes,

Anyway, I'm off to the gym now, to keep fit, no longer for a desired look,

I dedicate this lil rap to the Body Gossip Book.

Fredi Kruga, Rapper & Producer

I Feel Great!

A very splendid morning to you. My name's Jonty. I'm male. I'm 36 (today for the last day). My skin is the darker end of white. My hair started disappearing many years ago, making me look much older than I am. I wear glasses (I've done nothing yet about this - I may go for laser treatment later on in the year) and my tummy started to expand beyond where it should have been in the 1990s and I've been overweight ever since.

The first thing I decided to attack (apart from a couple of moles I had on my thighs which I cut off with scissors in the bath, in one case with total success and the other case with partial success) was the belly. All the other things are cosmetic issues (although my bad eyesight is a problem when I swim and I have no glasses and I can't see where the edge of the step is on the way to the pool and so on). I started on the Eurodiet. They gave me their stuff FREEEEE, which is pretty cool, because it's about £11 per sachet otherwise. (They were hoping to use me for some publicity but I think they've given up on that idea now.) They're from the same family of diets as those of William Banting in the Victorian era and, more recently, the Atkins diet. In other words they put no upper limit on how much you can eat and drink in a day, but they do bring the carbohydrate level crashing down to nearly nothing. In fact in the early stages you're not even allowed fruit (fruit contains fructose; fructose is a type of sugar; sugar is a carbohydrate). You get your Vitamin C and other vital nutrients from the packets of powder they give you which are to have water added. The food that you can eat limited amounts of is things like asparagus, beansprouts, cabbage and fennel. You probably wouldn't want to eat unlimited amounts of that stuff anyway. My weight started to come down, but every now and again I'd socialise and break the rule about no alcohol. Having broken that one my inhibitions would go down and I'd start eating whatever food there was with gay abandon. I remember having a meal with my friend Mark in Sandwich which ended up with my ordering a massive twelve slice chocolate pizza, just because I'd never heard of one and it sounded almost illegally delicious. It was but Mark said it looked too sweet and wouldn't eat any. I HATE seeing food go to waste and so I ate the lot. While I was polishing it off I remember saying to Mark how awful it would be if, at that moment, the hotel door came flying open and it was Liam Loftus from Eurodiet. "So, Jonty," he'd say in his Geordie accent whilst nodding assertively, "how's the diet going?" I'd have to mutter through mouthfuls of carb-ridden baked white bread, sugar and melted chocolate, "Oh, haww, yawwwngulp fine, thanks."

The overall journey was downwards but it was very slow. My top weight had been well in the 90s and I started the Eurodiet on 89 kg. With all the ups and downs, my top weight each week was always 86 kg, normally just after I'd just had a drunken get-together with someone. My target is 75.4 kg so that's not ideal. I then discovered Pharma Nord. They make vegetarian-friendly capsules with a combination of green tea and conjugated linoleic acid (CLA) in them. This helps you burn your fat away more quickly. I bought some of those and they wanted people to write in with stories that could help them in their publicity. I did and they seemed very interested. A really, really nice guy from there took me to breakfast. We discussed ideas of publicity on them - we may still do it. Eurodiet had said cut the carbs; this lot said don't worry about that but having these tablets plus exercising will help. So there were two different ideas, but Eurodiet had said drink green tea as well. I was then given FREEEE consignments of CLA-GT tablets. They asked if I wanted free consignments of any of their other nutritional supplements and I said I liked the look of their Alpha Lipoic Acid ones (also vegetarian-friendly). I get those FREEEE as well - rather jolly, don't you think? I now have no diet. Eurodiet works if you can stick to it but that's not easy to do every day. Sticking to it on the majority of the days plus doing lots of fast walking and medium-speed swimming virtually every day plus having these tablets every day seemed to send the weight down. I hit a week where my maximum weight wouldn't go above 83 kg, even after a night of socialising. I then hit upon other things as well. If you have a Dunn's River Nourishment drink in the morning, or combine a Novartis Nutrament Drink, a Gillian McKeith Vit C bar, a Lucozade Energy Bar and a Slimfast drink, you've had pretty much all the nutrients you need for the day. Carry on exercising and having the Pharma Nord pills, of course, but, after breakfast, drink as much liquid as you like and any type you like (green tea; alcohol; Coke Zero; hot chocolate; mineral water - whatever you want) but eat no solid food. Your body's got all it needs and is fooled into feeling full, but you're not eating. Also put pure essential oils of fennel and grapefruit on your trousers or socks and the smell will act as a natural appetite-suppressant. This has proved to be the best diet so far. Why the complicated combination of the McKeith bar, the Lucozade bar, the Nutrament and the Slimfast when you could just have one can of Nourishment? The reason I sometimes go for that more complicated one is that it's less fattening and really, really makes you feel full. "Fool-Feel-Full-Fuel" I call it! The result of all this: despite finishing off Easter with a lunch of an entire Easter egg my mother'd given me and a whole bag of fudge she'd given me, now, two days later, my weight is 78 kg, which is the second best since I've started and very close to what it should be. I hope my diet will bring me down to where I should be within a few weeks. Eurodiet's finished now but the good things it started I've carried on in other ways. I've also gained an interest in this topic and researched every diet from ones that say "No alcohol or fat" to ones that say "You must have red wine and cheese" to ones that say exercise is more important than what you eat etc., etc. I've been fascinated and surprised at what the two dos and don'ts that they all agree on are. Rule 1: Never eat white bread. They all say that. That seems to be worse for you than alcohol or sweets! Number 2: Always drink green tea. That seems to be very very common. If there were a third rule it'd probably be another don't: don't have fried food.

Next problem: the thinning hair. I went to an Australian who said they could turn it from the way it looks now to still looking thin but less so and it'd involve an operation and a scar (but pencil-thin) and £5-10k of my money plus VAT. I gulped. Then I thanked him very much for his time. I then went to see a Chinese specialist. They offered me treatment for less than £400. I accepted. This involves my getting nice, relaxing massages and acupuncture (so I'm not allowed to give blood for six months after it stops) and eating Sheng Fa capsules and putting Fabao 101G hair tonic on my head a lot. (I've also learnt that the chlorine from all the swimming I now do damages your hair so I put vinegar and pure essential oil of lemon on my hair after swimming). Most people say I've wasted my money but some say they can see an improvement. The Chinese doctor recently said my circulation was bad and gave me some other pills.

I went to a lady who set up a booth measuring people's cholesterol etc.. I was very pleased: my blood pressure is elevated but no longer classed as high; I was in good working order apart from my good cholesterol, which was a little low, so she recommended I buy soya lecithin.

So I got up this morning, washed, shaved, used my whitening toothpaste (which I've checked is vegetarian - it's Rembrandt, the best whitening one out there), put some Fabao 101G on my head and breakfasted on a Lucozade Energy Bar, a Gillian McKeith Energy bar, a Gillian McKeith Vit C bar, a Nutrament, a Slimfast, two alpha lipoic acid tablets, three teaspoons of soya lecithin, six CLA-GT tablets, eight Sheng Fa tablets and thirty Chinese circulation tablets.

And I feel great!

The best to you – Jonty

Jonty Stern, TV Personality

Body Gossip

"You were bloody gorgeous!", I said, as I looked at a picture from twenty five years ago.

If only I thought it at the time. I had so little confidence, was always finding flaws. Hair, too fine. Nose, too big. Lips, too thin. "If only I could loose a couple more pounds", even though I was a size eight.

Why oh why, no matter how beautiful I looked, deep down inside I never felt 'good enough'. An ugly duckling, longing to be a swan.

The other day I met a lovely woman around my age, in the ladies while putting on our lippy; as you do.

"Oh my god, I hate getting old!", she said. "I look in the mirror these days and hardly recognise the face staring back at me.

I told her my story, the twenty five year old photo. "I'm exactly the same", she said.

"I've always hated the way I look. Hated being a size sixteen starved myself for months just to drop a couple of pounds. Hated my hair! All through my teens 20s, 30s, 40s. Then I got cancer Now putting on weight means that I'm healthy, and having hair at all, is a bonus."

It made me feel sad and ashamed. Then I felt angry, angry at all those lost years of youth that so many beautiful women have used up not feeling good enough.

So, I have made a pact with myself. Tomorrow I will look in the mirror, see the face looking back at me and say;

"You are bloody gorgeous!"

I may not believe it entirely. But at least it's a start!

Carol Harrison, Actress and Writer

Designed to be Different

Like most women I have good days and bad days but I've always tried to have a healthy attitude towards my body.

I appreciate my body and believe if I look after it, it will look after me. It's all about moderation. My motto in life is, "a balanced life, is a happy life". It saddens me that so many people have major hang ups about themselves and that they have become a prisoner of what society says they should look like. It's utter nonsense! We are designed to be different!

Being you is the best you can be, so we should celebrate our differences.

Alesha Dixon, Musician and TV Presenter

Body & Mind

As a professional sportsperson, my body is my livelihood and I probably view it in a different way than most...

...For me, the most important thing about my body is not how it looks but how well my body performs. Football has always been my passion and my body has taken me from the playground in Beckton to sold-out stadiums around the world. I never forget how privileged I am to have made it but I have had to be disciplined and I always make sure my body is well looked after. I eat healthy and I don't drink or smoke.

One thing I've learned throughout my career, I believe, is relevant to everyone, though. You can't achieve your potential unless your body and mind are working in harmony. No matter what you do, or whatever walk of life you are from, it's your body that allows you to be who you are. We all need to accept our bodies, and to be kind to them, in order to be the best that we can be.

Jermain Defoe, Footballer

Airbrushing

No one will ever look like the models on advertisement billboards or the celebrities on the front covers of glossy magazines – not even those models and celebrities themselves, because these pictures have been tweaked and manipulated until the last spot, blemish, ripple of skin or asymmetrical feature has been eliminated.

Despite common knowledge of airbrushing, these images still have a huge impact. People of all ages still look in the mirror and think how they don't compare to these 'ideal' bodies. These negative thoughts are so powerful that women say they are willing to exchange years of their life, family and friends for the 'perfect' body.

The advertising media is just one part of our society's obsession with impossibly perfect bodies. We urgently need to open up the conversation in schools, open up the catwalk to a range of models that showcase the diverse beauty of our society, get advertisements back to reality and shift the focus from thin to healthy. Sharing the stories in this book is an important part of the cultural conversation we need to spark.

Jo Swinson, MP, Chairman of the All Parties Parliamentary Group on Body Image

A Weighty Issue

Oh my god! You've lost so much weight! You've lost soooo much weight!

People say when they haven't seen me for a while.

I haven't lost ANY weight. I'm exactly the same size as I was the last time I saw them.

So when they scream 'OH MY GOD! You've lost soooo much weight!'

what I hear is… 'Oh my God! I remember you as soooo much fatter!!!'

Well um thanks, that's great. I'm not as fat as you remember me.

What I think they mean to say is, 'you look great, gosh your gorgeous, damn you're sexy, I'd forgotten how gorgeous you were!'

But, no. People think the highest complement to tell any lady larger than a size ten is 'you've lost weight!!!' They come striding in, in heavy hobnail boots throwing around what they consider to be a compliment. 'You've lost SOOOOOO much weight.'

When I meet an old friend with a big nose I don't yelp, 'Wow, that Conk's shrinking, I'm sure its getting smaller!'

If I bump into a mate with a squint I don't say 'gosh those eyes are nearly pointing at the same postcode!'

If I meet a man with a tiny cock I don't say, 'that ointment must be working! Your penis could take my eye out!'

I don't say anything, But I do tell people they're looking fab. Because generally they are, and you know what? The more you tell people how great they look, the better they do!

You know the most beautiful sentence in the world? 'Darling you look wonderful! Can I buy you a drink?'

So, why is it that weight is up there for public debate and comment. Why is it ok to comment so openly on people's weight?

My god you've lost weight!

Don't lose anymore!

You're so skinny! (I'm a 12, I'm not skinny, I'm normal, and not tabloid normal, proper normal! My Normal).

'You've lost weight!' Like it's a prize! The best thing you can say to any woman. Hey, you can never be too Rich or too thin. Well you can actually. You can be a big, rich, dead, skinny corpse.

So please, when you see me, don't go there. Support me, love me, but back off judging me.

And when I say I haven't lost any weight. Please don't argue with me and insist I have! I'm a woman, I weigh myself every day. I know exactly how much I weigh to the ounce. So please don't keep insisting I have when I bloody haven't! You're insistance doesn't make it true it just makes you irritating. Because Most of the time I feel really good about my body, dam sexy, until someone starts talking about it in terms of pounds. Back off. And you know what I love best about my body? MY ARSE, hell yeah! My GLORIOUS ARSE. I am so proud of it. It's a woman's arse, its bloody lush my arse. Even I want to bite it. My arse is arsetastic!

Especially when I'm naked. I think I look great naked… Its only when I put clothes on I can feel like an amorphous blob.

Because after years of battling I'm fine with me, I've found the right shape for me. My BMI is healthy. I'm not too fat and I'm not too thin. I exercise regularly and sometimes, I do put on a little weight and sometimes I lose it. But its never in the hope that someone I love will greet me and comment on whether I have or haven't. That's for me and my doctor. Tell me that I look great, tell me that you love me, tell me that you missed me. But all that other stuff? You can shove up it up your arse!

By Lizzie Roper, Comedian and Presenter

Listen With Your Eyes

I paint my mouth with lipstick
Cos I have something to say
And if you look into my eyes
They're lined in charcoal grey
But I dream of times when my
Naked face will have its day
When hours in front of mirrors
Ain't the price I have to pay.
I love a bit of glamour
The glitter and the bling
Sometimes the rhythm gets me
And I shimmy as I sing,
Inviting you to judge me
By my skirt's length and my swing.

But listen with your eyes and
You won't hear a single thing.

By Mis-Dee, Singer/Songwriter

Love Yourself

I am a staunch advocate and supporter of all Body Gossip is trying to do because I know how many people's lives are ruined, or at the very least, diminished by their own detrimental self-image.

The 'ologists always say, don't they, that if you don't love yourself, how can you possibly expect others to love you? I strongly believe they have a point – which is why we must learn to love ourselves whilst at the same time trying to do the best for our bodies. In a world which seems to have gotten the whole body image thing out of proportion, we must try to redress the balance.

In my own case, my own personal ghost that's haunted me for many years, is my fight against being overweight. I have tried and failed many times to beat it, and probably made it far worse by the trying.

I always reached for a diet to exorcise my ghost. If you'd told me then, twenty years ago, that diets make you fat, and that 95% of dieters always put the weight back on again – and more, I wouldn't have listened. Because I bought into what was ultimately a self-destructive and punishing regime. Only now, many years later, do I understand the profound effect yo-yo dieting had on my figure – and my mind.

Mind you, it didn't help doing it all in the public eye!

When I appeared in the Celebrity Big Brother House, I was hailed as "Big Blubber". One writer in the Daily Mail said: "Anne Diamond's children must be ashamed to have a mother with such a gargantuan backside."

253

Well, you certainly need a thick hide to withstand that sort of attack, don't you?

Look, I know that anyone famous has to learn to take of all that sort of stuff in their stride. But it certainly taught me a thing or two about society's attitude towards obesity.

Compared with other celebrities and household names who were caught snorting coke, visiting massage parlours and having affairs with John Major, I had committed the sin of all sins. I had put on weight.

Believe me, it's hard enough to lose weight – once you've put it on – without society throwing brickbats at you, and beating you down with your own failed efforts.

I got so fed up with self-righteous holy men and women telling me that losing weight is "not rocket science, you know. All you have to do is eat less and exercise more!"

Because that sort of advice has landed us with an obesity epidemic. It simply has not worked.

It's not that it's not correct. Of course it is – we all know that energy in must equal energy out. But that is not enough. Not nowadays. Not in a world where we all live more sedentary lifestyles and we are all encouraged, bribed and brainwashed into eating more food, and some of it absolute junk.

Society has to evolve a more compassionate attitude towards those who are already suffering from obesity.

"I have always been fat", wrote one member of my weight loss support website, BuddyPower.net. "My mum says she had to prick extra holes in my bottle as a baby as my face would turn blue with the effort of trying to get the milk out. I was put on my first diet aged 8 - a vile Complan meal replacement thing, torture. I grew into a fat child, then a fat teenager, followed by being a fat twenty-something and I'm now a fat thirty-something. I have tried every diet imaginable, but am still around 6 stone overweight.

"I am generally contented, I have a very happy, loving and supportive relationship, two great kids, a job I love and plenty of good friends. I'm just not happy with me. I was diagnosed with Type 2 Diabetes in February and have struggled to reduce my blood glucose levels with diet and medication. I know I need to lose weight for the sake of my health and for my children. My husband loves me but I know he's terribly worried for me and dare not mention my weight in case it upsets me more."

She's desperate for help. She's not daft, but she can't do it on her own — and if you've ever been there, you'll understand that.

I have been there.

Oh yes, I have been there, done that, got the extra-large T shirt and even made the video. I have done every diet in the land — and put on yet more weight at the end of it

Once it piles on, it's hell's own game getting rid of it.

After the horrible headlines, I immediately starved myself and exercised like a mad thing.

I lost so much weight so quickly that everyone told me I should make a fitness and slimming video. So I did. But to celebrate its release, the publishers took me to a slap up lunch, and I never looked back.

On piled the weight again. And again, and again, after every diet and every gym subscription. All the weight again — and then more.

When I got to 15stone10lbs, I was scared. I knew that just around the corner lay diabetes and the increased risk of cancer, heart disease, stroke and a shortened lifespan — you know it.

The realisation that you are now one of those horrid statistics is heart-stopping. Even worse is the acceptance that you're almost useless at beating it.

That's when a little bit of you dies inside.

That's when you stop going out as much as you used to. That's when you don't go swimming with the kids because the only swimsuit that fits you looks like something meteorologists use to make weather balloons. So you just watch them from the poolside. It's when you wake up most mornings dreading having to get dressed into clothes you hate, and you go to bed every night feeling a failure because you ate a Malteser.

That's when I heard from a friend of a friend of a friend who'd had a gastric band fitted – and the weight was cascading off her.

Until then, I'd thought weight loss surgery was something that only weird Americans and Sharon Osbourne did.

So started my colourful history with weight loss surgery. To cut a long story short – I went to Belgium to have it done, because I thought it would be cheaper and they boasted no MRSA in their hospitals. And they put it in the wrong place – around the bottom of my oesophagus instead of around my stomach. No wonder it didn't work.

I just didn't lose weight, like I was told I would! I felt as hungry as before and when I ate, I couldn't feel any restriction whatsoever.

I felt awful. I'd gone all the way to Belgium, had the bloody operation, all of the worry, all of the fear, all of the expense – and nothing.

In the end, I just concluded, as all fatties do, that I was a big failure – it was all my fault and I was now beyond redemption. So I was going to be a sixty year old fat lady after all.

That's when I agreed to take part in probably the only TV programme I have ever, in my long TV career, totally regretted. It was called Celebrity Fit Club and it was utterly ghastly and symptomatic of everything that's wrong with the media's perception of obesity and those who suffer it.

So why did I agree to take part?

Because it held out the last glimmer of hope for me. The producers promised me it was all about fun, togetherness and team work, and would give me unprecedented access to the top weight loss experts in the world. Every contestant who'd ever been on before had lost stones in weight. It worked, they said.

Of course now I understand that it didn't. Nearly every single contestant still struggles with their weight! I had a miserable time. Especially when the Sunday papers then revealed I'd had a gastric band and therefore shouldn't be in the programme at all. The resultant furore, and my leaving the show amongst strident headlines, sure taught me a lot about attitudes.

More importantly, I got thousands and thousands of letters from fellow sufferers who just wanted to stay in touch. Which is why I set up my weight loss support website – BuddyPower.net. All of the members have fought obesity and their own body image problems in their own way, and are still fighting. No-one's complacent, but they have certainly learned the compassion message.

Fatties are so used to being abused and name-called, that they deprecate themselves.

You can even see it in the "user names" of my Fat Happens members. Although it's done in fun, some members give themselves horrible nicknames (like "FatAssGirl", "Lardy Lin" or "Porky"). Many have admitted to me in private emails that it masks an underlying despair.

I asked them what was the worst thing about being fat. Try and read these without feeling for their humiliation:

*Getting wedged in between your chair and the lecture table and not being able to move until everyone had left the room!

*Splitting a pair of jeans I was trying on in a shop.

*Getting stuck in a swing in the park!

*Needing an extension belt for aeroplanes.

*Being asked to pay for two airline seats.

*Having a friend's dining chair collapse underneath me.

*Going to the doctor with a rash/infection underneath my folds of fat.

*I broke the lateral trainer at the gym and wanted to die.

*Having blood pressure taken - and the arm strap is too small.

*I can't shave my legs properly.

*When on a camel ride on holiday with my boyfriend (that poor camel) they had to put sand bags at my boyfriend's side to balance the weight out.

*Being told (after collecting sponsor money) that I wouldn't be able to make a tandem parachute jump because I was too heavy.

*Being told by a "friend", it's a shame you're so fat, because you have a really pretty face.

*Envying every other woman you ever meet.

*Promising every morning you'll be "good" at dieting and weeping every night that you weren't.

We cannot show too much compassion. We just have to ensure it is channelled into constructive programmes that will really make a difference.

Learning to love ourselves would be a great first step. And that is the underlying message of the Body Gossip movement. None of us are perfect, but while we try and live our lives and even better ourselves, it would be just great if we could be nice to each other, and ourselves too.

Anne Diamond, TV Presenter

Trippin' Off the Chocolate Biscuits

I turn on the TV and what do I see
Another Skinny Minnie staring back at me
Grinning and gloating, almost mocking me
As I sit here contemplating on this chocolate biccy!

It's beckoning me, begging me
Yearning to be eaten
But I try to stay strong
For THIS WAIST LINE MUST BE BEATEN

I flick over the channel
Oh great! Top Model instead

These chicks look malnourished
Almost like living dead!
Well some of them look alright I suppose
Let me try not to be so harsh
The insults fly around my head
Like fingers to sweeties...fast!

OK let's check out Maury
Normal people...hooray
Not really trying to hear the story line
Not concerned with what they say

But most of them are normal
Normal sized, some big and some small
And watching them reminds me that
Perhaps the skinnies are heading for a fall...

...Fall because they lack body weight
Body density, body mass
Their breasts look practically non existent
And they sure ain't got no ass!

As I look at the biscuit packet
I think this girl could do with most
Finish that, then on to some cakes
Concluding with several rounds of toast

A couple of bottles of fat coke
Then three or four packs of Haribos
Quite a few bags of potato chips
Then maybe some chocolate just so she knows...

...what time it is, it's 'eating time'
It's called, giving you some shape
Rounding you off, filling you out

Forcing you to eat all that's on your plate!
OK maybe that's a little extreme
Let's have a look at that magazine
I can almost guess what's going on
From cover to cover and in between

I open it and just as thought
Its added fuel to my already burning fire
Stick thin, drawn in, just gaunt, drawn in
And to this I'm suppose to aspire?

Flicking through I sigh sadly
I shake my head in despair
This lingerie model's pelvic bone
Is eclipsing the underwear

She looks fragile, she looks so weak
Pretty face with NO sex appeal
Any man she wears that lingerie for
Will have to be 'genteel'

That's gentle but stretched out and softened
Because that's the only way she could play
To put that lingerie to good use
For more than one round? There's no way!

I carry on turning over the pages
The odd normy dotted here and there
But there's something awkward about how they pose
As if they're far too self aware

Probably were told before the shoot
'You need to lose some weight'
No encouragement or embracing of the fact
That being under weight is soooo late!

I continue on to the problem pages
About 4 out of 5 are about self image
Not confident enough or happy with size
And not much positive words about self image

Once again promoting the media ideal
Of what looks good, what looks great
Based upon what? Is a question asked by many
Who is dictating is the real debate!

I finish reading through the mag
And glance back at the biccies
I know I shouldn't really
But it's like my fingers are sticky

Sensibly I think it through
And consider what they are doing to my thighs
But I proceed to indulge in another, think about the summer
And then stifle my greedy mind cries!

Sherryl Blu, Radio Presenter and Poet

Burlesque

April 9th 2010, I slowly stepped onto stage, wearing a purple corset, black bra, purple ruffle knickers and a feathered suspender belt. I was about to perform burlesque for the first time and I was extremely nervous.

It had taken me nearly all my life to build the confidence to do this and I didn't want to mess it up. I finally felt like I was a sexy young woman not just a frumpy mum. My daughter, Holly was born July 2007 and I gained so much weight from pregnancy. I hid my body in shapeless clothes and walked with my head down. I broke up with Holly's dad when she was four months old, I felt like damaged goods and that I would never look good again.

I battled with post natal depression in secret, eating junk for comfort, stuck in a cycle of feeling fat and frumpy but doing nothing to improve my situation. I needed a fresh start, something radical to kick me out of the rut, so I packed our belongings and moved us to Leeds.

I decided I needed help, so when I saw a leaflet for counselling, I took the plunge and phoned. It was practical help like introducing me to other young mums in the area and encouraging me to take time for myself to look after myself. Slowly I started to eat healthily and exercise every day. The exercise made me feel fantastic and it stopped me comfort eating because I was reaching highs through working out. I got down to a size 14 but to be honest I wasn't bothered about the dress size, I could've been any size, I felt great. I woke up every morning feeling positive and ready to take on the world.

As my confidence grew, I felt able to wear figure hugging clothes and took time to find things which I felt good in. Eventually I started to go out with friends again and I relished getting dressed up. One such night was a burlesque night that a friend took me to. I was completely enthralled by the gorgeous ladies on stage, all of them so confident and sexy. I had to try it for myself, I felt confident and ready to show everyone how gorgeous my curvy body was.

So I practised, came up with my stage name (Gem de la Creme - good enough to eat) and bit the bullet. I tickled and teased my body with an ostrich feather and responded to crowd's applause by slowly taking each item of clothing off, giggling as I heard whoops and cheers.

I LOVED IT! People found me sexy because I found myself sexy, my confidence was the turn on not just the striptease. I never performed burlesque for acceptance or approval of others, I performed burlesque for myself.

So I performed this traditional style of burlesque for a while, enjoying it but never fully satisfied, I felt there was something lacking. Until one day I came across stories of Victorian sideshows. The bearded lady, the pony girl and the elephant man were people with unusual bodies who were exploited for money by travelling circus owners. The strangest story was that of the pig faced lady, a bear which was shaved and dressed in women's clothes and dragged around fairs for a public obsessed with 'Freaks'. It struck a chord in me and I couldn't get the idea of a pig faced lady out of my mind. I knew I had to do this. I had to make a statement that to some I'm a freak or a pig but I trusted my body to be sexy even in a pig mask.

So I set to work at finding the costume and practising the routine. I wanted to make it as graceful as possible to really shock audiences. I'm only onstage for 2 minutes 47 seconds but I make sure that every nano second counts. I strip off my elbow length gloves, my stockings and my corset. I'm left standing in a tiny pair of knickers, star shaped pasties and pig mask, proud of every inch of my body.

99% of the time I get really positive feedback when I perform pig faced lady. There has been the odd criticism but people are entitled to their opinion.

After spending years dieting, obsessing about my weight, I've learnt that the only way to be attractive is to believe that you are. Anybody who has a go at you for your size or shape are the kind of people who will find anything to have a go at. Why waste your time trying to please them when you can be enjoying your life without stress? Every woman is beautiful, no matter what size they are.

Gemma Carlier aka Gem de La Crème, Burlesque Dancer

That Naked Girl from Camelot

My name is Mieke Dockley, but you probably know me as the 'Naked Girl from Channel 4's Camelot'.

Picture the scenario: You're an aspiring actress. You want to get out there, to live your dream and learn your craft. Your agent calls you. Channel 4 want to see you for a role that will be seen by millions! This could seriously help you on the slippery showbiz ladder! Oh, one thing – You'll have to be totally starkers.

What would you do?

My friends are very keen to point out that I have a sort of 'glamour-model-esque' look. I have long blonde hair, I'm slim with proportionate curves. Heck, I even have a footballer boyfriend! When they found out I'd landed the role in Camelot some friends were quick to criticise. "You said you'd never get them out for the lad's mags!" they said. "But" I thought "I'm not".

I'm happy with my body and know I'll only be young once. I eat – In fact I once got told off for eating a bowl of pasta directly prior to a shoot. Apparently you're not supposed to eat for 48 hours beforehand. I told the director I'd pass out if I did that and to leave me with my munch! Ultimately, the only person you have to answer to is yourself – I didn't think the scene in Camelot was sleazy or particularly gratuitous and I know I'll look back on it and feel proud I had the guts to do it.

I want to be able to say to my grandchildren "look how hot Granny once was!"

Mieke Dockley, Actress and Model

My Body Image

As a buxom, amateur burlesque dancer on Simon Cowell's TV hit show Britain's Got Talent 2009, I was so scared of what (Mr Nasty's) words would be to me…

Instead, his words were "I adore you Fabia" which changed my life forever.

It was in fact the minority of the BGT viewers who set up a hate campaign against me, say I was a fat s**g. The worst comment was "If I were her son, I'd kill myself".

Dealing with comments like this because of being a sexy, curvy, voluptuous woman was so negative; I decided to turn it into a positive. I kept dancing, did my newspaper, TV and, radio interviews with grace. I understand everyone is entitled to their opinion but I guess they were in shock that a curvy woman would be entertaining the master of the entertainment industry with such a positive feedback.

I certainly flew the flag for curvy women nationally and, worldwide! My job to prove a point was done.

Yes, I have stretch marks on my tummy because, I've had my son, I also have cellulite, isn't that just being a woman?

At the age of 21, I was a size 10 UK, over the years I've gained weight due to medication I take daily for bi-polar disorder. Being pregnant in 2004 I gained weight and had gestational diabetes; I controlled it by using insulin 4 times a day. Since giving birth to my son, the diabetes has not returned. I am now back to the weight before pregnancy.

I embrace my curves I'm a curvaceous size 18/20 UK, I use shape wear under my dresses to enhance my curves. I'm curvy and proud of my body image!

Gok Wan's book called "Work your Wardrobe" is my body bible; it has brilliant fashion advice for curvy, voluptuous and buxom women. Some people call us "Real Women" but, every woman is real…

Gok Wan used to be of a larger frame, so he knows how curvy women feel, that's why he has such a huge fan base of women. He understands but he listens and he's very helpful and very kind too.

Gok Wan knows how it feels to be called fat! He too turned a negative into a positive.

Whilst I was on BGT the media were also calling me "Flabia", I thought to myself, that's a very inventive name, I wonder how long it took that journalist to come up with that name. I laughed my head off!

Being a curvy burlesque dancer got me more media attention than any other contestant on BGT 2009. I had a traumatic story to tell, they were interested in why my weight gained over the years.

I told my story in my autobiography, to help others who have suffered like me.

I may not look fit but I go to Jakuri fit to flex class, Zumba and I teach burlesque beginners classes too. So it's not as if I'm sat on my couch all day long eating.

My concern is with (PERFECTION). Why do we have to fit in to a certain category? Too fat, too thin, too ugly, big bum, small bum, too short, too tall, nose too big, ears too big, boobs too small. The list is endless. I for one am fed up of opening a glossy magazine and the models are so air brushed they don't even recognise themselves after the photo shoot.

A friend of mine was talking to me about her 13 year old daughter who has already asked for plastic surgery on her breasts!!! A tummy tuck and a nose job. She's just a child. What's happened to the youngsters of today? At that age, I had never heard of cosmetic surgery, only emergency surgery.

Dying to be beautiful comes to mind. Do they know that a general anaesthetic is very dangerous? They may not even wake up after the surgery they have paid for to look more beautiful.

The only surgery I've had is a C-section. I will never have cosmetic surgery – I had a bad experience from having a flesh eating bug, 24 hours after giving birth, I ended up in the intensive care unit.

I recently bought a copy of Vogue Italia and I was thrilled when I saw the title "Curvy". I did a double take to make sure what I was reading was real.

The fashion industry is catching up with the demand for more voluptuous women on the catwalks, TV adverts and magazine shoots too.

I've been signed to www.curvymodels.co.uk for fashion, advertising & high class glamour modelling.

I'm thrilled to be part of Body Gossip and more importantly shouting out about the campaign. I would like to thank Ruth, the founder of Body Gossip, and also Natasha. Without them, Body Gossip would not be around for people to express their feelings about body image, eating disorders and society today.

Please BODY GOSSIP. X

By Fabia Cerra, Dancer

Miss England

When I was a little girl I had no body issues, I would happily run around half dressed in the sunshine. I had no idea then that one day I would be singled out by my peers for being different.

My crime was that I was curvier than the average girl at school. I was taller, I had a bust, I had a narrow waist and rounded hips and I was persecuted daily for these crimes.

I truly hated the way that I looked, I wanted to fade into the background, I wanted to go about unnoticed and most of all just get through at least one day not being tormented for just being me.

I thought that if I ate very little and exercised at every opportunity, I would be skinny and flat chested just like them.

Thankfully my mum sat me down and gave me a good honest talking to. She told me that the other girls were just jealous of me because they secretly wanted what I already had! I thought she was mad! She also told me that no matter what, I would never be skinny. I just wasn't made that way, I was always going to be curvy. I had a decision to make and that was accept me for the curvy person I was or spend the rest of my life trying to achieve the un-achievable and to be disappointed each time I passed a mirror.

I decided that I wanted to be happy and I wanted to do something positive about it. I wanted to be a positive role model for young people as there were not any role models for me to aspire to when I was growing up. TV and magazines seemed only to portray thin models and celebrities and most of these had been airbrushed so much that the images that I was seeing were unobtainable anyway.

I decided to enter Miss England to highlight that beauty comes in a bigger package than a size 8!

I won my regional heat for Miss Surrey and the media went crazy!

I was photographed by the worlds press and interviewed by TV stations around the world. I flew to New York to appear on the Tyra Banks show and I even got my own Wikipedia entry under plus size model!

The best thing that happened was the E-mails that I received from people telling me their stories and how by seeing me and what I was doing had inspired them to accept themselves for who they were.

I did not win Miss England. I did come 1st runner up. I guess Miss England were not ready for a plus size beauty Queen!

It did not matter to me that I did not win, I had achieved what I set out to do and I proved that beauty comes in all shapes and sizes.

After Miss England things went quiet for me, the UK fashion industry was not ready to change its ways and modelling work was not coming my way. As soon as I could I approached Ford Models New York and in August last year I signed with them. I now live in Manhattan and I have not stopped working. I fly all over the world doing photo shoots. My dream of becoming an international model has come true and every day I aspire to be a positive healthy role model to others.

I now don't just walk past a mirror loathing what I might see, I always stop and take a good look at the gorgeous, voluptuous young woman looking back at me. This is not the end of my story, it is just the beginning.

Chloe Marshall, Plus Size Model with Ford Models, New York

Diving Into the Safety of the Water

I was very fortunate as a young girl, I didn't grow up with any real body image issues; it wasn't something I really picked up on as my mother and friends didn't have them. I was very tall and slim for my age and both my mother and grandmother had always been fit and slim so diets weren't present in my consciousness. I was fit and healthy and played sports at school. I was pretty embarrassed by my teeth; they were really goofy as a result of thumb sucking, but by the age of 14 braces were already working their magic. The only physical thing that bothered me was that I wanted bigger breasts, actually I just wanted breasts full stop! I was rather small and flat in that department and most of my girlfriends at school had all developed ahead of me. I used to dread swimming with friends, standing around in swimsuits and would stand with my arms folded until we were diving into the safety of the water.

Diving into the safety of the water.

Odd looking back at that sentence now, as it's diving into water that changed my body and my life forever. I was on holiday aged 14 years old when I dove off rocks into the sea, hitting my head on rocks and breaking my neck, leaving me instantly paralysed from the chest down. My head hurt and I knew something bad had happened but I didn't know the extent of my injuries were until I had been carried out of the sea and realised I couldn't move my legs.

I spent the next 10 months in a spinal unit where the days, weeks and months passed by in a haze of bed rest, school lessons, and physiotherapy. The rehabilitation staff were amazing but no one really knows what you're going through emotionally and not much attention is paid to body image adjustment. I can still remember the first time I started to see my body again after my accident. Since breaking my neck I had been in head traction for 6 weeks which effectively meant my head was pinned down to the pillow, I was unable to move my neck or head at all. I used a handheld mirror to look at my surroundings on the ward and to look at my face; I can't explain how reassuring it was to study my face and see that it hadn't changed though so much of my physicality was now changed forever.

I could see my legs when the nurses came to wash me and when the physiotherapists came to stretch my legs; they would lift my legs 90 degrees and stretch them up. My first reaction was sheer horror at how unbelievably hairy my legs were, and it was black hair! I'd never had hair growth like that on my legs previously. After I stopped shrieking the nurses explained that it was a reaction to the steroids I'd been on in the first week or two after my accident. Unfortunately while I was on bed rest I was also on blood thinners so they couldn't shave my legs. I was delighted when after 12 weeks I was finally allowed up to attend hydrotherapy in the pool and two brilliant nurses removed all the excess leg hair! Funny how it's the little insignificant aspects of our bodies that can bother us so much.

For the first year or two after my accident I was very underweight, looking back I think I felt rather vulnerable and unsure of my body, it still felt a little bit like a stranger to me. Everything looked familiar, freckles in the right places on my legs, but at the same time they weren't the same legs, I wasn't in the same body.

In rehab everyone wore tracksuits and trainers, that's fine when you've no self esteem or body confidence for a short time but at some point you have to re enter the "real world" where image and appearance matter. I learnt very quickly that the way I dressed affected the way strangers responded to me as a wheelchair user. I vowed never to dress in a way that could ever be mistaken for a disabled stereotype and as soon as I was discharged from hospital I was out shopping to find clothes that looked good sitting down.

I was very fortunate that, because both my mother and grandmother were professional dress makers, I was very well informed about cuts of patterns and fabrics. I also knew how to dress well for my new body shape and had my mum on hand to alter things or create upholstered evening gowns for events. She has always designed my event dresses with built in corsetry so I feel well supported and confident, it's great not to worry about fabric slipping or ill fitting clothes that accentuate the parts from which I'd rather detract attention.

So now 20 years on with all the changes in my body how do I feel?

In brief, fine. I like my body, it's in good shape despite the lack of muscle tone. I've still got very long legs, the softest feet imaginable, and a great pair of breasts that I coveted as a teenager!

What don't I like so much?

In my teens and twenties I never had to worry about my weight, I was always a 10. Then when I hit 30 I seemed to put on weight overnight which was a bit of shock. I tried to exercise expecting the weight to fall off but I hadn't realised quite how hard it is to lose weight when you can only move 30% of your body. I guess that makes me quite frustrated when I see people complain about their weight when all they need to do is eat less and move more.

I don't really like how big my shoulders and upper arms have become, my biceps are pretty large for a woman. Whilst I appreciate the strength of my biceps and triceps and I am forever grateful to have the use of my arms, I do wish it wasn't so hard to find clothes to accommodate them. Jacket & blouse sleeves are often too tight which is really frustrating. Designers aren't grading clothes accurately which means if I try a larger size it's too big on the bust and the waist but still too tight on the sleeves because they haven't increased the sleeve width.

I'd also love to have stomach muscles so I could have a taught and toned stomach, but I have to accept that is unlikely to ever happen as most of those muscles are paralysed. There is no point in beating myself up for something I have no control over but when I get overly concerned by appearances I remember that I'm lucky to be alive, lucky to have the use of my upper limbs which provide me with the ability to live a free and independent lifestyle. On a more shallow note I also remind myself of an excellent quote from Pulp Fiction: "It's unfortunate what we find pleasing to the touch and pleasing to the eye is seldom the same". Yay for soft stomachs!

However I have to confess I'm frustrated with the public perception of disabled bodies. There is an over prevalent assumption that we are all deformed, scarred or broken; this simply isn't true. It also contributes to why I've continued to model for 17 years and why I have appeared nude in a poster campaign and in a television drama; to remove the mystery of disability. It's also why I speak out in the press about the representation of disability in the media. I want other disabled people to feel they are being represented and for there to be greater diversity in the media as well as a respect and appreciation for people's physical differences in society.

In spite of any of those little issues, I'm happy with my body, it's not perfect but I appreciate it. I see so many women who do have "perfect" and able bodies who are desperately unhappy because they can pinch an imaginary inch on their waist or hips. I'm inclined to find that a little sad, life is far too short to worry about 3cms of flesh which no one else notices. It is these little issues that we focus in on and obsess about, believing everyone else notices too and thinks less of us. I've yet to meet a man or a woman who looks at the body of a loved one with a harshly critical eye, we are all our own worst critics.

Look at your body in the mirror, see every muscle you can move, touch your skin and be grateful you can feel the sensation, and watch how your body responds to messages sent by your brain. It's an incredible privilege. Our bodies change throughout our lifetime, be it through ageing, pregnancy, illness, disability, diet, exercise or surgery. Embrace its current form and focus on the aspects of your body that you do like. Most importantly, try to relax and be kind to yourself and remember to laugh through life! People always look great when they're laughing....

Shannon Murray, Actress and Model

The End of a Long-Term Relationship

At what age did I first step on a pair of scales?

Unlike today's kids that start dieting from embryo age, I don't recall even thinking about my weight until my mid-teens. Not until I was sweet sixteen and had just come back from months as a kitchen assistant on a Kibbutz. I returned looking like a tanned, stocky peasant, having lived off bread and chocolate spread because the canteen food was so dire (the weevils in the rice were so big, I'd named a few as pets).

All was well until the tan disappeared. I'd read in Cosmo the 'right' weight for my height. Apparently, mine was not it. From then on, the scales and I started a love/hate relationship. I felt they lied to me when I was sure I'd lost weight. I even tried dumping it for a younger, more reliable model.

Whatever, like an abusive boyfriend, I know I was always hoping it would change!

Often, I'd rebel outright, and tell it to 'get lost'. But every time it would hang around in a corner, waiting for just the right moment to lure me back. It knew from experience that one day my jeans would feel loose, I'd tentatively hop on eager to see proof of the lost pounds... and I'd relish its embrace. But before long, it would start upsetting me all over again, and I'd be checking it out daily, once more at its beck and call.

Having said all of that, I suppose I also have to reluctantly thank the scales for my book, Making it Big. People often ask what was the inspiration. I can pinpoint it to the exact day. I got on the scales one morning and watched the arrow climb higher than Everest. I felt mountainous – a naked jelly. Desperately removing ear studs, I reweighed. No better. I knew for certain I'd never get into the outfit I was looking forward to wearing. I remember thinking: 'If only the extra pounds made me as thrilled as when I lost a few. As I miserably brushed my teeth, I started to fantasize about what society would be like if it was reversed... a world where big was 'in' and skinny 'out'.

We would wear WHITE because it would show off all the lumps and curves. We would go to Skinny Farms to put on weight and be hand-fed a constant diet of fairy cakes whilst we lolled about on a chaise-long, saving calories.

Perhaps Max Factor would bring out a silver pen to highlight our stretch marks, whilst the celebrity rags would be full of pictures of the famous in size 20 bikinis. Woe betide the slim legged actress, her cellulite-free thighs would be shamefully ringed in red! It also prompted me to realize that how we feel about ourselves is very manipulated by advertising, glossy mags and movies.

If they all combined to make curves really fashionable, I believe our mindsets could be altered. After all, Twiggy at sixteen was indeed a twig. Today, we don't see that. The same size model wouldn't stand out on the catwalk as anything different. In fact, she might even be called 'Branch'. (And in a few more years of this growing madness, 'Tree-trunk'!) What upsets me most, though, is that a normal size 10-12 for our teenage girls is no longer considered ideal. They all strive to be a size 6-8. And with it, the young male perception of a 'hot' body is also corrupted.

Truth is, there is no perfect size. Once you realize the amount of unrealistic images and photo retouching around us, you understand it's all about brainwashing and mindset. In fact, despite its role in helping me to write a book, I've decided I'm going to dump my scales once and for all. It's finally over. It's going in the skip.

This time, I actually mean it.

By Lyndsay Russell, Author of best-selling novel Making It Big

The Unbearable Lightness of Doreen

"Chocolate never tasted as good as slim feels," Doreen our leader announces from her makeshift pulpit over the hubbub of approval and shuffling chairs.

"Today ladies you have lost on average a whole pound each – now give yourselves a clap," we all smack our hands together forcing a grin, while clinging to the shadowy abyss of eternal obesity. Tonight, in the draughty old St Mary's Village Hall I have won an award for losing my pound and as Beryl Cook's ladies look on, I walk to the front, once more the fat kid at School, patronised and pinned with a badge emblazoned with, 'I'm a Lifelong Loser!'

Every Thursday night at 7.30, along with 43 other desperate fatties, I pay £6.00 to face my food demons while sitting on nasty plastic chairs and breathing in stale air. Here I can share my hopes and fears with other sufferers while believing that one day this will all be behind me and I will be slim and therefore happy. Listening to Doreen I can almost see those fat closet doors swinging open and me reclaiming my life in size twelve jeans. I've been down this road many times before, but this will be different and with a heart full of optimism and a bag full of low fat Snack Attack bars I cling to the wreckage of hope.

The weigh-in has taken place, and Doreen is ready to begin her sermon. This bleak gathering of middle-aged blubber is transfixed and hungrily gobbling up every crumb the leader drops. We are seeking slimming salvation and knowing in our podgy, fat laden-hearts that Doreen 'our leader' holds the golden key. This Goddess woman was once like us, but she found the path and now wants to lead us there. "You can be as happy with your bodies as I am with mine," she says; "I lost two stone and changed my life."

Doreen begins with a tantalising glimpse of before and after photos - her life as a disgusting worthless pig (aka me now, tonight) then weeks/months later when she's rejoined the human race to wear off the peg dresses and little pastel cardis. Doreen, who enjoys her post-fat life as a Gold Leader with Lifelong Losers, sticks pictures of pies on the board while screwing up her nose in horror. We nod in agreement as she berates us for our appetites, pacing the floor, taunting with tales of her own steely control, tight tummy and 'passion for small portions.' Doreen transcended us mere mortals several pounds ago when she cast out her vile flesh by sticking 'religiously' to 'the programme', "not a diet dear – never say 'diet'."

Laying slim hands on narrow hips, delicious Doreen is now talking of holidays sun-kissed with sparkling water and salads. She waxes lyrical on Christmases of nothing but low fat turkey equalled only by the orgasmic delights waiting in a carton of low fat cottage cheese on Boxing Day.

The woman is a Lifelong Loser martyr, even her Easter bunnies are carved from fresh fruit, the only chocolate that's passed those perfect pink lips was in 2005 when her husband walked out and she binged on a Malteser. Allowing herself a cheeky almond slice on the decree absolute, Doreen's followers can only dream of such will-power. We are not worthy, we are fat and have no self-control. We EAT at Christmas, we EAT on holiday and - for people like us - Easter Weekend is a dirty orgy of chocolate bunnies filled with sickly fondant and self-loathing.

Having communicated to us the extent of our lardiness and absence of self-control, Doreen is now winding up the slimming sermon. She raises her arms to the heavens, evangelical in her zeal as our tubby minds wander to the 'Snack Attack Diet Bars' piled high and screaming 'eat me'. Guarded fiercely and flogged mercilessly to us wannabe thinnies, these crisp, profanely priced slimming snacks come in three flavours, contain a mere 110 calories and cost £1.50 each.

"Finally, do you want to lose 2 -3 pounds next week?" She asks, dragging us from the slimming snacks and going for a climactic finish. "...Do you?" she looks at every woman, toying with feelings and hopes and appetites. What slimming secret is Doreen going to impart to her followers tonight? Silence as, white witch-like, she breathes of 'magic,' and 'celebrity' and 'slim' then, with a flourish, presents a slimming artefact the like of which we have never seen before.

"A fabulous set of shiny 'Magic Celebrity Scales' ladies," is held aloft as an audible gasp of desire fills the room and bubbles like melted chocolate. Double chins quiver in anticipation and greedy eyes stare covetously at the bright shiny object, all porkers mesmerised by the glint and the promise that merely by weighing our food on these, our fat will wash away and our self-esteem will rise to Doreen-like proportions. There's a whispering rumble as it slowly dawns on the calorie-obsessed congregation that, 'If we have these then we have all the power' 'buy the scales - save the world' 'we will be slim forever and ever Amen.'

All this for a mere £25.00.

"Only a few left," she whispers, licking her lips porn-star slowly, raising one eyebrow and clutching the Celebrity Scales to her breast like an Oscar.

Suddenly Doreen is rushed by Beryl Cook ladies, stage diving and rugby tackling her to the ground, grappling blindly for the Holy Grail. But Doreen's been here before, she carries a backup crate in her Honda for such occasions and within seconds, Milly the tea lady is despatched to Doreen's silver four-door to single-handedly relieve it of its holy burden.

Later, as I hold my 'Magic' scales and climb into my car I'm sated with low calorie lust and brimming with hope for the week to come. I've shed a pound in weight and £33 from my purse, I can be happy like Doreen one day. I know what I have to do. I have to use my new scales every day, but more than this – I have to think like Doreen, eat like Doreen...be like Doreen, she has all the answers, because she's slim.

But leaving the car park, scales safely belted in the passenger seat, 'Lifelong Loser,' badge pinned firmly to my breast, I notice a crack in the curtains of St Mary's Village hall. Light is spilling through the opening and I spot a lonely figure sobbing and pushing peanut explosion flavoured 'Snack Attack' bars into her mouth...three at a time.

I'm shocked, I thought being slim meant never having to say you're sorry. I thought thin meant happy, fulfilled, loved.

I drive on, away from the village hall and think that perhaps our Gold Leader doesn't have all the answers after all.

So I take off my Lifelong Loser badge, dump the Celebrity Scales and stop at the chippy.

I don't want to be thin and live like Doreen...I want to live like me.

Sue Watson, Author of Fat Girls and Fairy Cakes

Dear Body

I have never had a problem with you, its other people who find you hard to accept.

I'm sorry for the times I let their words influence me. And, in moments of insecurity, forgot the little six year old body, a mass of tumbling gangly limbs and tangled hair, who fought so hard not to wear her plastic hand and cut off the fingers in defiance. I'm sorry I forgot how to fight for you.

And for the days when I focus simply on my reflection, forget all the good your are doing beneath my skin. My beating heart. My lungs filling with air. My ovaries ready to grow a baby. My voice ready to speak my truth. And the little secret well that you keep filled with tears, ready to spill down my cheek with joy or possibly sorrow.

You are the expression of my soul and you communicate my feelings to the world beautifully. When I am happy you smile and dance and when I'm sad or lost you manage to get up and keep walking. I was amazed that after my daughter's birth, when I felt too exhausted to breath, you kept on living and filled my breasts with milk. And though the cord is cut, I am bound forever by love and blood to the baby who grew inside you like a precious flower.

I'm so sorry that I ever doubted your desirability, being desirable is not about how you look but how you feel and being me is a fabulous adventure. So thank you for your individuality, for your tenderness and awkwardness, your pale skin and the blueness of your eyes. And for those moments of accidental grace that are quite unexpected. And thank you most of all for being a woman.

Cerrie Burnell, TV Presenter

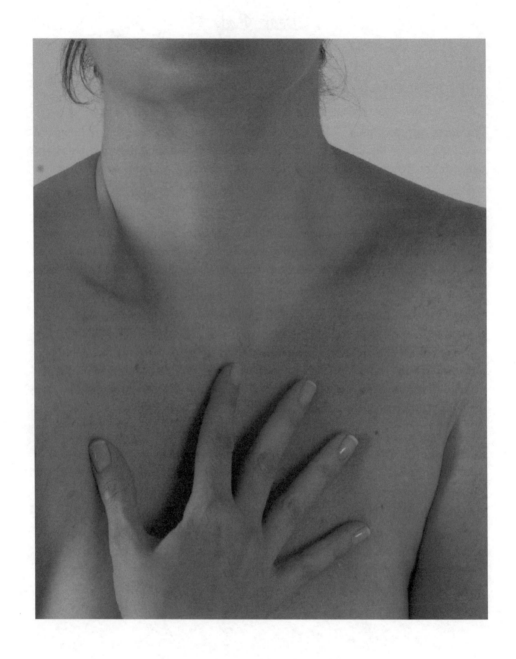

Afterword

'DEAR BODY...'

The stories in this book have shown the ways in which we struggle with, or celebrate, or ponder, or abuse, or modify our bodies. Yet, however much we may resent our bodies occasionally, our body is the only one we have.

We received so many 'letters to my body' as a response to our call for stories and they sum up our tempestuous relationships with our physical selves perfectly. The letters in this chapter are full of the perspective of people who have taken a step back and learned to accept themselves, perceived 'flaws' and all.

The Only Body I Have

I've:
Loved with it.
Told lies with it.
Ate too many mince pies with it.

Dressed it in some questionable clothes over the years.
Poisoned it with drugs.
Filled it balloon like with fears.

Cut it. Bitten it. Watched bits of it sag.
Walked it. Scolded it. Taught it how to nag.

Spent hours looking in the mirror criticising.
Different parts of it every year despising.

Yoga'd it. Toga'd it.
Made it run when it wanted its bed.
Put it through aerobics until every part was red.

Broken little bits of it on several occasions.
Blamed the flabby bits of it for struggling relations.

Called it too short.
Let it be bought.
Sold it down the river.
Taken vodka to extremes without warning my liver.

Dyed its hair. Painted its eyes.
Tried every product possible in efforts to disguise.

Dehydrated it. Berated it.

Burnt it in the sun.
Sat on it. Picked it.
Prayed I'd get a better one.

Tired it. Squashed it.
Failed to de-freckle with lemon bleach.
Scratched it. Starved it,
to be weights always just out of reach.

Bitched about it in its company.
Hated it with all my heart.
But now that it don't work no more
I wish I could go back to the start.

Eloise Williams, 38

Dear Body...

Have been watching a lot of the 'Dear Body' videos on YouTube but cannot bring myself to make a video or inflict it on others...so a few words and photos will suffice. Here goes... Dear Body... My Eyes...I love you...some say they are the gateway to your soul, they sparkle when I'm happy and cry when I'm sad. Sorry for not looking after you properly. Not removing mascara when I go to bed and looking like a panda the next morning!! For inflicting pain on you on the rare occasions I have slept in my contacts and then had to remove you with a plunger action the next day. My Lips...They pout, they pucker, they smile :) A little too large for my liking but hey, more to snog with. Mwwwahhh My eyebrows...are desperate for a pluck...yes, I said pluck!! Or a wax, whatever my pain threshold is at the time. My nose...it helps keep my glasses on my face, what more can I say! A tad too big, but good for smelling. It has a little moley thing on it, I'm learning to like that spot.

My Hair...oh dear, where do I start? I apologise hair for the many years of bleaching, dyeing, straightening, curling and not giving you enough nutrients to shine. I will try harder. Oh I do like the red at the moment though. My Boobs...No picture thank god, well not any that I can post on here! When I was at school we used to do the pencil test. If you can hold a pencil under your boobs they have drooped!! I can safely say I can hold a pencil case up now. Sorry boobs for not wearing the right size bras, I will endeavour to make getting measured as priority in the future.

My Feet...Uggh...feet. Sorry feet for squashing you into tight, too high, very inappropriate footwear, but I cannot promise it won't happen again. My Legs... Very long, very slender, I like my legs. Thank you legs. My Bum...I apologise for sitting on you far too much recently and will take you with my legs out a little more often. One day I will get you back to the bum I knew and loved. My tummy...Sorry tummy for not feeding you properly, for putting you through such stress and discomfort. For inflicting pain on you with a tattoo, but I do love the tattoo. Tummy, you are a reminder of my pregnancy and of the birth of my wonderful Son. I will try to be mindful of the changes you are going through and accept you whatever shape or size. I will look forward to jiggling you again.

In conclusion, body, I will treat you with the respect and love you deserve and look forward to having you around whatever your size for a very long time. xxx

Jackie Tanner, 43

I Apologise

For washing you relentlessly, then scorching you dry,
Leaving you in strengtheners to burn and to fry,
Brushing and combing, a bob then a Platt,
Dying you this colour, then dying you that.
I can only apologise.

For coating you in cosmetics as in vain I try...
To preserve youthful appearance as years slip by,
Vibrant colours splashed across lips and eyes,
Sometimes for beauty, sometimes for disguise,
Again, I apologise.

For piercing all those holes in my early days,
Filling them with studs or cheap diamantes,
Poking and prodding to keep them open wide,
Mopping up the blood as it trickles down my side.
I apologise.

For coating you in wax, then ripping you free,
Lovely smooth skin for others to see (and some just for me),
Overused blades used to slice through the stubble,
Severed spots always leading to trouble.
I apologise.

For exposing your charms on the sandy beach,
The sun hitting places it wouldn't normally reach.
Thinking to myself as the burns become clearer,
'I'm sure it'll be ok once I've applied Allo Vera'.
But anyway, I apologise,

For staggering around determined to look tall,
In dainty shoes at least 1 size too small,
The pain of blisters nearly making me feel sick,
A few skin coloured plasters should do the trick.
I apologise.

For excessive use of alcoholic lubrication,
Usually intended to bring a joyful sensation,
For the embarrassing scenes in recovering from it,
Violently expelling simultaneous wee and vomit.

I apologise (particularly to my boyfriend who had to clean up).

For failing to resist the lure of fast grub,
Big Macs, fried chicken, a massively filled sub,
Chips and pizzas are just some of my excesses,
No wonder each year I need a new wardrobe of dresses.
I apologise.

In search of a figure that satisfies my desire,
I just stop eating, put out my fire,
I balance my health on the edge of a knife,
No appetite for food, no energy for life.

Now I know you deserve more than an apology.
Now I know you deserve respect.
Now I know
Sorry!

Anonymous

Dear Kathryn

Dear Kathryn,

I am writing this letter to let you know how much you have neglected me over the last year. You have starved me almost to death. Giving me less and less food every day. Making me live on a sugar free jelly with only 3 calories and water. You hated me, never thanked me for what I was doing for you. You would exercise me until I couldn't do any more but you pushed me and pushed me until someone caught you. You called me names and would punch me to try and get rid of the fat you thought was there. You starved me until all of me almost shut down. I have kept you alive for 14 years and to thank me you neglected me and made me suffer. What have I done wrong? I don't understand.

Love From,

Your Body

X

Dear My Body,

I am so sorry I have treated you like that. I don't know why I let that horrible voice in my head take over. I really miss all the things we did together like horse riding, shopping and spending time with my family and friends. I will tell you now I will exercise in moderation and I will never starve you again. I realise now all the things you do for me. I can't believe I have made you suffer and have treated you so badly. You have and will keep me alive and let me do all the things I love to do. I have now learnt the valuable lesson of how to love you again. I can now see you are not fat and don't deserve to be starved. It really upsets me to know I have treated you so badly. I am so sorry. Please forgive me.

Love From,

Kathryn

X

Kathryn Kerr

About Body Gossip

Body Gossip is a campaign which promotes diversity, acceptance and realistic beauty by showcasing real body stories from the public, in the form of theatre shows, short online videos and this, the Body Gossip book.

Body Gossip invites everyone to write and submit their body thoughts to the campaign website, before working with a celebrity cast to bring the pieces received to life. In doing so, Body Gossip allows the public and celebrities to stand shoulder to shoulder in the body image debate and give the often silenced masses a much needed opportunity to have their say.

In addition, Body Gossip's award-winning education programme, 'Gossip School' has worked with tens of thousands of teenagers, giving them a crucial foundation of self-esteem by delivering confidence classes in schools, colleges and universities throughout the UK.

To find out more, or to submit your body gossip story, go to:

www.bodygossip.org

www.facebook.com/bodygossip

www.youtube.com/bodygossip

www.twitter.com/_BodyGossip

Body Gossip is run by volunteers. Please help us to tell more of your amazing stories by visiting www.buzzbnk.org/bodygossip/sofa

About TTP

TTP are one of the UK's leading specialists in addiction and disorder therapy, working to help those suffering with some of the issues you will read about in this book.

TTP work with Body Gossip to offer on-going support for issues such as eating disorders because, whilst the act of writing your story has been shown to be cathartic and can be an empowering first step towards recovery, often more help and expert guidance is required.

If you or someone you know is interested in finding out more, you can contact TTP using the details below.

TTP, 140 Harley Street, London, W1G 7LB

Tel: 020 7060 5884

Email: Harleystreet@ttpcc.org